THE NORDIC SERIES
Volume 11

The University of Minnesota Press
gratefully acknowledges the financial
assistance of the American Scandinavian
Foundation and the National Endowment
for the Humanities, under the Scandinavia
Today program, toward publication of
this book.

The Welfare State and Beyond

Success and Problems in Scandinavia

Gunnar Heckscher

University of Minnesota Press • Minneapolis

Published by the University of Minnesota Press,
2037 University Avenue Southeast, Minneapolis, MN 55414
Printed in the United States of America.

Library of Congress Cataloging in Publication Data

Heckscher, Gunnar, 1909-
   The welfare state and beyond.

   (The Nordic series; v. 11)
   Bibliography: p.
   Includes index.
      1. Scandinavia—Economic conditions. 2. Scandinavia—
Social conditions. 3. Scandinavia—Politics and govern-
ment—1945-   . 4. Welfare state. I. Title.
II. Series.
HC343.H4 1984   330.12'6'0948   83-21883
ISBN 0-8166-0930-6
ISBN 0-8166-0933-0 (pbk.)

The University of Minnesota
is an equal-opportunity
educator and employer.

For
Gunnar Hultgren

Contents

Preface

The so-called welfare state emerged in a number of industrialized countries after the First World War. It was seen as a sort of compromise between capitalism and socialism. The aim was to abolish injustices and hardships to the common people which appeared to accompany the capitalist system and which had been exposed by its critics. But this should be done without any "social revolution" in the accepted sense and indeed without changing the essentials of the economic structure. The market economy should be preserved, but with modifications introduced in the interests of social justice.

For a long time, both between the two world wars and thereafter, the establishment of the welfare state created euphoria. Here, it appeared, was the answer to all social questions, or at least to most of them. The fortunate citizens of welfare states would live happily ever after. Eventually it became obvious that this type of society was no more immune to problems than any other. Different conclusions were drawn from this discovery. Some observers maintained that the welfare state did not go far enough and that it ought to be transformed by the establishment of true socialism. Others, on the contrary, held that it had gone too far and that it was necessary to revert to a more orthodox capitalist system.

This book is an attempt to analyze and discuss some of these problems. It neither defends nor condemns the welfare state, nor does it aspire to resolve any of its problems. Consequently, it is likely to offend the advocates of socialism as well as those of traditional capitalism. This cannot be helped, but it is my ambition that the book might help both of them to develop their own thinking.

For reasons explained in the introductory chapter, the Scandinavian countries—Denmark, Finland, Norway, and Sweden—are presented as examples of welfare states and their problems. It should, however, be emphasized that the objective is not to write a descriptive study of Scandinavian society as a whole, but to present an essay on the welfare state as exemplified by experiences and developments in Scandinavia.

In 1979 I lectured at the University of Washington in Seattle on problems of the welfare state in Scandinavia and on its parties and pressure groups. The project for the present book arose out of these lectures, and the original intention was to publish it in 1980 or 1981. Because of unforeseen circumstances, I was unable to prepare the manuscript in time, and I am most grateful to the University of Minnesota Press for its patient acceptance of the long delays. These delays may not have been without their advantages, however. Much has happened in the past four years to clarify the issues, and it may be that the analysis has benefited from the observation of recent developments. Also, I owe sincere thanks to Victoria Haire for her strenuous efforts in editing the manuscript.

Gunnar Heckscher
Uppsala, September 1983

The Welfare State and Beyond

Success and Problems
in Scandinavia

Why Scandinavia?

When the pugnacious chairman of the Danish Federation of Labor, Thomas Nielsen, retired at the age of sixty-five in February 1982, he stated in a newspaper interview that he "belonged to a victorious generation. . . . What we didn't even dare to hope for has happened. . . . The fight for the daily bread is over. Now the question is one of distributing prosperity." This, in a nutshell, describes the Scandinavian attitude toward the welfare state. And it is much more explicit than the attitude in a number of other countries whose experience in fact differs very little from that of Denmark, Finland, Norway, and Sweden. Iceland, while also a Nordic country, is left out of this book because it represents a very special case.

Up to about the middle of the 1970s, Scandinavia—or the Nordic countries, a more accurate term since it leaves no doubt that Finland also is included—attracted international attention as the most typical welfare states in the world. Much was written about the welfare phenomenon, not only in the Nordic countries themselves but elsewhere as well. Much of it was complimentary, but some of it was negative. Relatively few comments tried to effect a fair balance of praise and criticism.

In spite of the changes that have taken place in recent years, the Nordic experience is still interesting to the outside world. Just as before, it is viewed either as a model that could at least in part be emulated or as a warning of possible dangers—or perhaps both. Traditionally, Western European labor movements have tended to embrace the former attitude, whereas Conservatives both in Europe and in other parts of the world more often remain critical. This, of course, is largely because on both sides they draw parallels to their own problems. William Beveridge and John Maynard Keynes in Great Britain and Franklin Roosevelt in the United States developed the ideas and practice of the welfare state at about the same time that these ideas reached Scandinavia. Both their partisans and their opponents found it useful to cite the Nordic countries as examples in controversies of the day.

In many respects Scandinavia was a testing ground for ideas that have come to the fore since the First World War. With apparent success the Nordic countries avoided the two extremes of unbridled capitalism and consistent socialism. Others did more or less the same, but with more vacillation and less conviction. From this point of view the Scandinavian experience remains interesting to others beside the Scandinavians themselves.

The present volume makes no attempt to describe the Nordic achievements in detail nor to present all or most of the relevant facts. The emphasis is not on description but on identification of problems. This does not mean that the aim is either to criticize or to defend. Rather, the "problem approach" is adopted to shed some light on a number of questions; whether the welfare state in these countries did or did not achieve what it attempted to do; whether the results attained are generally held to be satisfactory; what important problems remain unsolved; and what types of solutions are being attempted. The current problems may have been there from the beginning and may not have been dealt with satisfactorily by the efforts leading to the establishment of welfare states. They may have been noticed only lately, having formerly been overshadowed by others that appeared to be more important or pressing. Or they may be inherent in the development of the welfare state.

Before proceeding with our discussion, we must ask, what *is* a welfare state? This semantic question would probably be answered differently by different writers. But it must be explained at least how the term is used in these pages. At the bottom lies a catchword of the great

French Revolution: liberty—equality—fraternity. It could be argued, although this is sometimes disputed, that liberty was attained rather early. Equality, in the economic sense of the word, was certainly not attained at the same time. And fraternity was hardly even mentioned.

Whereas the open, liberal society established in the nineteenth and early twentieth century in the Western world had given considerable liberty to its citizens, the welfare state was intended to create equality. Like liberty, equality could as a matter of course never be absolute. Everybody should be entitled to certain minimum standards in their lives, and equality of opportunities should be granted to all as far as was possible. Equality of results was not even in the offing, but great changes were envisaged nevertheless. The means employed should be solidarity, a term which in Scandinavia has taken the place of fraternity. The welfare state claims to promote solidarity among all its citizens and eventually among the citizens of all countries. In this respect it differs from the state of affairs existing under "capitalism," a term which has been used only occasionally and only opprobriously. The relation of the welfare state to "socialism" is more dubious. Sometimes the two were held to be identical, particularly when it was intended to make the term socialism less frightening. On other occasions the terms have been kept quite separate.

One of the leading Swedish Social Democrats, Ernst Wigforss, created his own slogan: "poverty is more easy to endure when it is endured equally by all." This was never generally accepted, probably because it appeared to be excessively pessimistic at a time when there seemed to be every possibility of abolishing poverty altogether rather than sharing it, at least in the Nordic countries. On the contrary, the idea was, to quote Thomas Nielsen again, to win "the fight for the daily bread" and establish a protective net, so that no significant number of persons would risk poverty, destitution, or, to use a term employed by the British sociologist Robert Titmuss, "a state of dependency." Everybody should be enabled to "earn life" (Titmuss's words) for themselves and their families. A minimum standard of living or level of income, a "subsistence minimum," was to be guaranteed. And it should be available as their due, not as charity. This would mean fundamental security. And the mininum standard should not be fixed once and for all. It would depend on the average level of prosperity of the people. Quite clearly, this must imply considerable redistribution of assets from the rich to the poor. Nevertheless, the welfare state should be founded on individual efforts, and competition would still be regarded as legitimate.

Thus the term "welfare state" can be taken to mean a state that accepts collective responsibility for its citizens and conceivably also for other residents within its territory. It strives to abolish poverty and give to all concerned reasonable security against falling unwillingly into destitution, which is more or less arbitrarily defined from time to time as a level significantly below average prosperity. Also, the welfare state attempts to create equality of opportunities for advancement.

It is impossible to deny that Denmark, Finland, Norway, and Sweden have come close to the realization of such ideals. In several respects they have been more successful, and successful at an earlier time, than most other comparable countries. Our first question, therefore, must be whether in their history and their traditions there were any particular elements favoring such developments.

The second question is concerned with ideas and ideals. What did the founding fathers of the welfare state have in mind? Did they, like Plato and Aristotle, set out to establish the perfect, the permanently perfect society, or were their ambitions more modest? Maybe they were content to abolish some of the most glaring imperfections of the society into which they had been born. Maybe they were too busy with practical problems to have much time for utopian ideas. Or maybe, on the contrary, they had a clear vision of what was to be the ultimate goal, although they were ready to advance step by step and in their own lifetime to come only part of the way.

Much of this question hinges on the founding fathers' attitude toward the economic system rather than toward other parts of the social structure. There can be no doubt that most of the Scandinavians involved, and probably the most important of them, had originally been very much influenced by nineteenth-century Marxism. On the other hand, few of them were revolutionaries in the accepted sense. Since the influences that reached them in the early stages came mostly from Germany, they became revisionist socialists, largely of Eduard Bernstein's school. Later, they were confronted by other economic ideas, notably those of John Maynard Keynes. They seem to have become convinced that a welfare state according to their concepts could be realized within the orbit of a mixed economy, with ownership of the means of production remaining in private hands. It should be enough to insist that democratically constituted organs of the state be given the necessary authority to exercise strong control over the practices of private managers. It appeared that the founding fathers were willing to substitute interventionism for socialism.

Already at this stage, which was reached in the decades just before and just after the Second World War, there was considerable controversy. The welfare state was by no means universally acclaimed at birth. Criticism came both from within Scandinavia and from the outside. Domestic critics concentrated on economic problems. They maintained that a comprehensive welfare system was beyond the means of the respective national economies. They consistently objected to the high taxes it entailed. Moreover, they insisted, it would adversely affect the capacity for economic development. They believed that when the danger of destitution was removed, people would no longer be willing to work sufficiently hard at their jobs, and productivity would suffer. Ordinary people also would no longer be interested in saving for a rainy day when they knew they could rely on the umbrella of social security. Consequently capital formation would decrease and investments necessary for economic growth would become more difficult to make.

Foreign observers using Scandinavian experiences as arguments in their own disputes interpreted them very differently. The most striking examples were to be found in the United States. Advocates of the New Deal like Marquis Childs presented the Nordic countries as some sort of paradise. Here, they said, was to be found almost complete harmony, where all extremism was banned and free organizations on all sides cooperated with government and with one another practically without friction. Obviously the welfare state could be realized without the dangers to civil and even economic liberties or democracy which had been said to be inherent in socialism. Surely it must be sensible to repeat the experiment in other countries as well. Meanwhile, critics of the New Deal in the United States and conservatives in Western Europe (although not always in Great Britain) took the opposite stand. To a large extent, they repeated the arguments of domestic Scandinavian critics, but sometimes they went even further, as when Dwight Eisenhower made a couple of statements that were bitterly resented in Sweden. Moreover, the critics thought that this kind of society was a terrible bore: in protecting everybody from danger, it also took away the excitement of life. The latter type of criticism came chiefly from the Latin countries in Europe. And finally, early critics of the welfare state, chiefly outside Scandinavia, maintained that its practices were "immoral," meaning that it was an excessively permissive society. There are indications that such criticisms, even though they may on the face of it appear to have some justification, are the result of oversimplification. It may well be that traditional (some would perhaps say Victorian) moral principles are on the decline in Scandinavia. This may or may not be a result of the establishment of welfare states—more probably not. But on the other hand, new moral principles based on ideas of sincerity and solidarity, and thus equally rooted in Christian thought, are perhaps emerging to take their place. What remains to be seen is whether these new principles are going to influence human behavior as much as the older ones. In this connection it should be remembered that the religious base is largely disappearing.

Domestic opposition was unsuccessful and eventually became silent. The Nordic economies, especially those of Sweden and Norway, developed beyond the most optimistic expectations, and it appeared that no social expenditures would be too great for their capacities. Taxes went up and up, but on the whole revenues were collected without too much difficulty. The productivity of labor did by no means decrease—if anything it increased. Industrial investments remained at a reasonably high level, partly because enterprises plowed down their profits in investments, but partly also because individual savings did not go down significantly. Above all, in general elections Nordic voters made it abundantly clear that social security was what they wanted and that political parties could oppose it only at their peril. Naturally political leaders got the message and behaved accordingly. Indeed it appeared that criticism had been counterproductive. Because pessimistic prophesies had proved exaggerated or wholly unjustified in the past, it was now assumed that no reliable arguments could be advanced against even the greatest ambitions of the welfare state or against innovations that went beyond it.

Looking at past developments in the light of the present, we must now ask ourselves some rather hard questions. Was the enthusiasm of domestic and foreign advocates of the welfare state entirely justified —could it be that the critics were after all more frequently right than it appeared when their criticism was first brought forward—or were both sides partly wrong and partly right, as so often happens in political disputes? Answers to such questions can be found only after studying the problems of the welfare state at a time when it was more or less definitely established. The experience of the Nordic countries in this regard should be particularly enlightening to others as well as to themselves.

But first we must ascertain how welfare states actually function in this part of the world. The structure of their social security systems is not the only important thing to be examined. It is equally important to investigate the economic implications, the administration, and the political issues.

As we have seen, the Nordic countries have established a solid system of protection against actual need. They demand government intervention against abuse of power by private enterprise. They endeavor to create and safeguard equality of opportunities regardless of social status. They demand that the price of these and other egalitarian measures be paid in the form of very high taxes. To what extent is all this compatible with traditional principles of economics? And we must go further. So far the Nordic societies have usually been able to distribute abundant and growing resources to their members. What will be their position when resources become significantly more limited and austerity is called for?

The situation today is, after all, very different from that of the 1920s and 1930s, when production and productivity tended to grow much faster than consumption. This was true throughout the Western world, particularly in Scandinavia and perhaps above all in Sweden. In such circumstances, when a slump occurred causing widespread unemployment, it was plausible to accept the program of John Maynard Keynes. That program called for increasing public and collective consumption as well as for more subsidies to social groups with insufficient consuming power, financed by levies on those who were better able to pay. The same policy was applied in the United States and Great Britain, and it was on the whole uniformly successful. But Keynesian anticyclical theory also presumed that public and collective consumption should again be reduced as soon as the business circle turned and more or less full employment had been achieved. Such reductions never occurred in Scandinavia and hardly happened anywhere else either. Instead, improved conditions were used to create and develop the welfare state, with continuing increases in both private and public consumption, both transfers and collective consumption. To the general public, this course of action appeared to make sense. Why not spend all that was being earned if it could be used for the benefit of the majority of the people?

Against this background, it is necessary to ask ourselves a question that is hotly debated not only in the Nordic countries but in many other democracies as well. Are the remedies of fifty years ago still relevant to the problems of today? Are the circumstances not only of present unemployment and similar problems but also of past developments sufficiently similar to make this possible? If the answer is "no," it is equally important to ask whether there is any other economic theory than that of Keynes which can form the basis of practical conclusions in order to remedy stagflation in the welfare state.

The interventionist nature of the welfare state affects the administration of government: administrative functions multiply and influence the situation of average citizens more and more. The role of government changes, becoming more complex and less intelligible to ordinary people. Individuals may rightly or wrongly believe that the insistence on equality and solidarity deprives them of a great deal of desirable liberty. Moreover, the welfare state may become what Robert Titmuss called "the pressure group state," although pressure is exercised not only, perhaps not even primarily, by the great economic enterprises he had in mind but by other organizations, some of which can also be called "popular movements": labor unions, cooperatives, and so on.

Consequently the welfare state, which assigns more numerous and more complicated functions to public authorities, also gives a new meaning to political democracy, making it at once more difficult to operate and more important to the well-being of individual citizens. For this reason, we must get some idea of how Scandinavian democracy works. The establishment of welfare states followed the institution of political democracy, and indeed the two are frequently confused with one another. This does not exclude the possibility that the character of politics, and the role of the voting population, may have changed as a result of the new relationship between citizens on the one hand and democratically constituted authority on the other.

In planning the welfare state, the "social engineers" perhaps believed that no social problems would remain unsolved once their edifice was completed. But even poverty has not disappeared completely.

There are a number of marginal groups, collectively called "the new poor," all of them minorities and most of them quite small minorities, which believe that their interests are disregarded. Sometimes their problems are of a different character than those of former under-privileged groups and concerned less with material needs than with status and behavior. In any case, these groups are the responsibility of public authorities, since private charitable organizations are being dissuaded more and more from participating in the welfare system. It must be determined whether such complaints of neglect are justi-fied or not.

In fact, as Robert Titmuss has pointed out in the case of Great Britain, it is difficult to determine what is a "social service," who benefits from its activities, and who is carrying the burden. The more the welfare state develops, the more obvious it becomes that social benefits by no means always mean transfer of resources from the rich to the poor. Much of what takes place consists of transfers of resources between different periods in the lives of the same persons rather than between different types of persons, and it deals with persons who are neither particularly poor nor particularly rich. One objective may indeed be to steer their consumption away from what they them-selves might have chosen to consume and into channels that on the basis of higher wisdom are regarded as more useful to them, although they themselves do not realize it. It must be determined to what ex-tent this is in accordance with the original ideas of the welfare state and to what extent it involves new departures, to be explained by motives other than those that were held to be justified in the past. Especially in times of austerity the competition between privately desired and publicly desirable objects of consumption takes on a great importance to citizens.

Equality of opportunities was a great slogan, and in the Nordic welfare states much has been done in order to carry it into effect. Educational reform was perhaps the most important single element in these efforts. But two questions arise in this connection. The first is whether broadening of educational opportunities has impaired the quality of education. Few things were dearer to the founding fathers of the welfare state than the hope that their children and grandchildren would be able to benefit from the educational opportunities that they themselves had been compelled to forgo. On the face of it, their am-bitions were fulfilled. But before taking that for granted, we must investigate whether the education now available to everybody meets the educational standards the founding fathers had hoped for.

The second question had wider implications. If the same kind of education is offered to everybody regardless of economic and social status, will all people be equally able and equally likely to benefit from it? Or will some of them still be in a favored position by virtue of belonging to families with more pronounced intellectual and cultural traditions than those enjoyed by the majority, and thus be better able to prepare their children for an intellectual education?

This opens the door to the further question whether equality of opportunities is a viable concept. Perhaps some people will always be in a better position than others when it comes to making use of the opportunities. So far, the experiences of the Nordic peoples indicate that for instance higher education still fails to attract any major number of young people from the homes of parents who have themselves completed only compulsory school. The attitude toward questions of this sort goes a long way toward explaining why in the present debate equality of results rather than equality of opportunities is becoming the idea of hard-core egalitarians.

The welfare state has on the whole been realized in the Nordic countries. It was met with great expectations. Have these been met by its performance? If the answer is an unqualified "yes," there is still the question whether this should be taken to mean that we now had better let well alone or that we could and should continue further in the same direction. If, on the other hand, the answer is at least partly in the negative, if the welfare state like so many other human efforts has failed to come entirely up to expectations, then two opposite conclusions are possible. One is that the welfare state became too elaborate and should be at least partly dismantled. The other is that reforms of the traditional social structure did not go far enough, that the welfare state was only a half-measure, and that the time has come for more drastic change.

The old poor laws and the traditional economic order had attempted to discipline human beings by threatening them with the stick of destitution and encouraging them with the carrot of growing incomes and rising status. The welfare state took the stick away, seemingly without any seriously damaging consequences. Could the carrot also be removed; to what extent has this already happened; have any interesting consequences appeared so far, and what other consequences could be envisaged? Problems of this type do in fact exist. Nothing can be gained for anybody by denying their existence. But this in itself does not mean that the establishment of the welfare state was a mistake. Problems are by no means necessarily insoluble. "Facts are like cows: if you look them in the face they are not so dangerous."

Traditions and Roots

It is not necessary to write an economic and social history of the Nordic countries in order to explain their growth and development as "welfare states." However, some salient facts of their historical development should be emphasized, particularly for American readers.

The Nordic countries are far from unique. Indeed, in many respects their histories are samples of Western European history as a whole. Denmark, especially, was closely related to Germany up to 1864. The Swedish "empire," including not only Finland but also Estonia, Latvia, and part of northern Germany, maintained a close friendship with France in the seventeenth and eighteenth centuries. Such cultural and political contacts were important to social developments.

It should be remembered that, at least for the major part of Nordic history, we are dealing with two countries only (Denmark and Sweden) and not with four. Norway was part of Denmark from 1380 until 1814, when it gained autonomy but not complete independence in a dynastic union with Sweden. Finland was conquered by Sweden during crusades in the twelfth century. In 1809 it was lost to Russia but managed to preserve a certain amount of precarious autonomy. Norway achieved full independence in 1905, Finland in 1918. Iceland, which otherwise does not concern us here, lost its independence to

Norway in the thirteenth century and reclaimed it from Denmark in 1944.

Both Denmark-Norway and Sweden-Finland were definitely part of continental Europe up to about 1800. At the same time the early Swedish steel industry was largely dependent on exports to Great Britain, and as usual commercial and cultural contacts were closely related. This was equally true in the case of Denmark. Adam Smith's *The Wealth of Nations* was published in England in 1776, and no more than three years later a Danish translation was available in Copenhagen. By that time, the original was apparently well known to the enlightened Danish public. In contrast to the United States, Western Europe was of course never wholly free from governmental paternalism and interventionism. This was particularly so on the continent, while early industrial development in Great Britain favored "Manchester Liberalism," at least around the middle of the nineteenth century. And Scandinavia belonged to the continent, relations with Britain notwithstanding.

According to European tradition since the Middle Ages, the state, that is the monarch, stood in a paternal relation to its subjects. The king governed the country; he did not just administer it on behalf of the people. This may be one reason why Europeans even today refer to the executive branch as "the Government" (le Gouvernement, il Goberno, die Regierung, regeringen, Regjeringen, hallitus), whereas Americans speak of "the Administration." Some freedoms were left to the "children," more so in Britain than elsewhere, and paternal responsibilities for their well-being were strictly limited. Still the principle was there, and it justified an almost unlimited amount of interventionism in the economic and social fields. The mercantilist period in European history changed the objectives of government policies without reducing their interventionist bias. Economic life and social relationships continued to be matters decided by the state, not by individuals. The more dynamic view that gradually appeared among the mercantilists involved if anything an *increase* in interventionism, since the objective was now to guide development and not just stabilize the existing order of things. All this happened before declaration of independence by the American colonies, a historic event which was at least in part a reaction against interventionism by a distant government.

There is no denying that in the Nordic countries there were certain feudal elements in the social system both during the late Middle Ages and during the sixteenth and seventeenth centuries. But they were definitely less "feudalized," if such a term can be permitted, than the main body of continental Europe. And although the national government was far from democratic, local self-government never entirely lost the strength it had gained in the Middle Ages. In this respect the Nordic countries were similar to a number of today's "developing countries." One should of course not assume that local self-government was democratic in the modern sense of the word. It remained in the hands of the more prosperous farmers (or peasants) in each parish. But it was largely independent of both the aristocracy and the central government, centralized government being impracticable for obvious reasons of communications and transport. And even those independent farmers who enjoyed some prosperity by comparison with their neighbors were far from economically secure or "rich" by other standards. Moreover, the enclosure movement of the late eighteenth and early nineteenth century (for reasons to be discussed on p. 29) developed in such a manner as to strengthen the independence of farms rather than compelling them, as in Great Britain, to sell out to the gentry or the nobility.

Especially in the early seventeenth century, the nobility had ambitions of gaining the upper hand in Nordic society, and these ambitions were reinforced by influences from northern Germany and the Baltic provinces of Estonia and Latvia, since noblemen in Denmark and Sweden often held land in these parts as well. In Denmark proper the role of manorial estates—which, however, were by no means held exclusively by noblemen—remained important and almost predominant well into the nineteenth century. Nearly three-fourths of the land was owned by major landlords. The southern provinces of the Scandinavian peninsula retained these characteristics for almost half a century after being ceded by Denmark to Sweden at the end of the seventeenth century, but later they evolved along lines similar to those of the rest of Sweden. In Denmark, on the other hand, real land reform did not occur until the middle of the nineteenth century.

In Sweden-Finland as well as Norway, in contrast to Denmark, independent farmers always remained in possession of most of the land as owners, as tenants of the Crown, or for some decades of the seventeenth century as tenants technically subordinated to great landowners although largely independent of them. In Norway there was little, if any, feudalism, and while in Sweden-Finland a few landowners tried to amass vast landholdings in the middle of the seventeenth century, such developments were checked already before 1700.

Different circumstances caused this deviation from the general European trend. Not only were farmers eager to maintain as much as possible of their independence, but the monarchy was equally determined not to become dependent on feudal lords. The Crown frequently sought the support of the lower orders in its struggles with the aristocracy, and the Lutheran clergy also often appeared as the ally of the farmers. These trends were particularly strong in Sweden-Finland, but the same tendencies periodically appeared in Denmark as well; and in Norway the conflict between Crown and aristocracy simply did not arise. When absolute monarchy was established in the latter half of the seventeenth century—1665 in Denmark-Norway, 1680 in Sweden-Finland—it was with such support and, which is perhaps even more significant, with the objective of curtailing the power of the aristocracy. Not only was this constitutionally important, but it had fundamental social implications as well.

Absolute monarchy remained in force in Denmark until the middle of the nineteenth century. In Sweden it was short-lived, disappearing after four decades, but the measures taken during this brief period had been drastic enough to put a definite end to previously existing feudal tendencies.

Aristocracy was of course by no means abolished. But in Sweden (and Finland) it was based mainly on something other than land ownership or overlordship. This was also the case in the Norwegian part of Denmark and to a lesser degree in the main part of the latter kingdom. To use French terminology, it was (or became) a *noblesse de robe*, a nobility of civil servants, of bureaucrats, of servants of the Crown rather than an independent social group challenging the Crown's authority by virtue of its own strength. Even in the period from 1720 to 1772, when Sweden experimented with some sort of parliamentary (although by no means democratic) government, it was the bureaucrats and not the landowners who controlled the Parliament. In Norway there was practically no landed aristocracy, but this did not mean that there were no class differences. The upper class consisted of senior civil servants, the judiciary, and the clergy.

Taking Denmark-Norway and Sweden-Finland as a whole, the

social pattern was thus as variegated as on the rest of the European continent, or even more so. Under the king, the highest order consisted of the upper strata of nobility, usually owning more or less extensive landed property but also holding high military, judicial, or other civil offices. It was, however, not a closed caste: individuals of merit in the public service, as well as royal favorites, were continually incorporated in their order.

Next came the middle ranks of officers and civil servants. In Sweden-Finland up to the end of the eighteenth century these were more or less automatically given hereditary noble status if they were not born into such rank. But this did not mean that they came to belong to the real aristocracy or became major landowners. Their membership in the nobility was to some extent a matter of political expediency, since it gave them (or their families) the right to sit in the Estate of knights (Riddarhuset), the highest in status and in many respects the most important of the four Houses of the Riksdag. In Denmark, where there was no parliamentary system of any importance after 1665, even very senior officials often remained commoners all their lives, and in Norway this was the rule rather than the exception.

At the bottom of the ladder were different varieties of farm laborers and minor tenants of the landlords. Many of the latter paid their rent wholly or partly in the form of labor on the manor of their landlord. Sharecropping also was practiced. In Denmark these tenants were almost indistinguishable from the serfs in northern Germany. In the cities there were corresponding groups of journeymen and servants, although numerically these were hardly very significant.

However, there were also clearly pronounced middle classes, and these were by no means negligible. Merchants and master craftsmen in the cities belonged to this category, in Scandinavia as well as elsewhere. Junior officers and civil servants were more important in the Nordic countries than in the rest of Western Europe, while lawyers, on the other hand, played no significant role in the North. The clergy displayed much social, cultural, and political influence. But the most important and most numerous middle class group consisted of independent farmers. They were far from rich but regarded themselves as immeasurably superior in social status to the farm laborers and small tenants. In Sweden-Finland, where the Riksdag of four Estates was always a powerful factor in the life of the country (except for the four decades from 1680 to 1719), they were increasingly able to safe-guard their interests by political means.

In both Denmark-Norway and Sweden-Finland there was a limited degree of what used to be called class circulation. This movement was mainly upward, and thus no real circulation, and of very modest proportions. But it was by no means unimportant. The leading min-ister in the Danish Government in the 1770s was one Ove Guldberg (later ennobled with the name Hoegh-Guldberg), a historian and theologian born in Horsens as the son of a minor businessman in that provincial city far from the capital. The merchant and landowner Niels Ryberg, one of the wealthiest men in Denmark at that time, was the son of a peasant. In Sweden, peasants' sons who attracted the notice of the rector of their parish could not infrequently get ac-cess to higher education, which normally would result in positions in the Church. The subsequent generations would then usually enter civil or military service and perhaps eventually be ennobled. The far-mer Henrik Jakobsson, living in the extreme north of Sweden during the first half of the seventeenth century, had a son who took the name Benzelius and became archbishop of Sweden—as did three of his own sons, one after the other. In the next generation the family was ennobled and took the name Benzelstierna.

Such class circulation presented no significant opportunities to major parts of the common people, but it meant that fresh blood was continually injected into the governing classes. There is no denying that the Nordic countries were examples of class societies, but at least there were never any rigid caste distinctions.

Nordic development differed from that of other Western European countries in other respects as well. Partly because the Roman legions had never reached Scandinavia and partly for other reasons, above all the fact that Scandinavia was located far from the center of Europe, there was practically no reception of Roman law in Sweden and not very much in Denmark either. The traditional legal system, similar to British common law in much of its content if not its procedure, had already been codified in the early Middle Ages, and in spite of nu-merous statutes added to the legal code the basic legal structure re-mained the same through the centuries. Moreover, even in the Middle Ages the Church of Rome had never succeeded or bothered to estab-lish the same kind of authority in these distant Northern countries as, for instance, in Germany. Canon law did not affect the normal life of the laity. The Reformation, which came both to Denmark and to Sweden in its Lutheran form early in the sixteenth century, was consequently a relatively painless process for all but those in the monasteries and the nunneries. Yet it was important in strengthening the power of the Crown, the king becoming the recognized head of the Church and taking over most of its landed property. At the same time it vitalized local self-government in the parishes.

To recap some of the differences in the development of Denmark and Sweden: the feudal element was definitely stronger in Denmark proper than in the rest of Scandinavia, since Danish peasants were on the whole living under the same conditions as those of the adjoining part of Germany. In Sweden absolute monarchy was short-lived and never wholly effective, whereas the Danish king relinquished no significant part of his power to parliamentary bodies during a period of almost two hundred years. The Swedish "empire" east and south of the Baltic was more definitely integrated with the mother country than the German lands belonging to the Danish crown. Yet this empire was already lost in the beginning of the eighteenth century, while Slesvig and Holstein remained in the hands of Danish kings for more than a hundred years longer.

Perhaps the most important fact about Scandinavian history is that its countries were largely exempt from revolutionary social change whether in the seventeenth century or following the French Revolution of 1789. This does not mean that they took no part in European developments during these periods. On the contrary, both of them were much involved in the Thirty Years War in the first half of the seventeenth century and in numerous other armed conflicts both before that time and for over a hundred years afterward. They were frequently fighting each other but sometimes other European powers as well. Moreover, they experienced numerous *coups d'état* and constitutional changes. These were, however, not as extensive as the upheavals in Britain in the seventeenth century and very different from the French Revolution and the havoc wrought to the European continent during the Napoleonic period. The changes in Scandinavia tended to be rather superficial and never affected the really salient characteristics of society as a whole.

Thus Nordic society, if not the Nordic governments, displayed extremely strong continuity. This had great importance for the future of these countries. The paternalistic and interventionist characteristics that they had shared with the other parts of Western Europe never really disappeared. The legal system, and to a considerable extent the economic system as well, of previous centuries remained predominant well into the nineteenth century and was still in force when the Nordic countries were confronted with the new conditions of an industrialized world. In this respect they were practically unique. Interventionism was never banned, "Manchester Liberalism" was never even approached in Scandinavia. Especially in Sweden considerable quantities of land, both agricultural and other, were always under state ownership. Other land belonged to the parishes of the Church or to the universities. Numerous farmers were tenants of the Crown or of their own parish.

During the period of early industrialization in the eighteenth century the governments in the Nordic countries, as in the rest of continental Europe, maintained strong control over privately owned industrial units. In Sweden this meant among other things that steel production was controlled and limited by strict regulations. Similar controls remained acceptable under changed conditions. When public utilities such as canals, railways, and waterpower came into existence in the nineteenth century, they operated under state guidance and largely under state ownership. In fact the state built and operated many of the trunk lines of the railway system. This was accepted as perfectly natural not only because the state alone enjoyed sufficient international credit to borrow the necessary capital abroad but also because state intervention was consistent with the traditional attitudes of private enterprise and of the general public.

The rudimentary welfare system that existed before the end of the eighteenth century was not unique to Scandinavia. On the whole, it was not very different from that prevailing in Great Britain. It depended on the parishes and was largely supported by the Church. Dating back to the Middle Ages, it provided some sort of social assistance, if only at an extremely low level and with scant respect for the individual rights and integrity of needy persons. At first, its basis was charity alone, but eventually legislative regulations were established — not out of any increased feeling of social responsibility but in order to protect the parishes and maintain some sort of equity in their relations to one another. However, the fundamental idea was that even the incapacitated and the unemployed should somehow be kept alive and provided with the absolute minimum of necessities of life.

Much has been written and said of the iniquities of this system, and, by today's standards it was indeed wholly unsatisfactory or even execrable. Still, there is no denying that it existed and that it could be transformed into a basis for something more acceptable. Most important, the fact that it was founded on local self-government, and that local self-government was particularly strong in Scandinavia, had considerable implications for the future.

An equally or perhaps even more unsatisfactory situation was that of health care and hospitals. This sector had no traditional basis other than the doubtful interest of some private charities, and until the latter half of the eighteenth century was almost entirely neglected — probably even more so in Scandinavia than elsewhere. In the vast majority of cases no care was available for the sick. Only occasionally the poor laws made it possible for them to receive some sustenance from the parish. With the arrival of the Enlightenment and the consequent interest in natural sciences, a medical profession began to come into existence. Its services were chiefly offered to the upper classes, but a few particularly charitable doctors and surgeons might give medical treatment to others as well. There was of course no nursing profession, but midwives occasionally performed more than their primary duties. Hospitals were established in Denmark, Norway, and Sweden before 1800, but they were few and far between, and again usually not available to the majority of the people. Real improvement did not occur until the latter half of the nineteenth century, and even then developments were far from rapid.

Education is a different story. Here both state and Church became active at a comparatively early date. Although some schools had been established earlier, it was at the end of the Middle Ages that educational institutions came to be regarded as essential. The universities appeared first, in Uppsala, Sweden (1477) and in Copenhagen, Denmark (1478). In both cases the objective was pragmatic rather than cultural. Future clergymen were to be educated in their home country and not have to go abroad, to France, Germany, and Italy, for their studies. Although this happened before the Reformation, it was part of an effort to maintain national independence of Rome in religious matters. In Uppsala the initiative was taken by the archbishop, and it was in his residential city that the university was established. In Copenhagen it was the king who wanted the university to be situated in his capital, thus to be independent not only of the pope in Rome but also of the archbishop, who resided in Lund, at that time a Danish city.

These early educational centers were not entirely successful, largely because recurrent wars (often between Denmark and Sweden) necessitated concentration in other fields. They were, however, maintained, although with low levels of activity. When the two universities were reconstructed a few decades later, the situation had changed. After the Reformation, the need for educating future clergymen in their home countries was even more obvious. But in addition the kings of both Denmark and Sweden had started to establish their civil services, necessary to them in their efforts to strengthen their hand in dealing with the aristocracy. Civil servants and judges could function successfully only if they had some education. The universities were, however, still seen almost entirely as instruments for definite practical purposes, not as cultural centers. To some extent the horizon widened with growing international contacts during the seventeenth century, but the main purpose of university education remained the same: training for definite careers, not basic research and cultural development. This was largely true even of endowed professorships, as when Johan Skytte in 1622 established in Uppsala what might be called the world's oldest still active chair of political science. Its function was on the one hand to train future diplomats and on the other to support philosophical ideas opposed to the Aristotelianism propagated by the Roman Catholic Church.

Secondary education was introduced later, in the beginning of the seventeenth century, and it too had a definite practical purpose: to prepare young men for the university. Primary education was the last to be developed. Here the role of the Church was particularly important, especially in Sweden but to a lesser extent in Denmark as well.

One of the fundamental principles of Lutheran Protestantism was that the Bible and other religious documents, above all Martin Luther's catechism, should be made known to all the people and not only to the clergy. However, the effect of translating the Bible into Danish and Swedish would be limited as long as only a small minority were able to read in any language. Consequently parish priests and their assistants early began to make sporadic efforts to teach the common people to read, if not the Bible then at least the catechism (which was more easily committed to memory). In fact they were obliged to pursue this activity in Sweden under the Church law of 1687. Yet it took a hundred and fifty years before the Swedish authorities were ready to make a universal effort to abolish illiteracy, and by then the religious purpose had become less predominant. Still, it remained the duty of the self-governing parishes to act for the state in primary education. In the meantime some development had taken place, and it was always public authority, state and church, that took the intiative and retained the power in the educational field. Private efforts also did appear, but only in a subsidiary capacity and with no more than marginal importance.

In Denmark the duty of establishing schools for the common people rested with the landowners, who almost systematically neglected it. But the reformers of the Era of Enlightenment did not forget about education. A great Royal Commission on education was appointed in 1789 (before the French Revolution had begun!), and as a result of its efforts a law on public education was passed in 1814. Not only was it proclaimed to be the duty of the state of provide basic education for all children, free of charge. Parents were also made responsible for sending their children to school, under penalty of substantial fines. This was pioneer work. It was not until 1842 that similar legislation was passed in Sweden.

While still backward in many respects, Scandinavia was not untouched by the great changes that took place in the nineteenth century. There, as in the rest of the Western world, if with a certain amount of delay, constant change, development, and growth gradually came to be accepted as normal instead of exceptional. History began to move faster than ever before in all respects: culturally, politically, but above all in the economic and social fields.

Political change in the nineteenth century was no more drastic than in some previous periods, but in any case it affected all the Nordic countries more or less simultaneously, breaking up traditional structures and ties. Denmark lost Norway as a result of having vacillated so much in the Napoleonic wars that it ultimately found itself on the wrong side. The effect of this loss on the mother country was surprisingly small, probably because Norway had not been of central importance to the Danish realm. In fact Denmark's loss to Sweden of several provinces in the Scandinavian peninsula in the seventeenth century had been a much more harrowing experience. And a later development, the breakup of the dynastic union with Slesvig and Holstein as a result of a national reawakening in Germany in the middle of the nineteenth century also had more lasting effects. But taken together, all these territorial losses made Denmark what it is today: a small, closely knit, compact country without ambitions in international politics.

Norway gained more than autonomy, in fact something very like independence, as a result of the change in Scandinavia's political structure that took place in 1814. The union with Sweden was a purely dynastic arrangement. A separate Norwegian Parliament, the Storting, was established as well as a separate Norwegian Cabinet, responsible—like the Swedish counterpart—to the king of Sweden and Norway but increasingly also the Storting. The new relationship involved serious friction almost from the beginning, and Norwegian nationalism developed more rapidly than expected. It was also allied to democratic or at least liberal ambitions. The union between the two countries on the Scandinavian peninsula was precarious, to put it mildly, and dissolution gradually became inevitable, finally taking place in 1905.

For Sweden the loss of Finland in 1809 was a very serious matter from the point of view of national psychology. Indeed this traumatic experience influenced Swedish thought for a very long time afterward. The union with Norway five years later was intended as a compensation, but things did not work out in that way. Sweden and Finland had really been one country, with a single governing and intellectual class speaking the Swedish language—Finnish was used mainly by the lower strata of the population. Many of their families were now divided. No similar community feeling with Norway could ever be established. The growth of Norwegian nationalism worked in the other direction, and it is not too much to say that the union of 1814 had already after half a century become a source of disappointment to the Swedes—the Norwegians hardly ever had any illusions about it. It involved more conflict than cooperation both politically and culturally, and economically it was in fact without major practical importance to either of the two countries.

The separation from Sweden of course involved highly difficult experiences for the governing class in Finland as well. Its members were indistinguishable from their counterparts on the other side of the Gulf of Bothnia. This is not to deny, however, that there had for some time been a certain unrest and dissatisfaction with being governed from Stockholm. In fact toward the end of the eighteenth century some officers in the army and a few members of the civil service had already begun to contemplate separation. When it came, it was, however, exclusively as a result of the fortunes of a war that had been scandalously mismanaged by the Swedish authorities and not through the efforts of the dissidents.

The new master of Finland was the czar of Russia, and initially the relationship to him was by no means wholly unsatisfactory. He played on the budding nationalist elements in the country and allowed considerable autonomy to his newly acquired Grand Duchy of Finland. Even later, Finland never became a part of Russia proper, although it enjoyed far less independence than did Norway in the union with Sweden. But the czars usually insisted on the same absolute power throughout their realm, in Finland as in Russia, and this was hard for the "constitutionalists" in Finland to take. Their opposition was determined, and much of the history of the country in the nineteenth and early twentieth century deals with the resulting conflicts. On the whole, Finland maintained its autonomy with surprisingly great success, especially after the revolts that took place in Russia in 1904-5. In the latter part of the nineteenth century nationalism in Finland appeared in another form as well, namely in demands for cultural recognition of the Finnish language. The language nationalists confronted their culturally Swedish-minded compatriots, and the agents of the czars sometimes managed to play them off against the constitutionalists, who were more frequently found on the side of Swedish in the language issue. This issue was by no means resolved when Finland finally gained complete independence in 1918 as a result of the revolutions that had taken place in Russia the previous year.

Thus, for the first time in history there were after the First World War four separate and independent countries in the Scandinavian region: Denmark, Finland, Norway, and Sweden. Contrary also to what had been the case for most of their past, none of them were much involved in European power politics, which made it possible for them to concentrate on internal development: economic, social, political, and cultural.

The most significant political development in the nineteenth century was the growth of Liberalism—in the European sense of the word, which is somewhat different from the American connotations. The Liberal movements in Scandinavia were strongly influenced by those of other Western European countries, especially Britain and France, but they developed independently. They concentrated on constitutional aims such as reducing the power of the monarchy and widening the franchise. Still, it can hardly be maintained that any of the four countries—not even Norway, which in many respects was ahead of the others—had grown into full-fledged democracies by 1900.

Denmark, Sweden, and Norway very definitely remained part of Western Europe, with the two former countries oriented toward Germany and to some extent toward France, while Norway always looked to Britain for inspiration. Even Finland had stronger ties with Western Europe, particularly with Germany, than it had with Russia, in spite of the overlordship of the czars. In the economic sphere, trade relations developed by leaps and bounds, and capital from England and Germany was invested in Scandinavia. New social trends came from both Britain and the continent. Throughout the Nordic countries, the Baptist and other "free" religious movements, originating in Britain, competed with the traditional Lutheran churches, and not without success. Socialism came from Germany, and the solutions suggested by Socialists as well as anti-Socialists all over Europe influenced Scandinavian administrators, politicians, and thinkers.

Despite all this activity, economic and consequently also social development was rather late in reaching the Nordic countries. The four countries can be said to have remained underdeveloped until less than a hundred years ago in the sense that their economic potentials were not exploited to anything like the same extent as those of Britain, France, Germany, or Belgium. Their economies remained largely agricultural well into the twentieth century. Even in Norway, which was a bit ahead of the others, this was the situation up to about the First World War. Thus they continued to be "poor" countries in the accepted sense of economic development and growth, but eventually they were able to benefit from the experience of other European countries whose industrial development had come earlier.

Industrialization was preceded by profound changes in agricultural production, which had already started to become more efficient at the very beginning of the nineteenth century or in the case of Denmark a few decades earlier than that. In that country, serfdom was abolished in 1755, several decades before the French revolution. Danish peasants in consequence became much more able to benefit from efficient production. Yet the great landowners remained strong enough to lead the way. In the other countries, including the Norwegian part of the Danish realm, serfdom had never existed, but on the other hand there were fewer great landowners.

Throughout Scandinavia the structure of landholdings changed. There was devolution of ownership from the state and to some extent from other major holdings, but most important of all the enclosure movement (consolidation of landholdings) caught on. In Denmark it was initiated by a number of enlightened landlords in the middle of the eighteenth century. The movement reached Sweden a few decades later, but there the initiative was transformed into compulsory legislation. In all the Nordic countries except Denmark there was also the possibility of colonizing land not previously used for agricultural purposes, although there existed no "frontier" in the American sense of the word.

Thus, neither the enclosure movement nor other agricultural technological reforms were carried out independently by the owners of small and medium-sized farms themselves. The driving force came from above, from great landowners or from the state. In fact there was often strong resistance from the majority of the farming population, which tended to hold on to traditional inefficiency. Interventionism was a progressive and not an obstructive factor. It also made it possible to pursue more or less consistent policies, and as a result the enclosure movement did not, as in England and northern Germany, result in the establishment of large holdings by absentee landlords but on the contrary increased the economic strength of the class of independent farmers. And while there were undoubtedly underprivileged groups within the agricultural population, and while it is equally undeniable that the size of these groups grew somewhat, the most important result of the changes was that the middle class of relatively small farmers was strengthened. This had important implications for future political and social development.

Although, as has been repeatedly pointed out, the industrial revolution was late in coming to Scandinavia, it would be a great mistake to imagine that there was no industry before the nineteenth century. Denmark, which produced no raw materials for heavy industry, had a long tradition of light industries such as textile and porcelain manufacture, as well as the production of sugar. But while agricultural development in Denmark was rapid and successful even before the beginning of the nineteenth century, and ahead of the rest of Scandinavia, industry was less fortunate. As a result of the Napoleonic wars and consequent blockades, traditional industries were virtually destroyed, and it took a long time before the new industrialism caught on. When this happened it was largely without connection with traditional production. Norway was better placed, since that country had indigenous resources for the production of both steel and glass. Even in Finland a certain amount of industrial development had taken place before the separation from Sweden in 1809.

But Sweden, as distinct from Finland and other parts of the Swedish empire, was an important element in Europe's industrial economy already in the seventeenth and eighteenth centuries. This was by virtue of its production of copper and steel, and to some extent of timber, all of which were largely exported especially to Britain. These industries were rigorously controlled by the state both in the application of general mercantilist principles and more specifically in order to conserve the forests, which before the use of bituminous coal—and in the absence of such resources—were indispensable for steel production. It was the destruction of its forests that had made Britain dependent on steel imports, a fact which was well known to Swedish policy makers. However, with the emergence of new technologies by which coal could be used instead of charcoal, and partly owing to the difficulties of foreign trade in the Napoleonic period, the British market was almost completely lost. There were extremely serious consequences for the Swedish steel industry, although it was by no means completely destroyed. The demand for timber also diminished; moreover in all sorts of industry Norway became an increasingly successful competitor with its neighbor on the peninsula.

Thus in the early decades of the nineteenth century industry throughout Scandinavia had been reduced to a very low level. It could not be restored—and it is important to remember that the question was one of restoration, not of creating something that had never been heard of—without adaptation to a more modern economic order.

In Denmark tendencies in this direction appeared early in the nineteenth century, but initially in banking, commerce, and shipping rather than in industry. In the last named field it was only production related to agriculture that recuperated at an early date. Progress in Norway started somewhat later than in Denmark but then marched on much more rapidly. The forest-based industries became really important around 1850, and the mechanical and textile industries had begun to prosper even some years earlier. The growth of shipping and fisheries was a very important element in the development of the national economy, besides also favoring the shipbuilding industry. During the latter half of the nineteenth century Norway was probably well ahead of the other Nordic countries in industrial development. And although in 1865 over 70 percent of the Norwegian population were engaged in agriculture and only 10 and 16 percent in navigation and commerce and industry, respectively, the corresponding figures for 1890 were 57, 16, and 23 percent. This should be compared with the relevant figures for Sweden. In 1870, 72 percent of the Swedish people made their living from agriculture, 5 percent from commerce and transport, and nearly 15 percent from industry. In 1890 the figures were 62, 9, and 23 percent, respectively. The proportion employed in services and the professions was always nearly twice as high in Sweden as in Norway. On the other hand, the growth of the total population was approximately the same in both countries, 18-19 percent in the relevant period (on an average 5 per thousand per annum, net increase). The growth of the Norwegian economy was an important cause of friction within the union with Sweden, both because Sweden feared Norwegian competition and because this growth stimulated Norwegian nationalism. Several of the national leaders in Norway were great shipowners: for instance, Christian Mickelsen, Gunnar Knudsen, and Ludwig Mowinckel.

It was not until the last three decades of the nineteenth century that Sweden experienced real industrial and commercial growth. In the steel industry this growth was made possible by the use of new technologies, partly imported from Britain and Germany but to some extent independently developed within Sweden itself. Slightly later, the forest-based industries grew in importance. Timber was no longer the most important element, but rather pulp, paper, matches, and similar secondary products. In all these fields opportunities for export were developed. At the end of the century it also became possible, again on the basis of new technologies, to make use of formerly unworkable resources of iron ore, which became a crucially important part of the Swedish economy.

Finland did not industrialize quite as early as the other Nordic countries, but its resources for lumber and pulp industries started to gain importance from the 1860s and were able to compete, often successfully, with those of Sweden. Although the country as a whole remained mostly agricultural well into the twentieth century, this forest-based production had already become an important source of growing prosperity and the main basis of Finland's exports a hundred years ago.

For both Sweden and Norway two other elements of economic development were related to geography. One of them was the supply of waterpower, which by the standards of those days appeared to be almost unlimited as soon as it became technically possible to utilize it in the form of electricity. The other was transport. Canal building never was important to the Swedish economy, partly because it developed too late, and in Norway canals were for geographical reasons never really viable. Shipping early became an important factor in the Danish and above all in the Norwegian economy, and Sweden followed suit. However, it was only with the coming of railways that Sweden and Norway were able to establish satisfactory transport for their industrial products.

The railway age began in the Danish realm, although not in Denmark itself, when the route from Kiel to Altona was completed in 1844. Another small railway line, from Copenhagen to Roskilde, was built three years later, and this was extended to Korsør on the west coast of Sjaelland in 1856. The age of extensive railway building in Denmark began in the 1860s.

In Norway the first small railway was built in 1854. It did, however, take ten years more before any major development occurred, and the great extension of the railway system did not begin until the 1880s. From 1884 to 1914 the total net was then doubled and included both the line from Kristiania (Oslo) to Bergen and that from Narvik to the Swedish frontier in the north.

The first railway line in Finland was completed in 1862, and during the succeeding decades more and more lines were added. Most of these were built in the southern part of the country, but before the end of the century the northern and southern parts had been joined by railway lines. Since Finland was under Russian overlordship, the railway gauge was—and still is—the same as in Russia and thus slightly wider than that of Sweden and other Western European countries.

With negligible exceptions the Swedish railways were built a few years later than those of Denmark and Norway. The first major line, between Stockholm and Gothenburg, was not opened until 1862, but during the rest of the century the system developed very rapidly and became a factor of crucial importance in the economy. Especially the mining and steel industries would have been unable to develop without this efficient system of transport.

Railways were largely constructed and operated by the state, but most of the industrialization was due to private initiative and financed by private capital. Some of the capital was foreign (mostly British, to a smaller extent German), but the major part came from indigenous sources. This was possible because in Scandinavia, as in Great Britain, the agrarian revolution had preceded the industrial revolution and generated an economic basis for further development.

Another important factor in economic development was the establishment of efficiently working private banks. In this respect Denmark and Sweden developed along more or less parallel lines. In Copenhagen the first private bank of the modern type was founded in 1856 under the leadership of C. F. Tietgen, who soon became the most prominent figure in the economic life of his country and was active in many fields, for example, in developing telecommunications. At that time there were already several smaller banks in Sweden, but these were of an older type and chiefly based on the issue of private banknotes. The first modern bank opened in Sweden, as in Denmark, in 1856; its founder was A. O. Wallenberg, whose family has remained important and at times almost predominant in Swedish economic life ever since. Norwegian development was less dramatic, but by the early 1860s modern banking was well under way in Norway as well.

As can be seen from the preceding paragraphs, economic modernization did not result exclusively from either private or state initiatives. Banking, commerce, and industry were in private hands, but not only the major railway lines but also waterpower were divided between private and state ownership. Much valuable land, especially in Sweden and Finland, belonged to the state, and private activities in the mining industry and utilization of waterpower were subject to strict regulation by the government. Public utilities in the growing cities also frequently were in the hands of self-governing local bodies or kept under their control. Thus even during this period of industrialization the interventionist tradition was maintained at least to a limited extent.

Modernization in agriculture, in industry, and in commerce brought new social problems to the surface. This was particularly true in the traditional part of the Swedish and Norwegian economy, namely, small or medium-sized holdings of agricultural land. The number of agricultural laborers and other landless or almost landless households grew faster than that of independent farmers, although the latter still remained in the majority. Industrialization led to rapid urbanization in Denmark, while Finnish, Norwegian, and Swedish industry remained more decentralized. But industrial workers were no better off in Scandinavia than in the rest of Western Europe.

New social problems generated new social and political movements. For most of the nineteenth century Liberalism remained the most dynamic force. But as in the rest of Western Europe it changed in character. Its primary concern, which formerly had been the protection of individual liberties, now was the struggle for real political democracy in the form of manhood suffrage (the idea of votes for women usually came later) and responsible parliamentary government in accordance with the British model. It also drew the consequences of the democratic ideology and allied itself with the budding labor movement by insisting on social reforms in order to deal with the problems generated by industrialization and urbanization. Whether the latter goals should be regarded as a part of the Liberal creed exclusively remains in doubt, however. In reality initiatives were taken by interested persons from different political groups.

Labor movements, mainly among industrial workers, took the form of both political parties (Social Democrats) and labor unions. They were becoming significant all over Scandinavia even before the end of the nineteenth century, but only after 1900 did they really begin to put their imprint on Scandinavian societies. They originated in Germany, but it should be emphasized that they quickly ceased to be dogmatic: the Marxist doctrine they initially proclaimed quickly gave way to more pragmatic attitudes. They were in fact more similar to the British than the German labor movement. The notion of working class solidarity, originally derived from Marxist ideas of class struggle, became a practical necessity and a reality in the course of numerous strikes and lockouts, resulting already in the last years of the nineteenth century in the gain of important material benefits for union members and industrial workers in general.

An early Socialist movement, led by Marcus Thrane, had appeared in Norway by the late 1840s, but this quickly proved abortive. In Denmark both labor unions and a Social Democratic party came into existence thirty years later, and they were so strong that they could not be put down by the authorities. Sweden was a few years behind, and in fact developments there were partly influenced from Denmark. The labor movement began in Norway during the late 1880s and in Finland at the very end of the century. In all four countries the labor parties were created and supported by the labor unions, which were strong enough to take action without political support in the field of labor relations. As a result, employers also had to organize in order to meet the challenges of strikes and other concerted actions by their workers. Cooperatives, both consumers' and agricultural producers' organizations, developed first in Denmark (during the 1870s and 1880s) but soon took hold in the other Nordic countries as well. In Denmark the original objective was to organize the small independent farmers and tenant farmers, while consumers' cooperatives in Sweden at first regarded themselves as part of the (industrial workers') labor movement, although they were not directly involved in the political struggles of the Social Democratic party.

In Scandinavia, as elsewhere, there was strong resistance to the labor movement. It was opposed by those who traditionally belonged to the governing class, including the more prosperous part of the farming population. But resistance was never complete. Liberal politicians early began to seek the support not only of working-class voters but also of their Social Democratic representatives and leaders. More important, however, the growth of pragmatic labor movements was favored by the lingering paternalism in Scandinavian political and social traditions. Thus the labor movement's idea that the state and the self-governing local authorities had to live up to major responsibilities in the solution of the social problems of industrialism never appeared to be unacceptable in principle. The growing strength of political democracy and thus of the votes of industrial workers and allied groups had the effect of making this idea politically expedient as well.

A basic factor in social development was emigration to America, from all Nordic countries but especially from Norway and Sweden. This emigration continued well into the twentieth century, and it was very considerable in proportion to the population. Before 1900 about 900,000 Swedes left their country, out of a total population that only in the last decade of the nineteenth century had risen to about five million. The corresponding figure for Norway is about

375,000 out of a total population of approximately two million. In both cases this means that over 18 percent of the population emigrated. Most of the Swedish emigrants were drawn from the agricultural sector. Some of them were landless agricultural laborers, but the majority were tenant farmers or small independent farmers who went across the Atlantic Ocean in the hope of acquiring larger and better landholdings. In the main this was also true of Norway, but in the latter part of the emigration period numerous emigrants were drawn from the Norwegian cities as well.

In retrospect it would appear that emigration was a positive factor in resolving the social problems of the Scandinavian countries. But many contemporaries regarded this population drain as a serious threat to national strength. In reviewing the causes of emigration, interest was focused on existing social hardships, and even those who otherwise held strong conservative opinions therefore came to take an interest in those reforms that would make their country attractive enough to hold back prospective emigrants. Some reforms that benefited the agricultural population were instituted precisely as a result of debates on emigration. Minimum living standards thus rose, if only to a very limited extent. Where industry was concerned, some legislative attention was given to problems of industrial safety, while it was left to the labor unions to work—not without success—for more acceptable wage levels. And modifications of the poor laws were helpful to the lowest strata of both the rural and the urban population.

Another important field of social development was that of education. Primary education was regulated by law and already by the middle of the nineteenth century had become compulsory for all children in the four Nordic countries. It took some time before such legislation became wholly effective, but this was achieved well before the end of the century.

In addition, there grew up a specifically Scandinavian type of voluntary popular education, the folk high schools. This was a spontaneous movement, beginning in Denmark in the middle of the nineteenth century on the initiative of the clergyman and thinker N. F. S. Grundtvig, and it soon spread to the other Nordic countries, with Finland lagging somewhat behind. The folk high schools provided opportunities for young adults among the population of farmers and industrial workers to study in residential schools for considerable periods of time—usually one or even two academic years. The subjects varied but usually included economics, politics, philosophy, and literature, and instruction was given by means of lectures and discussion. There were no examinations either for entrance or at the end of the study period. The folk high schools were widely developed already in the last decades of the nineteenth century, and they had far-reaching importance. Their alumni played considerable parts in all the popular movements, particulary the labor unions and the Social Democratic party, and the folk high schools, together with other arrangements for popular education, enabled young people from the working classes to rise to responsible positions in these movements and to take an active part in both local and national politics. This is one of the reasons, and perhaps the most important one, why Scandinavian labor leaders were from the beginning drawn from the rank and file and seldom recruited from outside, as happened in so many other countries. Most of them were not ideologically motivated intellectuals but members of the working class itself, with personal experience of the hardships and ambitions prevalent there. Without a doubt, such experience fostered pragmatic attitudes.

Until about the beginning of the First World War, the Nordic countries remained relatively poor and underdeveloped in terms of economic and especially industrial progress. But they had reached what in modern parlance is called the take-off point not only with regard to the structure of their economies but also in their ability to meet the challenge of emerging social problems. Emigration to America continued up to 1914, but after the First World War it became negligible, an important indication that the Scandinavian countries had undergone a fundamental change for the better. From the 1920s on, spectacular economic development took place especially in Sweden. It primarily involved traditional export commodities such as iron ore, steel, paper and pulp, matches, and so on. But to these were added a number of secondary and tertiary products using steel, such as ships, ball bearings, and telephones. With the widespread use of electricity, the supply of waterpower became increasingly valuable to the economies of Sweden, Norway, and Finland. Denmark was one of the world's leading suppliers of animal foodstuffs. In addition, not only industries drawing their raw materials from agriculture but also other manufactures became increasingly important to Denmark. Norway had already become one of the leading shipping countries of the world by the end of the nineteenth century. Its mechanical industries grew by leaps and bounds after 1905, and the chemical products of "Norsk Hydro" became world famous about the same time. As usual, Finland was less fortunate. Its forest-based industries flourished, but other growth was still held back by lack of capital, by remaining scars from the civil war of 1918, and by a precarious geographical position at the edge of the Soviet Union.

It should be noted that in all four countries economic growth was directly related to exports. It was consequently dependent on the economic situation in the Western world as a whole, and the world crisis of the early thirties hit Scandinavia as hard as other countries, causing widespread unemployment. The general standard of living had been relatively low even in the 1920s, while capital accumulation was considerable throughout the early decades of the twentieth century.

Simultaneously the political and social strength of the labor movement had increased all over Scandinavia by the beginning of the 1930s. There had been serious setbacks such as the failure of a general strike in Sweden in 1909 and the outcome of the Finnish civil war nine years later. But these setbacks were short-lived. Both labor unions and Social Democratic parties were able to recuperate rapidly, and in all four countries the labor movement was powerful although not dominant by 1930. The doctrine of solidarity had been able to survive temporary failures and was bringing increasing success.

Labor relations were still often troubled by major strikes and lockouts, but both labor unions and employers' organizations were beginning to rely more and more on negotiation and less on open confrontation. Cooperatives, not only those of the consumers but also those of producers in agriculture, which were favored by official agricultural policies, had become an accepted and powerful element of the social structure. One of the characteristics of the Nordic countries had become their reliance on lawful and law-abiding economic and social organizations. These acted as pressure groups but were also willing to cooperate with public authorities.

Thus historical developments had created the society that impressed Marquis Childs, which he described as "Sweden—the middle way" (he could just as well have said "Scandinavia" instead of "Sweden") and which he held up as a model to Americans in the New Deal era. One could also say that it was the kind of society that in the years before the Second World War was being transformed into the Scandinavian welfare state. The transformation was largely the work of the labor movement, but not exclusively; other social groups and political parties also made significant contributions, and none of them put up any lasting resistance. With little opposition, the doctrine of solidarity was accepted and extended from the working class to society as a whole.

Among the Nordic countries, Denmark became the first welfare state. Already in the late 1920s the Social Democratic Cabinet of Thorvald Stauning and K. K. Steincke embarked on an ambitious policy of social insurance. Resistance from Conservatives and agrarian Liberals, which was vigorous initially, was overcome in less than ten years. Similar policies were proclaimed and realized in Sweden by the Social Democratic Cabinet of Per Albin Hansson, Gustav Möller, and Ernst Wigforss, with considerable support from the agrarian party. Norway was not far behind, and the same trend was visible in Finland until it was broken by the war with Russia in 1939-40 and 1940-44.

There was very little of Marxism in these Social Democratic policies. As mentioned in the previous chapter, they enthusiastically embraced the economic ideas of John Maynard Keynes, which seemed to be particularly applicable in these countries, where economic progress had resulted more in capital formation than in increased household consumption and where it was consequently not very difficult to reduce the local effect of the worldwide slump—or appear to do so—by means of public spending and by increasing the buying power of the less favored classes in society.

It is only natural that those who were responsible for the policies of the late 1920s and early 1930s up to the beginning of the Second World War took considerable pride in what had been achieved in their countries and were apt to regard it as their own handiwork or at least that of the social movements of which they were a part. They had seen and often personally experienced poverty and even destitution as they appeared in Denmark, Finland, Norway, and Sweden in the first decades of the twentieth century. They had been criticized and sometimes personally vilified in the course of their efforts to do something about these evils. They could point out that an almost insufferable situation had changed for the better in the Nordic societies. What had been achieved elsewhere did not concern them. Such developments were after some time almost universally acclaimed. Political debate concentrated on the question whether they were caused principally by social reforms or by economic progress. There would be no point in repeating such arguments here.

In retrospect it is more interesting to focus attention on another question, which was almost entirely forgotten at the time. What was the part played by general international experience, and how important was national tradition in thus utilizing economic progress for the purpose of social reform, that is, for establishing reasonably satisfactory conditions for the Scandinavian peoples, including their large previously underprivileged groups? It has been repeatedly pointed out above that industrialism in the modern sense was late in reaching Scandinavia. In some respects this put the Nordic countries at a disadvantage. But there were beneficial effects also. Scandinavian historians and political thinkers had made observations of developments in England and on the European continent for a very long time. Moreover, not only Friedrich Engels and Karl Marx but also John Stuart Mill, Otto von Bismarck, and Benjamin Disraeli had considered them most carefully. Their writings and activities were well known in Scandinavia. None of them had devised solutions that appeared quite acceptable to reformers in the Nordic countries, but at least there were many attempts at analyses which could give food for thought.

The slowness of Scandinavian development had other effects as well. The tradition of paternalistic interventionism had never been completely broken, and it could be used almost directly as a basis for democratic interventionism. To the Nordic peoples, the ideas and practices of the welfare state seemed to fit in with what they had learned long ago to accept as normal and satisfactory behavior by public authorities. These practices did not seem very revolutionary even to those formerly favored groups—or classes—that had to pay the bill. The solutions to social problems that were applied in the Nordic countries were by no means wholly original. Similar policies had been developed in New Zealand, and models for some of them had been derived from Great Britain. But Scandinavia was for many reasons a particularly fertile soil for the growth of welfare states.

Ideals of the Welfare State

The two hundred years from the eighteenth to the twentieth century are unique in the history of humanity. In the Western world at least, there was constant material progress, and apparently the sky, or indeed outer space, was the limit. Obviously the situation was very different in Africa and Asia, but to Westerners, their own part of the globe was all that really counted.

Scandinavia was no exception to the rule. It is true that progress came later there than in many other Western countries, but international contacts were intense enough for their experience to induce great hopes among Scandinavians. When the winds of change came to the North, the rapidity of material progress was spectacular. The result was a different society—industrial rather than agricultural or commercial, dynamic instead of static.

On the whole, even the common people benefited from the very beginning, if only to a limited extent. Although their living conditions appear to have been unbearable by today's standards, they were in many respects an improvement on those of their parents. And as usual improvement brought rising expectations.

These were emphasized by the rise of political democracy. Formerly underprivileged social groups, who formed the majority of the population, gained political power, and it was almost self-evident that they would insist on using it for their own benefit. Accepting the democratic process as an alternative to social revolution, they expected results, and these results would be the creation of a society different from that of "capitalism." In Scandinavia, their approach was pragmatic rather than ideological, but this does not mean that class consciousness was absent.

The leaders of the new radical political and social movements of the time were drawn primarily from the working classes. Some of them were journalists, this being a group which for a long time has been in the vanguard of Nordic politics. The political role of lawyers has always been far less significant in the Nordic countries than, for instance, in France or the United States. The representatives of the emerging powerful social groups were no mere agents. They had themselves mostly risen from the rank and file, and thus shared its experience of actual hardships, if not directly, then at least through their parents. Thorvald Stauning, prime minister of Denmark for a total of fifteen years between 1924 and 1942, once described how he became a Social Democrat: "I read *Social demokraten*, which at that time advanced several instances of injustice in society, the treatment in workhouses, etc. This impressed me very much when I was a boy. And conditions in my home were also extremely poor. My father was first a journeyman cartwright, then a general laborer, and there was much unemployment. . . . These circumstances left a permanent mark on my notion of social conditions . . ." And the Swedish social reformer, Gustav Möller, journalist and for three long terms a Cabinet minister, never ceased to refer to his mother's life as an example of the misfortunes of the working class in the new industrialized society. Many of his colleagues could fall back on similar experiences of their own.

It is necessary to be aware of this background in order to understand the policies and the ideology of Social Democrats in Scandinavia. It gave them a strong impetus (admittedly based on resentment) directed toward immediate social improvement. "Socialism in our own time," the slogan of British Fabians, was what they sought to achieve, not total change two or three generations later. It is no mere coincidence that Sydney and Beatrice Webb were more attractive to them than Marx and Lenin.

It is not easy to analyze the arguments used in favor of a "welfare state" in Scandinavia. Indeed, the word was rarely used. In Denmark, there was hardly any comprehensive slogan, and in Sweden, Per Albin

Hansson spoke of "det goda folkhemmet," the good home for the people. Nor is it quite certain that there was any clear vision of what the new, good society was going to be like as a whole. The reformers themselves may frequently have held opinions somewhat different from those advanced in order to gain support for their proposals from at least some of their avowed opponents. In retrospect, the welfare state has been credited with merits differing more or less from original expectations.

And, finally, it must again be emphasized that Scandinavia was not unique. The debate on similar issues taking place in other parts of the Western world influenced the Danes, the Swedes, and the Norwegians of the 1930s. The threat from Fascism and National Socialism was also very real. On the one hand, nearly all Scandinavians regardless of party allegiances abhorred these movements. But on the other hand, they had to admit that both in Italy and particularly in Germany there were at least in the beginning some notable achievements, and these were duly observed and sometimes influenced Scandinavian policies. Finally, general egalitarian tendencies were part of the European tradition, especially that of European Liberalism since the French revolution.

It is not difficult to recognize the protest element of the welfare ideology, its criticism of previously existing societies, particularly since this is so closely related to the debate taking place elsewhere in the world. The patriarchal (or feudal) society, it was agreed, belonged to the past. It had been unacceptable in not recognizing the dignity of man, but at least in theory there had been an element of responsibility. Capitalism had offered more scope to individuals of different social origin, but it was called ruthless, irresponsible, and unjust. "Equality of opportunity" was held to be no more than a sham in most cases. And moreover, capitalism had been inefficient in that it did not prevent poverty and unemployment. For these reasons, it was regarded as necessary to establish a new society, combining the best elements of previous ones while abolishing their injustices and irresponsibilities.

The reformers were basically idealists who believed as Rousseau did, in the natural goodness of man. They also shared with the Liberals—with whom they often cooperated in practice—an optimistic belief in almost unlimited progress, especially in continuing economic growth. Progress meant material, economic progress. This progress, in their opinion, had been held back by faulty institutions and by the capitalists' insistence on immediate profit. As Gustav Möller put it during the crisis of the 1930s: "No citizen should suffer need. We have sufficient powers of production, and it could only be because of bad will or insufficient organization that we should be unable to see to it that what is being created is sufficient for all."

It has already been said that the approach was pragmatic rather than ideological and that the aims were practical and immediate. Still, the ultimate goal was the creation of a classless society, not through violent struggle, but by raising the economic standards of the working class to the levels of the upper classes. For this purpose, it was essential that material security should be available to everybody. Elements other than material ones were sometimes referred to, but only in passing and more or less halfheartedly. To this extent the reformers were dialectical materialists in the Marxist tradition.

Material security was held to be valuable in itself as vastly improving personal well-being. This was natural to a generation that had looked stark poverty in the face. In addition, it was regarded as a prerequisite of responsible democratic government. To those who had seen the rise of Mussolini and Hitler, this also was practically self-evident. But security should not mean the disappearance of individual responsibility. One of the Swedish Social Democrats put it thus in a book dedicated to Gustav Möller. "Modern social welfare must aim at creating social security for citizens. But in realizing such a program, it is important not to neglect the claims on their personal responsibility." This remark was made by Bernhard Eriksson, a steel worker who had risen to be minister of social affairs and later speaker of one of the Houses in the Riksdag.

The welfare system should, consequently, follow the principles of help to self-help. Said Alva Myrdal in 1944: "It is just as logical that individuals, directly or by means of mutual insurance, should carry the main responsibility for risks during the productive part of their lives when the capacity for work could and should be the basis of their maintenance, as it is illogical to demand that they should carry such responsibilities during unproductive periods."

There was less interest in legislating for a minimum wage. Sydney Webb's idea of a "social minimum" was referred to in Denmark, but only as an argument in favor of social security. On the whole, it was regarded as the function of labor unions, rather than of politicians, to maintain an acceptable wage level.

All this, then, was practical, pragmatic, plausible. It was the very essence of reformism, or if one prefers the communist term, revisionism. It is interesting to note that the great Danish reformer K. K. Steincke had already in 1933 placed Fascists and Marxists on the same level: "Look at the pitiful enthusiasm of the upper classes for Fascism, and the equally foolish one of a small part of the lower classes for the dictatorship of the proletariat." Among other things, the policies of Social Democrat reformers were intended to give the lie to Marxist criticism of political democracy. Later in life, Steincke said of himself that he "never had anything like the same interest in politics as in legislation and administration." His system of social reform, he said, was "radical and conservative in the mixture necessary to avoid both reaction and Bolshevism." The policies of Scandinavian Social Democrats of those days involved repairing the defects of capitalist society rather than allowing it to continue, as Marx had assumed, on the road to catastrophe and revolution.

A consequence of this approach was that reforms had to be cautious and gradual, rather than bold and immediate. One of the Social Democratic economists closely allied to Gunnar Myrdal (Richard Sterner) wrote in 1944: "To make the standard of living rise as much as we want it to, it is indispensable that society does its part for rapidly making production more efficient." And in the same year, a Swedish labor union leader (Ragnar Casparsson) claimed that the Swedish union movement was "enormously" superior to that of Finland, not only because it had been able to organize workers more completely, but also "because Swedish industry is more highly developed and consequently able to pay higher wages." But other factors, he said, also had to be taken into consideration: "The unions are more likely to be successful if their program of action is in accord with the sense of justice of the general public. An organization operating without regard for the fundamental views of others could possibly achieve temporary success. But it can never become an important factor for general progress and social emancipation." Of Thorvald Stauning it was said that his views were always a little ahead of those of his contemporaries, but no more than to make it possible for him to pull them along.

It is futile to ask whether this was "socialism." Such purely semantic questions did not interest the Scandinavian reformers. They were *accused* of being Socialists by their opponents, but they took no special pride in the name. In fact, as often as not they insisted that their objectives should be acceptable to all sensible and responsible politicians, regardless of ideology. In this regard, they were similar to their British contemporaries, one of whom (Philip Snowden) used to say that he had been more influenced by the Sermon on the Mount than by Karl Marx.

The basic principles were humanitarian, and they could be applied in many different fields. Steincke quoted de Tocqueville and agreed that while poverty appears less and less evil to the mere observer the longer it is observed, it becomes worse and worse for those who suffer from it. And who could deny that it was desirable to abolish poverty and its consequences? Who could deny the merits of "social justice?"

Abolishing poverty and achieving social justice meant many different things. Housing standards were most unsatisfactory; the state and local units stepped in with new policies. Unemployment was a constant danger; employment policies and unemployment insurance made a considerable difference. Working hours were limited by law. Old age pensions had been introduced some time ago, but they were so low that they did not provide a living for those who had retired, and employers rarely provided pensions for their employees of the working classes. Health conditions were poor, and medical costs were often beyond the means of the common people. The answer was to continue along the lines of "socialized medicine," introduced earlier but never fully developed. In addition, the need for preventive medicine was increasingly recognized, especially in the case of children.

Also, there was a general feeling of insecurity in the working classes. It is interesting to see which elements of social reform were listed in the 1924 election platform of the Swedish Social Democrats. It included an improved system of workmen's compensation, health insurance, maternity insurance, unemployment insurance, old age and disability pensions, and industrial welfare. This was not all new, nor were the Social Democrats the only ones to advocate some of these reforms. But there is no doubting that such ideas loomed large in their minds.

The argument, however, was not exclusively humanitarian. It could also be said that reforms of this type could make society more efficient even from the point of view of industrial productivity.

This was particularly true in the case of economic policies. The reformers believed in the possibility—and desirability—of unlimited economic growth. In fact, growth in their opinion was hampered by the inefficiency of traditional "capitalist" policies. More equitable distribution of incomes and more expansive economic policies would, the reformers believed, stimulate the economy.

Their reasoning can be briefly summarized as follows. The existing productive strength of industry was not being used to full capacity because of insufficient demand. By increasing the buying power of the less favored elements of the population this could be corrected. Equally, unemployment involved waste of the most important means of production, human labor. Therefore, it was desirable to find employment, at normal wages, for unemployed workers by means of public or subsidized undertakings, even if this involved a temporary underbalancing of the state budget. Indeed, since one of the evils to combat was a *de*flationary trend in the economy, underbalancing—which had an *in*flationary effect—was desirable in itself. A significant element was housing. The building industry was important not only as a source of employment for laborers, but also in stimulating demand for other industrial products. And at the same time public activities in housing solved social problems by raising the standard of living of the common people. Another example was agricultural policies. Subsidizing agricultural production could make better foodstuffs available to the working classes, at the same time increasing the buying power of the agricultural population. And there was no need, it was agreed, to keep wages down in the circumstances of the 1920s and 1930s. On the contrary, the "economy of high wages" tended to increase productivity and efficiency in all different fields of industry.

Obviously, this is a simplification of the theory. It corresponded nicely with the policies J. M. Keynes recommended for a depression. In the case of a boom, contrary measures should have been adopted. But it should be remembered that the simplification was natural under the circumstances. There was a depression in the late 1920s and even more in the early 1930s, precisely when Scandinavian Social Democrats were putting their policies into effect. In this respect they used an approach similar to that of the New Deal in the United States, but somewhat earlier than Franklin Roosevelt was able to take action in the American economy. Moreover, in the 1930s autarchy rather than exchanges was characteristic of the world economic situation.

Other, less generally accepted arguments were also advanced. If the working population was relieved from material insecurity, it could be expected to concentrate more wholeheartedly on work and thus become more efficient. Material security for all would also facilitate planning for the best possible distribution of all social resources. Reducing working hours by no means necessarily meant reduction of work output. On the contrary, working time would be more efficiently used by the workers, while industry would be encouraged to introduce labor-saving devices and improve organization. Moreover, a working population enjoying material security and a reasonable amount of leisure time constituted the best possible foundation for responsible democracy. And strong labor unions with real influence, not only on wages but also on working conditions, could be expected to pursue responsible policies, avoiding strikes and lockouts.

This type of argument was particularly plausible in the fields of health and education. Universal health protection and access for all to good treatment in case of illness should make workers more efficient, and ultimately reduce the need for hospitalization. Such effects could be expected particularly in the development of preventive medicine. The same must be true of improved industrial safety measures.

The particular emphasis in the 1920s and 1930s was on social insurance. As early as 1926, Gustav Möller wrote: "From the point of view of Social Democrats, after the realization of universal suffrage, nothing can be more urgent than to create a system of social insurance giving a real sense of security to the citizens of the country. . . . *Such a system will be satisfactory only if it prevents destitution from crossing the threshold of homes where illness, accidents, old age, or unemployment have made their entry.*" And the benefits provided for this purpose should be given as of right, not as charity. Indeed, this was a fundamental principle of all modern Scandinavian welfare systems. Its *rationale* was respect for the integrity of all citizens, even the most destitute.

The Danish system of social insurance, adopted in the beginning of the 1930s on the initiative of K. K. Steincke and based on ideas presented by him ten years earlier, was compulsory and based on health insurance, old age pensions, and a number of other integral benefits. It was highly controversial almost from the beginning and made its author one of the most hated men in Denmark, primarily because the element of compulsion was at that time not generally accepted by the public. But in retrospect the most important novelty of the system was that it was universal, and not—as in most other Western countries—limited to wage earners and salaried employees.

In Sweden the system developed differently. Health insurance remained voluntary for a long time, and the same was true of most other parts of the social insurance system. This did not mean, however, that the cost was borne exclusively by the insured themselves and their employers. The state and the local units subsidized the insurance organizations to a considerable extent, not only by taking care wholly or in part of their administrative expenses, but also by contributions to the actual benefits. Thus their members were entitled to receive more than what could be calculated on the basis of their own fees. This idea was at the time more widely accepted by the public than was compulsory participation, but nevertheless there was always a tendency for the lowest income groups to remain outside the arrangement, since they tended to regard even relatively low fees as beyond their capacities. As a consequence, the Swedish system developed along lines similar to those in Denmark, although for a long time without the administrative simplicity characterizing the Danish plan.

In the middle of the 1930s the "population question" came into focus in Scandinavia, especially in Sweden and largely as a result of contributions to the debate by Alva and Gunnar Myrdal. Swedish birth rates had been falling since the end of the First World War, clearly because of more widespread use of contraceptives. Traditionally this was regarded by Radicals as a good thing, while Conservatives deplored it. But the Myrdals changed the ideological pattern, pointing out that the composition of the population was likely to change in a manner unfavorable to the development of a balanced social and economic structure. The reason for the fall in the birth rate, they argued, was the insecure and otherwise unsatisfactory situation of families in modern industrialized society. Only by giving families greater security against unemployment, by improving their housing standards, by relieving parents of a considerable part of their economic responsibility for children, and by taking measures for the benefit particularly of smaller children, could society hope to reverse the unfortunate trend.

The population question became a motivating force for developing social welfare and for increasing the responsibilities of the public sector. One of the novelties introduced as a result of this debate was universal child subventions. It was characteristic of the new plan of welfare and social security that benefits should be made universal rather than selective. A system of steeply progressive taxes made it possible to follow this line without danger of injustice. Millionaires and paupers alike received child subventions for their offspring, but the millionaires paid practically all of it back again in taxes.

At a slightly later stage, mainly after the Second World War, education came into the picture. Broadening educational facilities should not only give personal satisfaction, but also—in line with the traditional attitude about education in Scandinavia—be directly productive. Educated people could be expected to work more efficiently in all fields, but more important, an equitable system that would abolish all economic barriers to higher education should improve recruitment in the "intellectual classes." Society could make better use of the capacities of all its members by mobilizing the "intelligence reserves," those who had the ability but had been denied the opportunity to educate themselves beyond the compulsory school minimum.

It should not be imagined that these new policies were from the first acclaimed by all groups in society. On the contrary, in Denmark, Sweden, Norway, and later in Finland, there was—as has been pointed out in a preceding chapter—considerable opposition from non-Socialist parties and their supporters. But this opposition was directed less against the general principles of welfare than against specific features, such as Denmark's compulsory system of social insurance or the new unemployment relief policies in Sweden. Considerable parts of the new legislation were adopted more or less unanimously in Nordic legislatures, and the controversy that did arise was often limited to details, such as whether old age pensions should vary with the cost of living in different parts of the country.

Some negative arguments of a more general nature were of course advanced. It was occasionally said that social security and welfare benefits encouraged people to be lazy. How could they be made to work sufficiently hard if they were able to survive in any case? It was also argued that the welfare system itself (like other economic policies based on interventionism) was a danger to the freedom of the individual and consequently, a hamper to economic development. Criticisms of this type were voiced intermittingly, but it does not appear that they really took hold either in the 1930s or in the period following the Second World War.

Much more important was the question of economic resources. Prosperity had come late to Scandinavia, and caution about public expenditure was a strong political tradition in all its constituent countries. There was genuine fear that expansive and expensive social policies were beyond the means of societies that until only recently had been among the poorest in the Western world. Such fears were manifested at nearly every point when the new welfare system was being introduced. But it is clear that such objections were directed less against its principles than against attempts to realize it speedily. Also, to the extent that the fears proved again and again to have been unjustified (because of the fortunate development of the economies), it came to be assumed that resources were indeed much more plentiful than before and could be expected to grow to such an extent that the main problem would no longer be their further expansion, but their allocation among different social groups.

As a result, the idea of the "welfare state" became generally, if not universally, accepted in all the Nordic countries, regardless of political affiliations. As a matter of fact, public opinion developed more rapidly than the opinion of politicans outside the Social Democratic parties. Critics of social security proposals were apt time and again to lose ground in the next political election, and this was probably the most important factor contributing to the more or less permanent predominance of Social Democrats in Scandinavian politics. Other parties learned the lesson, if often belatedly, and became increasingly eager to show that they were no less "progressive" than their opponents.

It can, of course, be questioned whether such acceptance of the ideas of the "welfare state" was real or only a matter of expediency. But even if the latter was at first the case, in the long run the new order came to be regarded as a natural characteristic of the Scandinavian way of life. And it can hardly be denied, even by the most "bourgeois" of observers, that this was largely because Social Democrats in the Nordic countries had been careful never to move too far ahead of public opinion.

In addition, it should be remembered that the ideas of "social justice" and of interventionist public policies in the welfare field were part of traditions existing long before the Social Democrats came into power. Moreover, Labor Cabinets were often temporarily (or even more or less permanently) supported by one or more non-Socialist parties such as Radical Liberals in Denmark and Agrarians in Sweden.

The experiences of the Second World War strengthened these tendencies. Denmark and Norway were occupied by the German Nazis, and people of all shades of political opinion, from Conservatives to Communists, cooperated in their resistance movements. In Sweden and Finland, national governments were formed, excluding the Communists but including all other major parties. The habit of cooperation across party lines in circumstances of stress and under the threat of catastrophe made for mutual understanding and also for recognition of the need for equitable distribution of the social product among all classes of society.

Thus, by the end of the Second World War—and even more definitely in the decade immediately following it—there was no longer any group of importance in Scandinavia which did not accept the basic principles of the "welfare state." Such disagreement as appeared for instance in the 1950s was related to the means of its realization, not to its aims.

Social Security
and Social Engineering

The social security systems of the Nordic countries are not identical. Denmark, as has already been pointed out, was the pioneer, and especially in the early stages the solutions chosen there were sometimes copied by others. But already before the Second World War Sweden had advanced as far as Denmark, and not infrequently along different lines. Having said that, it is equally important to emphasize that on the whole Scandinavians do approach the main problems in the same way, and quite often it should be enough to describe the system of one of the countries as being fairly representative of all four. This is particularly so because of the important role played by investigating committees, which often cooperate across national boundaries. When a comprehensive report has been prepared in one of the countries, its conclusions influence public debate and legislation in the others. Sometimes reports of one country are even more or less completely copied by its neighbors.

Some differences between the systems are purely technical or related to the administrative structure. The level of compensation may also differ considerably from country to country, and there are even some differences of approaches and ambitions. To the extent that such differences seem to relate to the principles of social security and welfare, they will be noted here. However, the purpose is not to provide a handbook of social service benefits but to discuss the problems of the welfare state, and from this point of view most differences are irrelevant. Thus it is frequently unnecessary to give full accounts of the systems applied in each of the countries.

Yet some divergencies appear to be more substantial, at least for the time being—development has not always proceeded at the same pace in all four countries. Moreover, recent changes in the structure of the economies, as in other Western European countries, have not applied equally or at the same time in all the Nordic countries.

Declaratory statements in social legislation are to some extent characteristic. Most traditional is that of Finland's law of social assistance: municipalities are bound to give such assistance to persons who would otherwise be unable to receive necessary maintenance and care. The Norwegian formula is similar. Assistance *should* be given to persons who are unable to maintain a decent livelihood or to take care of themselves, but *may* also be supplied to persons who are compelled to adapt themselves to a difficult situation. The corresponding rule in Denmark is that those who need advice or economic or practical assistance because of their own situation or that of their families should be given support for their development, for the re-establishment of their earning capacity, or for care, special treatment, or education. And the new Swedish law of social service, passed in 1980, goes further. The aim should be not only to establish economic and social security but also to contribute to equality in living conditions and active participation in the life of society.

Apart from such more or less ideological differences, it can be said that some fundamental principles are common to the social security systems all over Scandinavia. Benefits are to be provided as a right, not as charity. For this reason, the most important parts of the system comprise universal rather than selective services, and these are largely provided automatically when certain conditions are fulfilled, without requiring any request from the recipient. The ambition is that it should be complete, so that no one should fall between the meshes of the welfare network. Only by this means, it is presumed, can citizens receive that absolute or almost absolute economic security which is regarded as one of the characteristics of the welfare state.

Security for what and against what? Is poverty the problem? If so, against what standards is poverty to be measured? In the Nordic countries (and most industrialized countries of Western Europe today), poverty in the sense of absolute destitution no longer exists. It is primarily because of general economic advance but in part also thanks to the development of welfare states that it has disappeared. But new concepts have also come into use. It is not unusual today to speak of "relative" poverty, meaning the lack of those amenities, for instance in housing, that are regarded as normal by most people. Poverty in this sense can of course never be completely abolished, for as the general standard of living rises, so does the level below which only "the poor" are able to exist.

Another objective, closely connected with the idea of "relative" poverty, is that of social peace. In a sense, this is the Marxist attitude: social problems are held to be unavoidable in a capitalistic society; social policies may prevent or postpone the collapse of capitalism. A prominent Danish Social Democrat, Ritt Bjerregaard, who was minister for social affairs at the time of this writing, has said that the function of social policy is to "mitigate the wrongs of capitalism and hide the causes of conflict in society"—while there can be no question of abolishing the underlying conflicts—since without effective social policies "we shall not be able to guarantee public peace and order." If differences between the haves and the have-nots become too great and too evident, she apparently argues, a revolutionary situation will arise. For obvious reasons, the operative word here is "differences." History indicates that the really destitute are usually not very active revolutionaries, but the reverse applies to those who without being destitute believe that they are the victims of grave injustices. The implication is that the haves also may profit from social policies aimed primarily at providing benefits to the have-nots. This may be the case in regard to certain labor market policies. The system of compulsory occupational injury insurance, for instance, relieves employers of liabilities which they might otherwise incur more directly and which could prove particularly onerous for small enterprises. Also, it has been pointed out by a British observer (Dorothy Wilson) that employers probably benefit from the vocational bias of much of the Swedish educational system, since this at least gives them a good basis on which to build their own training programs for new employees.

If, on the other hand, equality is regarded as the overall objective, there is no denying that a great number of problems arise. One of them relates to aliens. All the Nordic countries, and in particular Sweden, have received a considerable number of immigrants since

1945, both as refugees and as "guest workers." But neither in regard to civil rights nor when it comes to social benefits are they put on a wholly equal footing with citizens of the host country. An exception is inter-Scandinavian migrants, against whom there is in principle very little legal discrimination. But this is in consequence of specific mutual agreements, and for instance Danish law expressly stipulates that such agreements are a condition of equal treatment.

By international standards, all four Nordic countries can now be called affluent. As in other industrialized countries, one of the consequences of affluence has been an increase in the percentage of the GNP expended on social services, together with a rise in the level of what is regarded as the minimum standard of living. But there are indications of more fundamental changes. The emphasis is increasingly on equality, probably because in the new circumstances, those of rich or even very rich societies, it appeared to "progressive" social reformers that the very concept of minimum standards was no longer a sufficient ambition. Again, the most typical example is Sweden. On the other hand, with the new and surprisingly unexpected economic difficulties that have surfaced in the 1970s and 1980s, it remains to be seen whether social policies may not again become a little less ambitious.

Social insurance is, of course, the basic element in the security system. It aims at covering certain definite risks, such as illness, accidents at work, unemployment, or old age. All Scandinavian countries have developed extensive systems of such insurance.

The traditional concept was that the insured should themselves pay reasonable fees, which, however, should be lower than what could be required by ordinary actuarial calculations. The difference could be covered out of tax revenues. In some cases (originally industrial injuries only), the fees were to be paid by employers, and then normal actuarial calculations would apply. The idea behind this system was that the payment of fees should make it clear that the insured had a legal right to the stipulated benefits. The benefits would on the one hand go beyond what the individual had the means to secure by his or her own resources, while on the other hand they should not relieve the insured of personal responsibility. Nonpayment of fees, if caused by neglect, would involve reduction or even complete cessation of benefits.

As it turned out, the major part of the costs often came out of tax revenues, the fees paid by the insured being of symbolical rather than financial importance. For this reason, there was a growing tendency to dispense with such fees in order to reduce administrative work. On the other hand, the Scandinavian countries are gradually approaching the system prevalent on the Western European continent, where employers' contributions cover a large part of the costs. One argument in favor of this change is that in many cases, such as those of occupational injury and unemployment, employers actually benefit from the fact that their employees are insured. Otherwise they might themselves be held legally or at least morally responsible.

The level of compensation is usually not related to fees paid by either the insured or their employers. In Sweden, it is estimated to range from 100 percent of the normal income in the case of occupational injuries to 65 percent (up to a certain maximum level) for old age pensions in the ATP system of supplementary pensions. Similar or slightly lower levels apply in the other Nordic countries. In certain circumstances, where insurance benefits appear to be manifestly inadequate, supplementary payments can be made through other channels.

To the extent that fees paid by employers or by the insured do not cover costs, financing comes out of tax revenues, from the state, from counties, or from municipalities. Taking social service expenditures as a whole, and including also those falling outside the insurance system, we see that in Sweden about 40 percent of the total comes out of state revenues, 30 percent out of county and municipal revenues, and 30 percent out of fees, mainly from employers. For the other countries no similar estimates are available, but it is likely that fees play a somewhat more important role in Denmark and Norway, while municipal participation is more strongly emphasized in Finland.

Health insurance is administered by local authorities under supervision from the central government. Coverage includes free hospitalization, or treatment as outpatients in hospital or otherwise by doctors or nurses free of charge or at low fees. Pharmaceuticals are free or provided at low cost. The insurance system also provides for sickness benefits in cash.

Details of the system vary considerably from one country to another, but the fundamental principles are the same. Insurance is compulsory and covers not only wage and salary earners but the population as a whole, including children and pensioners. It is independent of payments by the insured, but cash benefits relate to the estimated loss of income caused by ill-health. The majority of hospitals are operated by counties or municipalities, but some are run by the state. Private hospitals exist, but especially in Sweden their number is very small and the number of their patients comparatively even smaller.

There is considerable discussion about the effects and merits of this very comprehensive system and the very liberal benefits granted. On the one hand, it is argued that it improves the health of the population as a whole, prolongs their working life, and reduces the loss of working hours by illness. On the other hand, it is said to be abused by unscrupulous persons who unnecessarily report themselves ill, thus creating problems of absenteeism. This criticism has been particularly vocal in Sweden, where benefits have been paid out from the first day of illness without any requirement of doctors' certificates except in cases where the absence exceeds a certain fixed period of time.

On the whole, both arguments appear to be exaggerated. It is true that the life-span has increased, but this applies in all industrialized countries and a great number of others as well. There are no real indications that the health of the population has improved more in Scandinavia than for instance in Japan, where no comprehensive health insurance system is in existence. In fact, absence from work by reason of reported illness increased rather than diminished up to the last few years. Conversely, recent studies indicate that this absenteeism is not to any major extent the result of actual abuse, but rather of a tendency to stay at home not only for major illnesses but also for common colds and similar diseases—which may be sensible, as they are usually contagious and reduce work efficiency.

Occupational injury insurance has existed for a long time and has taken the place of workers' compensation, the duty of employers themselves to pay compensation directly to workers for injury sustained at work. Consequently it is financed entirely out of fees paid by employers and applies mainly to wage and salary earners, although self-employed persons are entitled to voluntary participation. It covers accidents at work, including certain illnesses caused by working conditions. In Finland and in Sweden it also covers accidents occurring on the way to and from the place of work. Especially in Sweden, occupational injury insurance is coordinated with the general health insurance system.

The most important consequences of replacing workers' compensation with a compulsory insurance system are that employees remain covered regardless of the economic strength of their employer and that costly law suits are avoided. It is true that the administration is cumbersome, and in more complicated cases it may take a long time before compensation is actually paid, while a generous employer might have been willing to act more expeditiously. But many employers are either unwilling or unable to show generosity; security is regarded as more important than speed; and after all, the administrative efficiency may improve. There is no real criticism of the system as such, although individual cases are often taken up by the press and other mass media.

Old age pensions form the largest part of social expenditure. It can be debated whether they should really be considered part of the social insurance system, since they are not financed in the same way as its other parts, but from the point of view of the beneficiaries there is little difference.

Pensions are caluclated in three parts. There is a basic pension, which is in principle roughly the same amount for all pensioners. Second, there are *additional* pensions for those who have no income or only a small income in addition to the basic pension. And finally there are *supplementary* pensions based on income earned during the active period of life. Those who receive full supplementary pensions are of course not entitled to any additional pensions.

The basic and additional pensions are financed out of state and local revenues, the supplementary pensions out of fees from employers. The amounts of the pensions are to a greater or smaller extent related to changes in the cost of living. These amounts vary from country to country. In Sweden most people, except those who used to earn incomes well above the average, would receive basic plus supplementary pensions equivalent to two-thirds of the average income during the fifteen "best years" of their working life. The percentage is somewhat lower in the three other countries, and there are other differences as well. Fundamentally, however, the systems are similar. Thus, the idea is to provide a minimum income for all pensioners, so as to protect them against abject poverty, while also letting them maintain a standard of living and a style of life more or less similar to what they were used to during their working lives. At the same time, it is assumed that the needs of a pensioner are somewhat more limited than those of a person in the workforce.

When the pensions systems were established, they were sometimes criticized on the ground that the effect would be a reduction in private savings. But it is very difficult to say whether the pensions system has had any appreciable impact on the propensity to private savings. On the face of it, no such effect has been ascertained. On the other hand, income levels rose rapidly in the same years as those in which present pensions systems were established, and it is of course quite conceivable that this would have resulted in higher proportions of private savings if old age security had not been guaranteed by the pensions. However, this can be no more than a likely or unlikely hypothesis.

In addition to the old age pensions provided as an element of social security, there can be voluntary supplementary pensions provided either by agreement with employers or by insurance companies in accordance with normal actuarial calculations. This possibility exists in all four countries but is perhaps of particular importance in Denmark and Finland.

Pensions other than old age pensions are provided for the physically or mentally disabled, for orphans or children with only one living parent, as well as for widows. By and large, pensions of this type are similar to the basic old age pensions. However, there are considerable differences between the four countries as to both their amounts and the calculations of relevant income.

Unemployment insurance, finally, is very different in each of the four countries. It is compulsory and provides universal coverage in Norway while it is at least in principle voluntary in the three others. On the other hand, unemployment insurance societies in these countries are closely related to the labor unions, and union members are generally supposed to take out this type of insurance. Since labor is very well organized in all Scandinavian countries, this means that most wage and salary earners are insured, while the self-employed are usually not. Those young persons who have not yet held any regular employment also remain outside the system. Financing is achieved by a combination of fees from the insured and their employers, on the one hand, and subsidies out of state revenues, on the other. In this respect, voluntary unemployment insurance corresponds most closely to the former system of social insurance referred to above.

In addition to unemployment insurance, there are other forms of unemployment benefits, except of course in Norway, where the insurance gives universal coverage. Financing of these benefits is accomplished by state revenues. They are particularly important to young persons who have not yet managed to find employment. Consequently they have come to play a greater part in recent years.

Unemployment is a condition with very serious social implications apart from purely economic need. Thus, so-called labor market policies aiming at creating, although artificially, employment opportunities in times of general or local recessions have come to be regarded as increasingly important. Even more important is the efficiency of the employment exchange systems and arrangements facilitating the mobility and retraining of workers. While these devices do not form part of the social insurance system, they are not unrelated to it. It is through the employment exchanges that opportunities for employment or rehabilitation are brought to the knowledge of persons seeking employment, but exchanges also are expected to provide necessary controls to ensure that insurance and other benefits are not paid out to those who neglect to make an effort to find employment. During periods of full or overfull employment these controls often became inoperative. Unemployment figures were low; it was possible to pick and choose employment; and employment exchanges found it difficult to insist on acceptance of just the jobs that they were able to offer at a given time. These tendencies did not entirely disappear when the situation changed, and although unemployment has become a much more serious problem than before in all four countries, there is still, especially in Sweden, the possibility that available jobs will be difficult to fill if the location or type of work is unattractive to those seeking employment or if they are not combined with suitable offers of housing and other amenities.

Difficulties of this type may be one of the reasons that only Norway, and not the three other countries, has introduced compulsory unemployment insurance. Such a system is, however, being seriously considered especially in Sweden, but also in Denmark and Finland. It may be inexpedient to attempt to establish it during a recession, but if conditions improve this may well be one of the first social reforms to be launched.

A number of social benefits are frankly gratuitous. However, it is not always easy to distinguish these from general measures, such as labor policy devices, on the one hand, and social insurance on the other. As has already been pointed out, some of them are simply intended to supplement social insurance. Others take the form of subsidies to various private organizations, such as study circles or sports associations, for services of presumed value from the standpoint of social welfare and policy. Another type of assistance that has been most controversial in a number of countries is fiscal benefits—tax reduc- tions for specific groups—but they have not been of major importance in Scandinavia, except perhaps in Denmark. On the other hand, cash benefits are often exempt from tax. This is one of the elements which together with steeply progressive taxes complicate the picture when the benefits are related to the taxable income of recipients, since it makes for serious "threshold effects" when incomes pass a certain level.

In the case of the *mentally and physically disabled*, the pension system provides the basic benefits. Certain cash benefits outside the system are also available. But perhaps the most important welfare element for this category of persons is rehabilitation and—in the most serious cases—institutional care. Here, the approach differs from country to country, and the level of efficiency even differs between municipal and regional agencies in the same country. It can hardly be said that any one of the Nordic countries has developed a consis- tent policy in this field, and isolated cases of serious abuse still occur from time to time.

Organizations of the physically disabled constitute comparatively active pressure groups, and especially in Sweden they have been in- sisting that their problems should be solved with the help of state and other public revenues without any major participation of volun- tary welfare organizations and agencies. Moreover, they demand— with varying success—that practical arrangements should be made to enable the disabled to lead a normal life, both privately and in their places of employment. The mentally disabled, on the other hand, are obviously in no position to exercise similar pressure, and it can hard- ly be denied that their position in society is a serious blur on the escutcheon of the Scandinavian welfare states.

A type of gratuitous subsidy that takes a sizable part of public revenues consists of *food subventions*. All Scandinavian countries are in the habit of making such subventions from time to time and of varying amounts. For some reason, however, they are seen as an element not of social but of agricultural policy. They are general subsidies not restricted to certain categories of consumers or graded according to income. They are undoubtedly of general social importance, since they cause a considerable reduction in the price of basic provisions which carry particular weight in the case of families with children. Another effect is that the consumer price index is kept down, which in turn affects the level of such wages and salaries, pensions and other benefits whose amounts are related to the index. But above all, they make it possible to maintain domestic agricultural production at a level that would guarantee a reasonable food supply even in times of war or danger of war. It is therefore sometimes jokingly suggested that food subventions should be considered part of the defense budget.

The greatest spending on social security, apart from old age pensions, is for children, and the most important part of that sector is *child subventions.* Such subventions, for children below the age of sixteen years (in Denmark eighteen years), in cash and taxfree, are provided by all four countries. Moreover, additional subventions are available for special categories of children, such as orphans, children of single parents and of pensioners, and so on. In Sweden, the maximum age for receiving child subventions is raised from sixteen to eighteen years if the recipient continues to go to school. Pensioners with children receive an augmented basic pension. Fiscal benefits in the form of tax reduction are allowed in Finland and Norway and to a relatively small extent also in the two other countries.

The introduction of child subventions in cash was originally justified largely on the grounds of population policies: the idea was to stimulate population growth. But already from the beginning there was also a more direct social motivation, namely, to improve living conditions for children and to assist families with children, whose standard of living generally tends to be appreciably lower than that of childless families. The latter motive has increasingly come to supersede the former even where the amount of subventions rises with the number of children in the family. In fact, it still appears to be true that families with several small children are definitely less well off than those who have none or only a single child.

Another important but to some extent controversial form of

benefits to families with children is that of *collective child care*: daycare centers, "latchkey" facilities (which provide care after school hours), and so on. In these institutions, parents pay a fee, but this covers only a minor part of the cost and the amount sometimes varies on the basis of the income of the parents. Such institutions are particularly widespread in Sweden, although even there demand far exceeds available accommodation.

Controversy over these institutions covers a number of problems. From one point of view, they are motivated by the interests of parents rather than those of children: they make it easier for both parents to be gainfully employed. Other arrangements, such as cooperation among several families, could serve the same purpose, but these are usually more costly for the individual and may not be subsidized by the public. On the other hand, as long as the available accommodation does not correspond to demand, those parents who are unable to find room for their children in daycare centers or other facilities, but who—as taxpayers—still have to contribute to the upkeep of the institutions, are apt to regard the arrangements as inequitable.

From the point of view of the children themselves, it is argued that participation in such an institution is educationally useful and develops habits of social contact. On the other hand, it is claimed that because of high personnel turnover and other failings the daycare centers fall short of their objective and become no more than warehouses for the storage of children. Critics also maintain that children who spend most of their day in institutions of this type are deprived of the feeling of security created in a family and tend to become rootless.

Another form of collective benefits for children is *the school lunch program*. When the program was first introduced, it was on the basis of observations indicating that the eating habits of many families were unsuitable for growing children. Today this argument is less valid, but in families where both parents are working away from home — and these are the majority—children may still fail to receive suitable nourishment in the middle of the day. At the same time it cannot be denied that some children are apt not to avail themselves of the meal provided at school, especially when this is less palatable than nourishing, that considerable waste is taking place, and that school lunchrooms are frequently both noisy and otherwise unattractive.

In connection with *childbirth*, special subsidies are paid, in Norway and Sweden within the health insurance system but with fixed amounts, in Denmark and Finland independently of the insurance but according to similar principles. In Denmark the subsidy is available only to persons below a certain income level. Probably more important are the free medical examinations of future mothers and small children; these, however, can be regarded as part of the health insurance system.

In the case of children living with only one parent although the other parent is also alive, *child support payments* frequently are in arrears. This used to cause serious hardship both after a divorce and in the case of children of unmarried mothers. All Nordic countries now provide for maintenance subsidies, from the state and/or the respective municipalities, which, however, are entitled to recover their expenses from the negligent parent. Until the years of the First World War, drastic measures were in force for recoverage, such as imprisonment in workhouses. These have been discontinued, and in fact a considerable part of the cost is never recovered and thus is financed from public revenues. There are also other special social arrangements for *single-parent families*, which are much more exposed to economic difficulties than others.

Free education is a Scandinavian tradition of long standing. But there is nowadays no agreement on what should be understood by "free" in this context. It used to mean that there were no tuition fees or only extremely low fees which could be remitted in case of need. But should we stop here, or does free education also include subsistence during the time of study?

Scandinavian students were less accustomed than those of the United States or even of Germany to "work their way" through schools and universities, partly because so many of them came from well-to-do families that were ready to pay for their upkeep, while the others were able to maintain themselves by means of scholarships and loans. This was acceptable as long as the student population was small; "well-to-do" families really had money to spare; and graduation normally could be expected to open the way to relatively well-paying jobs. In all these respects the situation has changed: the student population has grown considerably, and available incomes for different social strata have become far more equal. It is therefore logical to include students' benefits, and not only the absence of tuition fees, among the advantages offered by the welfare state. Thus there are special arrangements for children and youths who continue their studies beyond the compulsory school system.

Housing is closely related to welfare, and in all the Nordic countries public housing policies over the last fifty years have developed more or less pronounced welfare elements. Rent control also has been justified chiefly with arguments based on social policy.

There have, however, been other important arguments as well. So-called Socialist tendencies, as distinct from social policy, have been characteristic of housing policies. Both national and municipal governments often have favored public rather than private ownership of dwellings. By the same token, rent control has been motivated not only by the desire to keep rents down for the needy, but also by the anxiety to prevent excess profits and speculation by the rich. It is often difficult to ascertain where one motive ends and the other begins.

There are two distinctly different items in public expenditure for subsidizing housing. One consists of general credits and subsidies granted to facilitate housing construction and major repairs regardless of who is to use the dwellings. The other one is based on the needs of tenants themselves. An intermediate type is credits given for the reconstruction of existing dwellings in order to adapt them to use by disabled persons.

The first type of housing subsidy has been particularly prevalent in Norway and Sweden, although by no means unimportant in the two other countries either. At least in the first two nations, most blocks of apartments and a considerable part of the separate or semidetached houses as well were constructed with the help of public grants, often by the municipalities themselves or by municipally owned companies. At one time there was talk of "the socialized housing market." Even in blocks under private ownership, rents are usually determined by what has been agreed in the case of publicly owned dwellings. Both for this reason and also because rent control measures remained in force for a comparatively long time after the war, rents remained low at least in Sweden. But in the long run credits and subsidies have lost some of their effect and rents have had to be raised considerably even in publicly owned dwellings. To some extent this is also the result of high standards of quality and equipment of dwellings. There is now considerable discontent, and tenants' organizations have had little success fighting not only private landlords but also public agencies and publicly owned companies in order to keep rents down. The whole system has become controversial, partly because it is very expensive, while there is no certainty that it will benefit those who are in real need of subsidies more than others.

A special problem is that of condemnation and clearance of tenements. Particularly in the affluent years of the 1960s and 1970s there was a prevalent tendency to insist that only the best housing was good enough and thus to tear down old houses which, though still serviceable in a modest way, did not correspond to current requirements. The new houses built in their place invariably called for much higher rents, which neither previous tenants nor young people in search of independent living quarters were willing or even able to pay. And modernization of old houses was no more satisfactory: often it even proved more costly than the construction of new ones.

In all four countries direct housing subventions are available to two categories of people: pensioners and families with children. In most cases they are provided for apartments, but at least in Sweden they can be granted for separate or semi-detached houses also. They are based on the assessed incomes of tenants and are calculated to benefit only those who would otherwise be unable to enjoy satisfactory housing standards. But there have been complaints that in their present form they are liable to be abused, so that even persons and families who would easily be able to pay out of their own pocket for suitable housing manage to have it subsidized from public revenues. Moreover dogmatic advocates of universal as against selective benefits sometimes maintain that the housing subventions run counter to the principles of modern social policies.

As has been made clear above, some benefits are entirely general in character; for example, child subventions are provided for all parents regardless of their income. Others are selective insofar as they are made available only to those below certain income levels. They may also be negatively proportionate to incomes. This is true for instance of the housing subsidies just referred to. Fees for collective child care may also be regulated according to income.

These benefits not only are given as of right, but also are based on formal and easily ascertainable qualifications. Yet there will always be cases that have to be treated on an individual basis. They are supposed to be taken care of by *social assistance*, which is administered by municipal authorities after more or less thorough investigation of individual circumstances. The actual cost of this part of social security is comparatively very low, even though it goes up during times of serious unemployment. In Sweden it can be estimated at approximately 1 or possibly 2 percent of what is expended for social welfare as a whole. Yet it is highly controversial and criticized from different sides.

Some critics maintain that the authorities are too generous, that social assistance is given in cases where it is not really necessary, and especially that it is given to drunkards, narcotics addicts, criminals, and prostitutes who are held to be unworthy of using up taxpayers' money. This attitude is rather widespread—in spite of the small importance to taxpayers of social assistance expenditures; notwithstanding that rehabilitation of the persons in question cannot take place without expending public revenues; and regardless of the fact that most social assistance is actually given not to asocial elements of this type, but to perfectly ordinary and law-abiding citizens in temporary difficulties.

From the other side, social assistance is criticized because it necessitates humiliating disclosure to the authorities of the private life of applicants and also because of the "stigma" attached to receiving this kind of help. "To be on social assistance" is according to this view often still taken, although without justification, to indicate improvidence, lack of responsibility, and lack of capacity for independent maintenance.

There is no doubt that the latter attitudes frequently appeared even rather recently and that persons in need sometimes refrained from applying for social assistance for this reason. Studies performed as late as the 1960s indicated that even then such inhibitions were common. Whether this is still true is more doubtful. Although no serious investigations have taken place, it may well be—but it is by no means certain!—that those who were born after World War II are less sensitive in this respect than their parents.

Social welfare is not exclusively concerned with the distribution of funds from public revenues or private charity. There is also the important element of *regulatory and curative* measures, which from many points of view can be regarded as equally expressive of public concern over social problems.

In the case of institutional social care, for instance in daycare centers and "latchkey" institutions, homes for the aged, etc., as well as in schools, where the responsibility rests with municipal or regional authorities, there can be comparatively great differences in standards. Especially in Sweden there has been a tendency to try to ward off such differences by central regulations and controls. In recent times, local self-government has begun to insist on greater independence. To some extent this is a result of the increasing scarcity of resources: local bodies have complained that the central administration compels them to increase expenditures in order to comply with ambitious regulations, at the same time insisting on strict economy. But there are also other causes. In Scandinavia, as elsewhere, there is growing impatience with administrative centralization, and this has its effects in the field of social welfare as well as elsewhere.

New attitudes toward sex together with the increasing independence of women has led all Scandinavian countries to legalize abortions, at first only after rigorous controls and for specific reasons, but later wholly or almost wholly at the will of pregnant women, provided only that pregnancy is not too far advanced. The legislative changes in question did not arouse great opposition when they were introduced, partly because illegal abortions were not unusual and involved serious danger to the health of women. Recently there has been some talk of reintroducing more restrictive policies, but prevalent opinion seems to be that the liberal system should be maintained. And this opinion is by no means limited to politically radical groups. It is interesting to note that in Norway the Conservative party, which came into power with a minority government in 1981, steadfastly refused to bind their members to support the abolition of free abortions although this was the condition stipulated by the Christian Peoples party for a coalition that would have transformed the minority into a comfortable anti-Socialist majority.

Another form of regulation is control of prices, rents, and so on. This was widespread during the war years and for some time afterward, but in the long run there have been increasing doubts about its efficiency. In its more pronounced and permanent forms it encourages black marketing, and even when only temporarily applied it tends to result in no more than a retardation of developments which may eventually prove unavoidable. On the other hand, all Scandinavian countries have taken measures to supervise prices and rents and to discourage speculative ventures, as well as to protect the interests of consumers and tenants. In the field of housing, tenants' organizations are very active. And although there is no real consumers' movement of the American type, consumers' cooperatives are extremely important and by their competition attempt not without success to keep prices down and maintain quality requirements for both provisions and permanent consumer goods.

Educational and medical services, as has been pointed out before, are mainly in the hands of public authorities. To the very small extent that private schools, private hospitals, and private doctors still remain active, they are subject to far going regulations and controls, both in regard to the quality of their services and in regard to their fees. Private doctors and dentists are usually associated with the health insurance system, which means that the direct fees of patients remain at a low level.

Child welfare and youth welfare form another that is dominated by regulatory controls. A minor example is holiday camps, which are sometimes organized by municipalities but to some extent also by private organizations. In the latter case they are often subsidized by the public authorities and always subject to administrative rules and supervision. It is generally agreed that activities of this type should not be operated for commercial gain. The principles of the child and youth welfare systems in Scandinavia are on the whole not very different from those obtaining in most other countries. Basically, of course, the idea is that children and other very young persons are unable to accept full responsibility for themselves, and that while this responsibility should in most cases rest with their parents, there are exceptions, not very infrequent, where society has to step in. This happens not only in the case of orphans but also to some extent with children of single parents, as well as when children are maltreated by their parents, when parents can be expected to exercise an influence which is not acceptable from the standpoint of the norms of society, and when children or youths are wayward or outright delinquent. In the last-named case, the functions of welfare authorities relate to the fact that those below a certain age are exempt from criminal prosecution and that even youths beyond that age should not normally be sent to prison. The relevant age limits are fifteen (in Finland sixteen) and eighteen years; in Sweden certain measures can also be taken by the social authorities in the case of youths up to the age of twenty or even twenty-three years. None of the countries has experimented with children's courts. The authorities charged with child and youth welfare are primarily local boards, elected in the usual way by municipal councils on a political basis.

In Denmark, child and youth welfare is financed out of state revenues, but in the other three countries municipalities are expected to assume most of the financial burden. Control is invariably exercised by regional and central state agencies, which may sometimes employ judicial procedures. The ordinary courts have no jurisdiction in child or youth welfare cases, although in a criminal case against a young person above the age of fifteen (sixteen) they may decide—in the words of the criminal code—to "hand them over to the social agency for care in accordance with the child welfare legislation."

Different types of action can be taken by child and youth welfare authorities. Parents may be offered advice and assistance by special advisers. Children may be placed with foster parents, with or without the consent of their biological parents. Children and youths who are delinquent may be put under surveillance. They may also, either in lieu of placement with foster parents or because of delinquency or actual criminality, be placed in institutions especially established for this purpose.

A debate on these problems is currently going on, and indeed public criticism is often very intense. From this point of view it used to be very important that authority rested mainly in the hands of locally elected boards, who had and still have great freedom of action. With the enlargement of municipal units, it is, however, increasingly difficult for the boards to deal substantively with each case in detail, and actual authority is gradually being transferred from the boards themselves to social workers employed by them. This means that professionals have taken over from laymen. While this may imply that cases are handled more consistently and on the basis of greater knowledge, for instance of psychology, there is no doubt that the public is often more suspicious of professionals than of laymen, since they are more easily able to identify themselves with the latter. Also, in an urbanized society—and all Scandinavian countries are today mainly urbanized —youth problems are both more difficult and more significant. The

Scandinavian peoples may, however, find some consolation in the fact that nobody else appears to have been more successful in solving them.

An equally acute problem concerns *alcoholics* and *drug addicts*. Here, Scandinavia suffers from the same malaise as most industrialized countries. Alcoholism does of course constitute a problem of long standing, and various measures have been undertaken in an attempt to solve it. Both Finland and Norway at one time tried to enforce complete or partial prohibition, although with scant success. Just as in other countries that made similar attempts, law enforcement proved practically impossible. Sweden for a long time applied a somewhat complicated rationing system, which on the whole proved enforceable. It was abolished, however, on the plea that it encouraged everybody to use all their rations and thus favored mild alcoholism, even though it might reduce the number of more extreme cases of abuse. In Denmark heavy taxation and consequently very high prices were held to keep consumption down, and eventually the three other countries emulated the Danish method. This appears to have been comparatively efficient at one time, but less and less so as the standard of living rose and more and more people were able to pay the higher prices.

In all the four countries, although less so in Denmark than in the others, temperance movements were very strong and still remain a force to be reckoned with by the political parties. To a considerable extent policies have been determined as a result of their pressure. It should be noted, for instance, that it was the temperance movement and not its opponents which demanded the abolition of the rationing system in Sweden.

Both with regard to alcoholics and even more when in recent times drug addiction has called for public attention, one of the most controversial questions has been whether treatment, and especially treatment in closed institutions, should be compulsory or based on the consent of the addicts themselves. On the one hand, it is argued that enforced treatment is rarely successful and that consent should consequently be called for. On the other hand, the protection of third parties is held to be so important that the interests of the addict should take second place. Actual policies have wavered between the two extremes, and it is impossible to state that either side has been able to prove its case.

In dealing with *crime and criminals*, the Scandinavian countries twenty or thirty years ago used to be in the vanguard of the reform movement. New, humanitarian policies were introduced on the grounds that crime was largely the consequence of faulty social conditions and that in any case a system of retribution and deterrence is unworthy of civilized societies. In the four countries—most particularly in Sweden, least of all in Finland—the accepted idea became that of treatment aiming at "resocialization" rather than punishment. As a result, more and more emphasis was put on supervision by social workers—or voluntary supervisors—without imprisonment, while prisons were reformed and made more fit to live in. Again, such ideas were particularly prevalent in Sweden, and persons especially of Finnish origin who had committed crimes in Sweden were anxious to serve their sentences there rather than in their own country.

These humane reforms were on the whole recommended by an intellectual elite rather than by public opinion. When the crime rate increased, probably for reasons unconnected with the penal system, there were widespread demands for harsher treatment of criminals or at least for more deterrent punishments and above all for greater security in prisons in order to prevent escape. The latter demands were largely complied with, although it became more and more obvious that escape-proof prisons are an impossibility in the circumstances of modern society.

In recent years, the fundamental principles of the idea of "treatment" have come under fire. Critics maintain that it is based on fundamental misconceptions. Nobody, they say, improves in character or becomes more likely to adapt himself or herself to the requirements of society by serving time in prison. If anything, contrary results are to be expected. Systems of surveillance without incarceration have proved no more successful. Consequently, it is argued, one should relinquish the whole idea of treating crime or an inclination to crime as an illness to be cured by appropriate treatment. No such treatment has yet been devised by human ingenuity. Humane conditions in prisons and other correctional facilities should be established, but this belief is motivated by general humanitarian principles and not by any hope of "improving" criminals. And while the idea of retribution is still rejected, it is held that the function of punishment should be to manifest disapproval of criminal acts, although not of the criminal as a person. This disapproval must be proportionate to the offense.

These different views are still the object of heated discussion. They are sometimes referred to as individual prevention and general prevention of crime, respectively—i.e., preventing the individual, by means of resocialization, from falling back into criminal habits, or generally preventing crime by making it clear that it is subject to disapproval by society. The growing frequency of crime, both against persons and against property, which is no prerogative of the Scandinavian countries, helps to focus public attention on problems of crime prevention. It also indicates that crime prevention in the circumstances of urbanized industrial society remains increasingly inefficient, whether it follows the general or the individual approach. Consequently, in actual practice the choice between the two alternatives is of only limited importance. Humane treatment of criminals is fervently advocated on both sides. Also, they both agree that imprisonment is at best a most imperfect instrument which should be avoided whenever possible. The advocates of general prevention favor fixed sentences where definite periods of imprisonment are imposed by the courts, while those who believe in individual prevention want to give prison authorities more leeway to determine the length of the sentence. Ironically, prisoners themselves usually prefer fixed sentences and do not believe in "treatment." But nobody goes to extremes, differences in the application of the penal system tend to be marginal, and neither side is able to present an entirely convincing case to the general public, which is of course much more reactionary and repressive than the experts.

It is not always easy to distinguish social welfare policies from general social and economic policies. Various measures that are taken with other motives than those of welfare, or where at least the welfare motives are of secondary importance, may have more decisive effects on the social security of citizens than measures taken with this security as the primary objective. This is particularly true if it is agreed that prevention (of social ills) is better than cure. Social planning, it is argued, cannot be distinguished from economic planning.

Taxes are a striking example. They are presumably levied in order to finance the activities of the public sector, whether in the field of social welfare or in any other field. But taxes also have direct social effects. The choice between direct and indirect taxes and the incidence of taxation are closely related to social policies and to the distribution of available incomes among different groups in society. The progressive income tax—and the concomitant tax on the margin —is even more obviously an expression of social ambitions. High taxes, regardless of how they are spent, normally have a leveling effect.

Some social benefits are taxfree, while others are liable to income tax. There is no real consistency as to which of these alternatives is chosen. To the extent that pensions are to be regarded as "postponed wages," it is reasonable that they should be subject to tax. Nor is it illogical that certain reductions take place in the case of pensioners whose incomes are relatively low, although not below the minimum for income tax. The case of child subventions is more dubious. When they were introduced in Sweden, it was argued that recipients of high incomes from other sources would in any case pay back practically the whole amount of their child subventions in taxes. With the present level of taxes on the margin, this may be even more true today. In any case they are taxfree, and to families in the lower or middle income brackets this is undoubtedly important.

In the *labor market*, the predominant question would appear to be how to get work performed and how much to pay for it in wages and salaries. However, a moment's reflection indicates that this is by no means all. How much unemployment can be acceptable? How important is the maintenance of labor peace, as against frequent strikes and lockouts? And what should be the correct division of functions between the organizations of employees and employers, on the one hand, and democratically elected parliaments, ministries, and local councils on the other? Here the four countries are by no means pursuing the same policies.

In Sweden labor unions and employers' organizations have so far been extremely jealous of their independence, and the idea of incomes policies has been emphatically rejected. It has been regarded almost as an outrage if a minister so much as indicates his opinion regarding the level that should be aimed at in wage and salary negotiations. (Of course the offense is regarded as more venial by the unions if the minister is a Social Democrat and by the employers if he or she is not.) Government is expected to do no more than nominate official mediators—not arbitrators—at the threat of a conflict. After the event, it will of course have to draw the necessary conclusions and perhaps raise or reduce taxes, especially indirect taxes, to offset possibly damaging effects on the national economy.

But in Denmark wage negotiations almost invariably fail to achieve agreement between the parties. When this has been established on each particular occasion, Parliament on the proposal of Government passes into law a draft settlement that was proposed by the mediator but found partly or wholly unacceptable to the negotiating parties. In Norway awards are also usual, although the role of the Government is less pronounced than in Denmark and Parliament does not come into the picture. In Finland negotiations may continue for a very long time without results, and major strikes are not unusual.

Another aspect of Scandinavian policies that may or may not be related to the emergence of welfare states is that relating to the *position of women* — "women's lib," or parity (jämställdhet) as it is usually called in the Nordic countries. Especially when seen as liberation, this has much to do with the access of married women to the labor market and their wages and salaries once they are gainfully employed. Equal pay for equal work is in principle completely accepted in all four countries. But it is sometimes difficult to define equality between different sorts of work. And while it is probably true that women have better access to gainful employment and are on the whole better paid in Scandinavia than in other industrialized countries, this does not mean that women's movements are satisfied. Furthermore, married women are more apt than men to work only part time. If this is really by their own choice or simply because even in these socially advanced countries men still refuse to take on a reasonable part of child care and other household work is hotly debated. Various measures have been taken, such as putting fathers and mothers on the same footing in the right to a leave of absence for child care. Results have so far been meager, but again it is not easy to say whether this is only because traditions die hard (although they will eventually disappear) or whether there are other, more or even less acceptable reasons.

A third question concerns *workers' participation in management* both in the private and in the public sector. This has been developed especially in Sweden. The accepted system gives extensive rights to employees' unions but not necessarily to the actual employees of an enterprise or an administrative agency. It is frequently said that it has led to more bureaucracy rather than to employee influence on important decisions other than those concerning working conditions and the working environment.

The need for *environment protection* in general has recently come to the fore and commands great interest. It affects housing policies and other aspects of social policy but does of course go much further. Establishing a reasonable balance between ecological considerations and those related to economic efficiency and employment is becoming an increasingly recognized problem. It can hardly be said that the Nordic countries have been more successful than others in this respect.

Immigration is closely related to labor market problems. For a considerable time a common Nordic labor market has existed, allowing citizens of one Nordic country freely to seek and hold employment in one of the others without requiring works permits. This has led to considerable mobility especially between Finland and Sweden. For several years this was more or less a one-way traffic, since Sweden could offer greater opportunities and higher wages, and there are still a considerable number of Finnish citizens working in Sweden and relatively few Swedish citizens working in Finland. With an increasingly hard climate in the Swedish labor market, considerable remigration into Finland has, however, taken place. Denmark and Norway have been less involved in such migration, although their citizens have the same rights as those of Finland and Sweden.

Especially in recent years the number of other immigrants has increased. To some extent these are "guest workers," mostly from Turkey and Yugoslavia, as in other Western European countries. Some of them are, however, refugees, and it is sometimes difficult to distinguish the two categories. Refugees also require jobs, and there may be other reasons than those of political dissidence that impel people to leave the country of their birth. Depending on political and other circumstances outside Scandinavia, there have been waves of such immigrants from the "Baltic countries," especially Estonia, as well as from Hungary, Latin America, Turkey, Lebanon, and to some extent "boat people" from Vietnam. The Nordic countries recognize no "right" of immigration, but on the whole since 1945 asylum has not been refused to any "political" refugees able to prove that they run the risk of persecution in their home countries. The situation of "religious" refugees such as Christians from Turkey and other countries in the Near East is more difficult since it is sometimes almost impossible to draw the line between those who really risk persecution and those who simply find living conditions unbearable at home and are attracted to the Nordic countries precisely by their reputation as welfare states. The latter reason is not admitted as a sufficient ground for immigration.

A practical question of no mean importance concerns passports. Such documents are no longer required for travel between the Nordic countries, and this rule applies not only to their own citizens but also to other nationals. Anyone who legally — or illegally — has entered one of the four countries thus finds it comparatively easy to proceed to one of the others. Immigration control is difficult on the border between Denmark and the Federal Republic of Germany, and illegal entry is consequently often possible there. A considerable number, perhaps the majority of those who entered illegally from Germany later continue into Sweden or Norway in the hope of finding jobs and/or of joining relatives and friends. A number of difficult cases have occurred when such illegal immigrants must be returned to their home countries.

While immigration regulations are not in themselves part of the welfare system, they do in fact bear a close relation to the practice and above all to the ideology of the welfare state. In Scandinavia, as elsewhere, labor unions look with a jaundiced eye at any major influx of workers from abroad. They believe that immigration increases the supply of humble and undemanding manpower and may thus stand in the way of demands for higher wages and salaries. On the other hand, it remains an open question whether the welfare state should accept responsibility for its indigenous population alone or whether its humanitarian principles should extend to others who seek by immigration to participate in the rights and duties of its people.

Sweden has recently taken a unique step in regard to the rights of immigrants. Foreign citizens who have resided in the country for more than three years are now entitled to vote in municipal and regional elections, and they were also given the right to vote in a recent referendum (on nuclear energy). It has even been suggested by the Social Democratic party — which has received the bulk of their votes in municipal elections — that they should be given the right to participate in parliamentary elections also.

The intertwining of economic and social policies is particularly strong because in Scandinavia more than in most other countries special emphasis has been put on the infrastructure of universalist services, rather than on selective benefits. It goes without saying that economic considerations, in contrast to downright welfare objectives, are more important the more general the measures taken. Not only Marxists, but even more the advocates of a mixed economy or of Liberalism, have become increasingly aware of this connection.

On the other hand, with higher standards of living and equalization of available incomes, the need for universal free services is less apparent. In these circumstances, it seems doubtful whether the consensus on social policies can be maintained. And certain categories, such as old age pensioners receiving only the minimum pension, families, and the disabled, are definitely more vulnerable than others and in need of special benefits, which call for selective rather than universal welfare.

On the whole it is, however, not so much pensioners as families or single parents with children who form the bulk of what has been called "the new poor." This term refers to those who are caught in the trap of the relationship between high progressive income taxes and means-tested benefits, or—perhaps more usually—have adjusted themselves to standards of living that cannot easily be maintained when something unexpected happens. Most frequently, the difficulties are triggered by illness, divorce, or other circumstances reducing the number of wage earners from two to one and calling for costly economic arrangements.

The financing of social policies, leaving social insurance aside for the moment, varies from one field to another. Some of it comes out of state revenues, some out of county, and some out of municipal revenues. The use of the two latter sources is important also because it results in considerable differences—"injustices"—between the inhabitants of different communities, and there is a dilemma between safeguarding the interests of individuals who find themselves discriminated against because they live in the "wrong" community and insistence on local self-government. None of the four countries have found a satisfactory solution to this problem.

As is apparent from this brief survey of social security measures in its four countries, Scandinavia is on the face of it by no means unique in the Western world. Practically all the elements of its welfare system are found elsewhere as well. In some cases the Scandinavian countries have been ahead of others, in other cases they have lagged behind them. What is perhaps unusual is the wide coverage of the Scandinavian system. Each particular arrangement may have its counterparts somewhere else, but the system as a whole is unusually complete. It is not easy to say offhand what the establishment of such a comprehensive social security system has meant from the standpoint of an egalitarian social structure. A number of issues must be considered, above all the extent to which subsidies really affect the economic situation of the majority of the population, but also the existence of minority groups subject to discrimination.

The economic situation of Scandinavians can be examined by reviewing two reports on living conditions. A report on Denmark (1976), Norway (1980), and Sweden (1979) has recently been published by the Nordic Council. In addition, a much more comprehensive report on Sweden (1974 and 1975) was published by the Swedish Central Bureau of Statistics (SCB) in 1977. These two studies are referred to here as the "1983 report" and the "1977 report," respectively.

The 1983 report gives index figures for the monthly wages/salaries of different groups of employees:

	Denmark (1976)	Norway (1980)	Sweden (1979)
All manual workers (professional employees = 100)	51	65	55
Industrial workers (professional employees = 100)	58	75	62
Women (men = 100)	63	58	63
Employees in major cities (the whole country = 100)	109	109	109

In ordinary political debate, much is made of such gross income figures, and it is maintained that these show how little actual equality has been achieved. But given the high rates of direct progressive taxation on the one hand, and widespread subsidies on the other, it should be obvious that such figures do not provide any relevant information.

The 1977 report goes into more detail. It deals not only with direct earnings, but also with "available incomes," that is, income after direct taxes have been paid and various subsidies received. It does not take into account such benefits as free education, free hospital care, etc., which can hardly be evaluated in monetary terms. Nor does it count the indirect tax burden, which also can hardly be reduced to exact figures. Nevertheless, the results are very revealing.

The 1977 report divides the working population into six "socioeconomic" groups of more or less equal size:

A1	unskilled manual workers (10.2 percent of the population)
A2	semi-skilled manual workers (13.7 percent)
A3	skilled manual workers (11.0 percent)
B1	clerks, assistants, etc. (10.1 percent)
B2	engineers and other specialists (13.6 percent)
C	employers and other self-employed persons, including farmers (7.8 percent)

In addition, 33.6 percent of the adult population were not gainfully employed. This group included students, old age pensioners, disabled persons, and persons (mostly women) working only in the home.

Let us first consider the average income from work for the different categories. The following figures are given in Swedish crowns. (At that time one crown was approximately equal to 0.20 U.S. dollars.)

		Individuals Working (1974)	*Individuals Working Full-time (1974)*	*Individuals Working (1975)*
A1	unskilled manual	21,700	26,800	25,700
A2	semi-skilled manual	28,700	32,200	32,500
A3	skilled manual	33,600	35,500	41,500
B1	clerks, assistants, etc.	30,400	34,600	37,000
B2	specialists	49,200	52,200	59,500
C	self-employed	26,200	33,000	31,000

The group of self-employed persons is very heterogeneous, and since it is at the same time smaller than any of the others it can be disregarded. Of the rest, unskilled manual workers have the lowest gross income, whereas engineers and other specialists are by far the best paid. The difference between these two extremes in regard to all individuals working was no less than 127 percent in 1974 and 130 percent in 1975. If only those working full time are taken into account, the differential is still as high as 83 percent. Since these calculations are based on different figures from those employed in the 1983 report, no real comparisons can be made. On the whole, the picture appears to be about the same in the two reports.

The Swedish figures for the average *available* income of all those gainfully employed in 1974-1975 are very different from those for gross income:

		Families (1974)	*Individuals (1975)*
A1	unskilled manual	28,600	21,500
A2	semi-skilled manual	29,000	22,500
A3	skilled manual	31,100	23,500
B1	clerks, assistants, etc.	32,600	25,500
B2	specialists	39,700	28,600
C	self-employed	26,000	18,000

Here also, the last group should be left out of consideration, since the figures are probably unreliable: estimating the net available income of farmers and similar small entrepreneurs is proverbially difficult. As with gross incomes, the first category (unskilled manual workers) has the lowest income and specialists the highest. But the difference between the two extremes is incomparably smaller: only 39 percent for family incomes in 1974 and 33 percent for individual incomes in 1975.

For some reason, no similar studies of the distribution of available incomes have been made either in the other Nordic countries or for any subsequent year in Sweden. However, the OECD in 1981 published a chart (see p. 83) showing the available incomes of individual workers—as a percentage of total wages—for twenty-one countries in 1972, 1976, and 1980. It appears that the percentages are particularly low in Denmark, Norway, and Sweden, although the situation is approximately the same in the Netherlands and in the Federal Republic of Germany. However, it should be noted that these figures apply only to a male industrial worker with two children and a wife who is not gainfully employed—whereas in most families of the Nordic countries both husband and wife work outside the home. Consequently, it is not unlikely that a study of family incomes would show somewhat different relationships.

Another chart published by the OECD (and reproduced on p. 84) shows the annual per capita personal consumption in the Nordic countries for the years 1970 to 1980, measured in U.S. dollars. The general trend appears to have been an increase in consumption from 1970 until 1979, especially in Norway and Finland but also in Sweden. During the last year included in the chart, consumption dropped sharply in Denmark and mildly in Sweden. This finding has interesting implications. When the Swedish Social Democrats were relegated to the position of an opposition party in 1976, they complained that the "bourgeois" Governments were pursuing policies favoring the rich at the expense of the majority of wage and salary earners. But it cannot be substantiated that any major changes of this type have occurred. After all, per capita consumption started to go down only after 1979 and less sharply in Sweden than in Denmark which at that time had a Social Democrat Government. And the latest figures that have been published for Sweden show that between 1975 and 1979 available incomes (in real terms) rose by nearly 1 percent for blue-collar workers and by 1½ to 2½ percent for white-collar

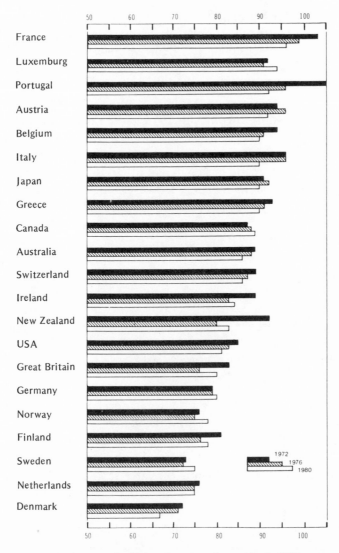

Available per capita income for selected countries in 1972,
1976, and 1980, expressed as a percentage of total wages.
Source: OECD, 1981.

workers in the lower income brackets. On the other hand, they fell
by ½ percent for senior (professional) white-collar employees. Thus
equalization apparently continued, if at a somewhat slower pace than
in the preceding period.

Just like other industrialized countries, Sweden and Denmark

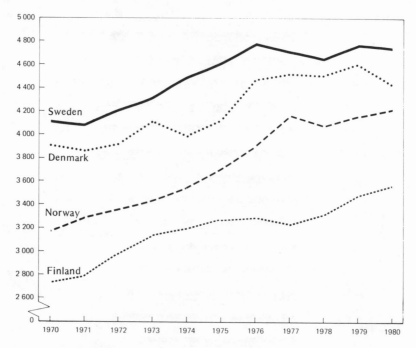

Annual per capita personal consumption in the Nordic countries, 1970-80, in U.S. dollars. Source: OECD, 1983.

suffered setbacks in economic growth and development during the late 1970s and early 1980s. Eventually the general standard of living was affected, especially for families with several small children. But such families had been less well off than other households even in earlier years. The 1977 report—but not the later studies—gave some vague information on this subject: it appeared that those who had small children often worked long hours and had unsatisfactory dwellings, although few of these families belonged to the lowest income groups (or to the highest income groups either). Most of those with older children, on the other hand, belonged to relatively high income groups, had shorter working hours, and usually lived in satisfactory dwellings.

According to the 1983 report, professional salaried employees in Denmark, Norway, and Sweden on the average worked longer hours than either industrial workers or other white-collar employees. They even seem to have been more likely to work at inconvenient hours; in this respect the 1977 report for Sweden does, however, give a different impression. Corresponding figures for Finland are not available.

A comparison was made in the 1977 report between native or naturalized Swedes on the one hand and foreign nationals living in the country (mostly of Finnish origin). Compared with the Swedes, foreigners in the country had more inconvenient, although not particularly long working hours and more strenuous occupations. They perceived themselves to be more exposed to the risks of accidents, noise, and other environmental discomforts. On the other hand, they were more rarely unemployed, and fewer of them belonged to the lowest income groups. This is explained, said the SCB, by the fact that the proportion of old age pensioners is smaller among foreign nationals. Their housing conditions were often less than satisfactory, and they did not own as much leisure equipment as others. Not surprisingly, they appeared to be a disfavored group. Some data for the same immigrant group in Sweden were given in the 1983 report as well. They are very indefinite but give a similar general impression.

Housing conditions are an important indicator for the standard of living. In all four countries they appear to be relatively good, as evidenced by the following figures from the 1983 report showing the percentage of the respective populations living in up-to-date dwellings.

	Denmark (1976)	Finland (1978)	Norway (1980)	Sweden (1979)
Persons over 19 and below 65 years of age	84	65	91	97
Manual workers	79	63	88	97
White collar employees	90	82	96	98
of these: professionals	97	87	98	99
Farming population	89	35	81	88
Owners of business enterprises	92	70	95	98
Persons living alone	68	52	79	92
Families with one or more small children	91	76	97	99

The very definition of "overcrowded" living conditions is significant. Overcrowding is supposed to exist wherever there are more than two persons (adults or children) per room, exclusive of kitchen and living room. Thus a family of two parents and two children should have at least three rooms and a kitchen. By these standards, according to the 1977 report 8 percent of the Swedish population between sixteen and sixty-four years of age were living under conditions of overcrowding. Most of these were manual workers, the differences between unskilled, semi-skilled, and skilled workers being relatively small. Even among unskilled manual workers, the figure was only a little more than 10 percent.

Household appliances were also plentiful. Ninety-five percent of the population had access either to refrigerators or to washing machines. For old age pensioners the figure was more than 90 percent, for unskilled manual workers more than 93 percent. Ninety percent of the whole population had access to washing machines and 75 percent to refrigerators. Significant differences were found between geographical areas rather than between socioeconomic groups. Household appliances were less plentiful in the sparsely populated regions in the north of Sweden. No comparable figures are available for the three other countries, but it can be assumed that the general standards are about the same in Denmark and Norway and appreciably lower in Finland.

Another indicator of living standards is the number of automobiles. The percentage of the respective populations owning or otherwise having access to an automobile is as follows:

	Denmark (1976)	Finland (1978)	Norway (1980)	Sweden (1979)
Persons over 19 and below 65 years of age	75	59	83	84
Manual workers	73	59	81	84
White-collar employees	81	66	90	88
of these: professionals	88	69	92	91
Farming population	90	64	90	96
Owners of business enterprises	94	86	92	91
Persons living alone	51	39	65	60
Families with one or more small children	86	74	93	95

With relatively small variations, the pattern appears to be the same in regard to telephones, TV sets, summer houses, and other types of leisure equipment. Comparisons between the 1977 and 1983 reports indicate that standards rose somewhat even in the late 1970s. In all cases, Sweden emerges as the most opulent and Finland as the least opulent of the four countries. Significantly, this affects the distribution of the standard of living among different groups as well as the aggregate situation. Swedish conditions appear to be the most equitable and those of Finland the least equitable. Thus, in Scandinavia there appears to be a definite correlation between prosperity and equality.

A remaining, unanswered question is how Scandinavia in these respects compares with other industrialized countries such as Great Britain and the Federal Republic of Germany, and indeed with parts of the United States such as California and Minnesota. There exists hardly any sufficiently detailed information for these, although it is likely that some reports will eventually be published for all OECD countries. In the absence of relevant data, one may, however, hazard the hypothesis that the Nordic countries will prove typical. The society that developed there in the 1970s is probably similar to that which emerged at about the same time—or slightly later—throughout the industrialized world.

A New Economic Order?

In many respects, the economic problems facing Scandinavian countries today are the same as those of most other industrialized countries. These problems are largely caused by an unwarranted expectation of continued material progress entirely without limits. To the extent that there is a difference between Scandinavia and the rest of the Western world, perhaps most of it lies in the choice of a few solutions different from those preferred by other similar countries. What, then, is the relationship between these problems and the establishment of welfare states? The answer can be summarized as follows: in Scandinavia these common economic problems appear in conjunction with conscious efforts to maintain egalitarian societies, or even to increase the emphasis on egalitarianism. In this respect, this part of the world is extreme, at least in comparison to most other countries, including those calling themselves Socialist.

First, some general observations. In any prosperous society, the role of durable consumer goods—"gadgets"—like motor cars, TV sets, etc., is of predominant importance. Necessities of life like food or even housing play a much smaller part in the economy of households than they did in the past. This is associated with a change in the way of life, namely, shorter working hours and more leisure. Much of the increase in standards of living appears in this form. And leisure is closely related to these durable consumer goods, as can be seen in

United States society, which appears to be dominated by the motor car—"love your car, love your family," a well-known American poster used to read. All this applies to the Nordic countries as well as to others.

Both industrial sophistication and the use of household gadgets call for a high consumption of energy. In the North, this tendency is even more strengthened owing to the harsh climate. With long and relatively cold winters, heating of private dwellings uses up much of the available electricity and/or oil. Of the four countries, Norway alone produces oil, and this is such a recent development that it is as yet impossible to assess its effect on the economy. Bituminous coal is not found in appreciable quantities in any of the Nordic countries. As a consequence, rising prices of energy have had a very strong impact in Scandinavia. Here, as elsewhere, they have had a double effect. On the one hand, they have raised the cost of living, causing cost inflation. On the other hand, they have raised the cost of industrial production, making industry less competitive and causing stagnation. "Stagflation," the combination of inflation in prices and stagnation in production, is thus at least in part a result of the new energy situation. In all four Nordic countries these trends are strikingly evident, even more so than in other parts of Western Europe or in the United States. This is not to say that all four countries show wholly identical traits or that developments have been going on at exactly the same pace in all of them. But as usual the similarities are greater than the differences.

Economic problems of this type differ fundamentally from those of the 1920s and 1930s. At that time recessions were largely caused by underconsumption, resulting from grossly unequal distribution of incomes, and they were characterized by falling prices, not by inflation. (Germany and Austria just after the First World War were exceptional cases.) In the present situation, however, habits of consumption have tended to vary according to expected levels of economic growth and of prices. Even apart from energy problems a salient fact was that expectations of growth gradually came to rise unrealistically but still determined consumption. The resulting imbalance involving greater increase of demand than of supply led to high prices, inflation. But since the cost both of raw materials, above all for the production of energy, and of labor rose equally or even more steeply, production and productivity did not respond to traditional price stimuli. Inflation continued but without overcoming stagnation. This was just another aspect of stagflation—which was regarded as next to impossible as late as in the 1960s. It could also, more simply, be described as a situation allowing people to live beyond their means.

Some current misunderstandings about Scandinavia must be cleared up at the outset in order to establish a reasonable basis for subsequent analysis. The four countries are not "Socialist" in the sense of Eastern European Socialism. Production—as distinct from the supply of services—is still taking place mainly in the private sector. Public ownership is of major importance only in the case of certain utilities and in some fields where the state has decided to step in when private enterprises were unable to cope with unexpected difficulties. The major part of banking is in private hands. The four countries all have "mixed economies," which in their case means that democratically elected governments, whatever their political color, have thus far preferred steering the private sector by various means rather than nationalizing it.

The relative role of the private and public sectors and the character of the public sector can be understood only after certain reservations have been made. In all prosperous industrialized countries, and by no means in Scandinavia alone, the public sector of the economies has for a considerable time been growing more quickly than the private sector. It can hardly be denied, however, that in Scandinavia the growth of the public sector has been spectacular. In Sweden, which is the most pronounced case, public expenditures as measured in fixed prices grew by an annual average of nearly 7 percent over a period of fifteen years. In 1979, out of a GNP calculated at 436 billion Swedish crowns, or a little over 100 billion U.S. dollars, the public sector was responsible for 286 billion Swedish crowns, or almost exactly two-thirds of the whole.

But what is the public sector? Half of it, or one-third of GNP, consists of transfers and thus reverts to private consumption. The other half consists of collective consumption: education, health and hospital care, national defense, and so on. In some of these areas the Nordic countries are in fact representative of the industrialized world as a whole. It is a well-known fact that the larger the per capita income of a given country, the larger is the share spent on health care. The following figures, expressed as percentages of the GNP, show the role of "general government consumption expenditure," which constitutes the main part of collective consumption (thus exclusive of transfers), in the four countries of Scandinavia.

	1977	*1980*
Denmark	21.9	18.3
Finland	18.9	18.6
Norway	20.2	18.9
Sweden	27.6	29.2

Clearly expenditure in this part of the public sector remains high all over Scandinavia. However, it is significantly higher (and rising) in Sweden than in the other three countries. But it should be noted that during the relevant years, from 1976 to 1982, there was a non-Socialist majority in the Swedish Parliament and non-Socialist Cabinets in power—while the labor parties either by themselves or as part of coalitions were responsible for the governments of the other three countries.

It is generally assumed that the public sector is less productive than the private sector. However, productivity in the public sector is not easily identified, let alone measured. And moreover this is true to a great extent also in the part of the private sector that produces services rather than goods, and this part is growing everywhere. What can be said with some assurance—and this is important enough—is that the public sector is not as sensitive to prices, and therefore less sensitive to demand. Productivity both in the public and in the private sector must be assessed very differently depending on whether it is judged from the standpoint of individual enterprises and services or that of society as a whole. And the cost to society, for instance of geographical concentration of industrial production, cannot be calculated in any definite terms.

Transfers in the form of child subventions, old age pensions, and similar benefits financed by taxes or corresponding levies are no monopoly of the Scandinavian countries. But they are undoubtedly a more prominent element in their social and economic systems than in those of most other nations. In fact they constitute one of the most important characteristics of contemporary Nordic society. By definition, transfers can hardly be advantageous to everybody. Originally they were meant to establish a sort of Robin Hood policy: take from the rich in order to give to the poor. The rich could hardly be expected to show much enthusiasm for the idea. However, not only the really poor but also the undefinable group constituting "public opinion" applauded the venture as justified by the duties of society to human beings in need. As time went on, transfers changed in character and lost much of their moral justification. In Scandinavia a large part of the transfers are not really transfers at all, since the benefits are paid for in taxes by the same people who are the recipients. In other cases they constitute transfers not between different classes of persons, but between different periods of life. The middle-aged, whose children are grown and who have reached maximum earning capacity, pay back in taxes what they once received in allowances for their children and at the same time help finance what they will eventually receive in old age pensions. It can hardly be said that transfers of the latter type are meaningless or that they lack justification. Good arguments have indeed been advanced in their favor. But they can be expected to have definite effects on the economic system. Household savings at least in theory become less important and there is less motivation to save when one no longer needs a savings account to provide for one's old age nor to give financial help to one's offspring. In fact the objective of transfers is to increase possibilities of consumption for those who would otherwise be compelled to reduce it, and they consequently almost by definition tend to increase demand and thus have inflationary effects. On the other hand, if one assumes that most people regardless of their income level are improvident to the extent that at any given time they consume all they earn, or even more, transfers could also be said to take the place of private savings which fail to materialize. All this is based on the assumption that transfers go to those who are either temporarily or permanently unable to obtain what in the given society is regarded as the necessities of life. In fact transfers do, however, expand the spending power of others as well and thus stimulate the tendency of society as a whole to live beyond its means.

The other half of the public sector, as has just been stated, can be called collective consumption. As with transfers, the justification lies in making certain assumptions about the behavior of normal individuals. Most of them are supposed to work—produce—in order to earn an income to be spent in the acquisition of commodities that they desire. But they might attempt to consume more than they produce, thus stimulating inflation, and their choice of goods and services could be unwise by the standards of those who "know better." Moreover, certain things could be made available more economically by being provided collectively rather than individually. In order to be justified, collective consumption does not necessarily have to be advantageous to each individual or at all times in his or her life. As long as one remains in robust health, one gains little by the public health system; and if one has no children, free education ceases to be a benefit once one's own education is completed. This is hardly an argument against collective consumption, however. Like transfers, it is intended to benefit those who are in the greatest need, in the interests of social justice, and to provide protection against dangers that individuals are unable to deal with on their own. The extreme example of the latter, of course, is national defense.

One characteristic of collective consumption should be pointed out at this time: it refers almost exclusively to services. Its growth therefore gives an additional impetus to the increase in importance of services in both the private and the public sectors relative to the production of goods. As has just been pointed out, this tendency is one reason why the productivity of the public sector cannot be assessed with any reasonable accuracy. And it is typical of the welfare state in Scandinavia that services are largely provided in the public sector, in accordance with what Gunnar Myrdal once called "socialization of consumption."

The basis of individual consumption, apart from that resulting from transfers, consists mainly of wages and salaries. Incomes of private individual entrepreneurs, and from stock dividends, are of no more than marginal importance. Wage earners and salary earners are the dominating element in the population: numerically, as in most industrialized countries; economically, as in all industrialized countries that have achieved at least a modicum of material equality; and politically. In the third respect, the Nordic peoples present a more pronounced example than most, presumably because of their traditional homogeneity. Religious and ethnic conflicts have been practically absent in Denmark, Norway, and Sweden, and even in Finland differences between Finnish-speaking and Swedish-speaking elements of the population have lost much of their social and political importance. Consequently it is the economic interests of wage and salary earners that constitute the dominant force in politics. Within the employee group there used to be a difference, sometimes amounting to conflict, between blue-collar and white-collar workers. As a result, they organized in separate labor unions, the lead being taken by the former group. It would be an exaggeration to say that such differences have disappeared, but their importance is undoubtedly diminishing. Well-paid blue-collar workers are not infrequently much better off than the lower strata in the white-collar group. With mechanization and automation, working conditions in blue-collar jobs tend to be far less different from those in white-collar jobs than they used to be. And while separate unions are still maintained, cooperation between them frequently takes place.

On the whole, unionization has gone further in Scandinavia than in most other parts of the world. In Sweden, it can be called more or less complete, and while exceptions are less rare in the three other countries, from the standpoint of wage and salary negotiations and their economic consequences nonunionized employees constitute a group that is practically without importance. As a result, wages and salaries both in the private and in the public sector are determined by employers' negotiations with the unions. A factor simplifying negotiations and above all making for relatively good discipline in the labor market is the virtually complete dominance of industrial as against trade unions. The employees of an enterprise or public agency in a given field are divided between blue-collar and white-collar unions—a third element in some cases consists of professionally trained white-collar employees. Within each of these categories all the employees usually belong to the same union, and disputes between different unions rarely create complications of any importance. Moreover, negotiations about both wages/salaries and working conditions take place on an industry-wide or even on a nationwide basis, leaving only the details to be negotiated with particular companies or agencies, and then on condition that disputes at this level must not result in strikes, lockouts, or similar open conflicts.

It might be asked why, under these circumstances, does the distinction between blue-collar and white-collar employees still remain in force. The answer is that this is largely a matter of tradition, but of traditions that still have some practical consequences. White-collar workers are employed and paid on a monthly basis and enjoy somewhat greater job security, whereas a considerable if diminishing number of blue-collar employees still work for hourly wages or piece-rates or under similar conditions of payment. Also, there are obvious conflicts of interest between the two groups over conditions of employment and working conditions. Finally, political attitudes remain different, with blue-collar workers predominantly Social Democrats and white-collar workers spread out over the whole political spectrum. Thus, while the difference in income levels is disappearing, other circumstances still preclude a complete integration of all employee organizations.

With the exceptions just noted, however, Scandinavian labor markets are characterized by greater unification and stability than those of most other countries, whether industrialized or not. Wildcat strikes in violation of law and agreements do take place, but not very often and only for relatively brief periods of time. Especially blue-collar workers' unions, but to some extent also those of white-collar workers, have adopted the principle of "solidarity in wage policies," meaning that even among their own members the wage differential ought to be successively reduced by giving priority to wage increases for groups of employees having the lowest income level. It has never been ascertained whether the rank and file of members are ready to give more than lip service to this principle, which originates with the leadership and has been applied in a number of negotiations during recent decades. (It would of course appear rather invidious for a faithful union member openly to oppose it.) On the other hand, most of the wildcat strikes occurring in recent decades have been undertaken by relatively well-paid blue-collar workers, who (not always without justification) have insisted that their particular employer should be able to pay higher wages than those agreed upon at the nationwide or industry-wide level. In this context, it is interesting to note that at least blue-collar workers' unions have almost invariably opposed the idea of incomes policies, that is, policies relating the wage level to the level of other types of income.

For a long time the Scandinavian countries have represented a seller's market in labor, to such an extent that the usual marketing forces have been almost completely put out of action. Both the fact that wage and salary negotiations take place across the board and not for individual enterprises and the related principle of "solidarity in wage policies" contribute to this state of affairs. It remains even in circumstances where full employment is not achieved. Labor—or labor organizations—being both politically and socially much stronger than capital, enterprises (both in private and publicly owned) find it difficult or even downright impossible to put up any solid resistance to their demands. Especially where international competition is very strong, companies are often fearful of open conflict, that is, strikes or lockouts, since these could result in almost immediate loss of markets and thus put them temporarily or even permanently out of action. Surrender to union demands may lead to the same result in the long run, but at least the catastrophe can be postponed, and in the meantime some miracle may occur.

Given this situation, mechanization and automation and other measures making it possible to reduce the labor force become enormously attractive to management, and the unions are not as powerful in influencing technological processes as they are in wage negotiations. Under these circumstances, it obviously becomes difficult to maintain full employment. But the welfare state regards it as a duty to care for the unemployed without inquiring whether unemployment might disappear or at least diminish if the wage level were kept down. The principle of "solidarity in wage policies," when fully applied, strengthens this tendency. Especially in countries like those of Scandinavia where industry is dependent on exports, this creates considerable difficulties.

A special problem for the labor unions is the growing importance of multinational corporations. For such enterprises it is both natural and relatively easy to establish production in countries where productivity is highest in relation to wages and benefits paid and to transfer already established units of production from countries where there is a pronounced sellers' market in labor. This is true of multinational corporation originating outside the Nordic countries, but also of let us say the Swedish ball bearing industry, SKF.

One of the problems the welfare state set out to solve was that of unemployment. "Full employment" was an accepted slogan all over the Western world in the 1930s. What does full employment mean? Obviously not that every able-bodied person should be gainfully employed every day of the year, holidays and vacations alone excepted. Especially in a dynamically changing economy there must always exist an "employment reserve," a number of persons who have had to leave a job before findng another one. Mobility of labor can be secured only at the price of a certain amount of "unemployment." One of the founding fathers of the ideology of the welfare state, Sir William Beveridge, maintained that 3 percent of the labor force was the lowest unemployment rate that could be achieved. In other words, "full employment" never could exceed 97 percent. Of the Nordic countries, Sweden long had the highest rate of employment because of industrial expansion. In the 1970s it was overtaken by Norway and occasionally by Finland. For considerable periods of time, the proportion of unemployment in the sense of persons seeking employment without immediately securing it was down to 1½ percent of the labor force of these countries, or about half of what Beveridge regarded as the minimum. This exceptional state of affairs is apparent from the following figures on unemployment in some of the OECD countries (expressed as a percentage of the total labor force). Since there is such a close relationship between employment and inflation, consumer price indexes (1975 = 100) are also given. The figures also show that both in Denmark and in Finland during this period unemployment rose to levels approximating or even exceeding those of other countries in Western Europe.

	Unemployment					*Consumer Prices*				
	1974	*1975*	*1976*	*1977*	*1978*	*1974*	*1975*	*1976*	*1977*	*1978*
Denmark	2.5	6.0	6.1	7.7	8.8	91	100	109	121	133
Finland	1.7	2.2	4.0	6.1	7.5	85	100	114	128	138
Norway	0.7	1.3	1.3	1.1	1.3	90	100	109	119	129
Sweden	2.0	1.6	1.6	1.8	2.2	91	100	110	123	135
Austria	1.5	2.0	2.0	1.8	2.1	92	100	107	113	117
Belgium	3.2	5.3	6.8	7.8	8.4	89	100	109	117	122
France	2.3	3.9	4.3	4.9	5.3	90	100	110	120	131
Ireland	6.3	8.7	9.8	9.7	8.9	83	100	118	134	144
Italy	4.8	5.2	5.5	6.4	7.1	85	100	117	138	155
Netherlands	3.6	5.2	5.5	5.3	5.2	91	100	109	116	121
U.K.	2.6	4.1	5.7	6.2	6.2	80	100	117	135	146
W. Germany	2.6	4.7	4.6	4.5	4.3	94	100	105	109	111
Canada	5.3	6.9	7.1	8.1	8.4	90	100	108	116	126
Japan	1.4	1.9	2.0	2.0	2.2	89	100	109	118	123
U.S.A.	5.6	8.5	7.7	7.0	6.0	92	100	106	113	121

Employment statistics are not always easily interpreted, however. In the first place, the size of the labor force is by no means a constant. Not only age distribution, but also social *mores* can drastically affect it. At the time when Sweden had the highest employment rate in the world, the proportion of persons gainfully employed in relation to the total population was lower than it is today. One of the main reasons for this, and probably the most important one, was that during this period the number of married women seeking work outside the home was much smaller. Ironically, at that time there was such a scarcity of labor that official propaganda—personified by the finance minister—systematically attempted to increase the labor supply by encouraging women to change their habits in this respect; and the new attitude toward women in the labor force reached its full effect at a time when the situation in the labor market had already changed and employment opportunities were no longer so plentiful.

Unemployment and scarcity of labor can coexist in the same country. In Finland, Norway, and Sweden, as well as in Denmark to a lesser extent, geographical distances are such that the demand for labor in one region cannot be easily satisfied by movement from another region, at least not on short notice. This difficulty also has gained increasing importance with the emergence of married women in the labor market. Quite apart from problems of housing, a couple is rarely willing to move to another place except on condition that both, and not just one of its members, can find acceptable employment.

In highly developed industrial economies such as those of Scandinavia, employment opportunities for unskilled labor continually decrease. But skilled workers—who *are* in demand—must have acquired specific types of skills that relate to specific types of employment. Thus, when structural changes take place in industry, there can easily be both unemployment and scarcity of labor in the same field, and even in the same industrial enterprise. This has been true of all the Nordic countries in the 1970s, and there is every indication that structural changes will be even more drastic in the 1980s. In such circumstances, the welfare state is finding it increasingly difficult to maintain its principle of full employment.

During earlier slump periods industry tended to lay off employees in upper middle age. For various reasons employers preferred to engage young workers. By means of legislation, as well as through pressure from the unions, such layoffs have been made much more difficult if not downright impossible, so that young people just out of school are now finding it anything but easy to get reasonably desirable jobs. The fact that somewhat older workers have acquired skills that are needed for highly specialized types of production, while the young ones are inexperienced, works in the same direction. The tendency for unemployment to be highest among the youngest generation is reinforced by the fact that during the boom immediately preceding the oil crisis of 1973 there was such a scarcity of labor that practically anybody was able to choose an attractive job even without previous training and without necessarily adapting themselves to traditional work discipline. With the altered situation those who banked on such possibilities have found themselves disappointed, i.e., unemployed.

Thus the figures given on page 98 are no longer relevant. And moreover, especially in Sweden official employment statistics are at present misleading. While officially only between 3 and 4 percent are counted as unemployed, at least the same proportion of the labor force are artificially kept out of the statistics by virtue of having "employment" in vocational training or retraining courses, relief works, and so on. To some extent this is the case in the other Nordic countries as well. Thus, these welfare states have much hidden unemployment, although it is of a totally different type from that existing in less developed, mainly agricultural economies. A similar trend occurs in a number of industries in both the private and the public sectors which produce against inventories during periods when demand for their products is slack, both in order to manifest their sense of social responsibility toward their employees (and indirectly to society as a whole) and perhaps also in the hope of being placed in a favorable position when the situation changes. If they are disappointed, such practices simply mean the postponement and in the long run perhaps a deepening of unemployment. And even in the opposite case they entail retarded reaction to improvements in the situation: increased demand for their products does not necessarily encourage them to increase their demand for employees.

Traditionally, unemployment appeared in deflationary, stagnating periods of the business cycle, whereas inflation combined with high rates of development and employment. In all Nordic countries today — and in a number of other industrialized countries — the tendency, as has been briefly pointed out above, is toward "stagflation." Inflation of domestic prices appears in an otherwise stagnating economy and is thus combined with unemployment. It can hardly be denied that this coincides with the attempt to establish welfare states. The question is whether there is a logcial connection between the two.

In a closed market economy, that is, one that is not at all, or only to a marginal extent, dependent on exchange of commodities with other markets (imports and exports), the mechanism of supply and demand works in a very simple way. If prices go up (inflation), either supply is increased or demand is restrained until economic balance is restored. Thus inflation tends to boost production. In a closed economy of the nonmarket type, such as those of Eastern Europe, the same result can be achieved by other means.

When imports and exports play a significant or even dominant role in the economy, these mechanisms do not work quite as simply as that, especially if—as in Scandinavia—the domestic market in question is too small to exercise more than a marginal influence on the rest of the world. When inflation is caused by increased prices of imported capital goods or raw materials, such as oil ("imported" inflation), in a market economy subject to no political or social pressures, or only to very weak pressures of that type, this can be offset by a corresponding reduction in demand for the goods and commodities in question, by a reduction in the cost of other means of production, such as domestic labor, or by allowing the labor force to be kept down by sizable unemployment. In this case inflation stimulates the economy only to the extent that domestic production can take the place of imports under viable economic conditions. Where inflation is caused not by external factors but by excessive domestic demand, the economy is stimulated only if this demand can be satisfied by domestic production, either directly or indirectly through an increase in exports, which makes it possible to import the required products. Both these situations, and especially the latter, call for a satisfactory level of productivity. Again, in a nonmarket economy similar results can be achieved by different means. At short range, monetary and financial policies can adjust difficulties in both types of societies.

The Scandinavian countries all depend largely on imports and exports for their well-being. As welfare states they are, however, unwilling to give free rein to the mechanisms relative to "imported" inflation. One of the characteristics of the welfare state is that the incomes of certain groups of the population are supplemented by "society" independently of their earnings. The tendency is to let the supplements rise in proportion to the price level, so that their demand remains unaltered in times of rising prices, including prices of imported goods. Another characteristic is the strength of employees' unions, which attempt to maintain as far as possible the real incomes of their members, thus making it difficult or impossible to offset "imported" inflation by reducing either domestic demand or other costs of production. As a result, at least "imported" inflation makes exported products more costly and less competitive, and production for export stagnates. To this extent the tendency toward stagflation is characteristic of welfare states, and Scandinavia is no exception.

Since the 1970s Denmark has been the Scandinavian country having the most trouble with such problems, followed by Sweden. In Norway, domestic production of oil has to some extent reduced the dangers of "imported" inflation. Finland at least for a time managed to keep down the cost of labor, thus maintaining competitiveness in its export industries. Growth of unemployment has been permitted in Denmark and to some extent in Finland, where this has, however, led to the temporary emigration of labor into neighboring Sweden under the auspices of the common labor market established by the Nordic countries. In Sweden, successive governments of different political colors have all attempted to resist any major growth of open unemployment. The success of their policies has been far from complete, and in any case the hidden unemployment referred to above has been growing.

It is sometimes maintained that the welfare state also tends to encourage voluntary unemployment: when incomes from social welfare approach the level of incomes earned by those doing regular work, there is little or no incentive to accept work at all. Recent Scandinavian experience does not substantiate such assumptions. It appears that the mere fact of being unemployed, regardless of income levels, has highly negative connotations for both men and women, both young and old.

In a mixed economy, where industry and trade for the most part remain in the private sector, taxes and related revenue constitute practically the only important source of income for the public sector. In fact, the total incidence of taxation roughly equals the cost of collective consumption plus transfers; it being understood that transfers themselves are also subject to taxation at least in part. Since collective consumption and transfers together correspond to about two-thirds of the GNP, tax revenues should on the average amount to nearly the same proportion. Statistics on the incidence of taxation are not always easy to interpret, but it appears that a little over one-third of this revenue originates from indirect taxes, less than one-fifth from direct taxes on private corporations, and the rest, or nearly one-half, from direct taxes on individuals, national and local. But since indirect taxes are also a burden on private persons, citizens would, on the average, pay at least half of their incomes in taxes. Even this, however, is not the whole story. Another complication is the proportion (or disproportion) between the working population on the one hand and those above or below working age on the other. The latter pay very little in direct taxes. Less than two-thirds of the Swedish population are between eighteen and sixty-six years of age, and within this age group a considerable number of young persons are engaged in study. Figures for the three other countries are similar, if a little less extreme. As a result, a skilled worker living in a locality where the local tax level is normal will pay almost half of his or her income in *direct* taxes alone.

The principle of "equitable" taxation, or in other words steep progression in direct taxes, is important to the extent that direct rather than indirect taxes constitute a substantial portion of the tax system. Progressive direct taxes almost by definition tend to put the burden on more successful individuals. Thus, they more or less discourage people from seeking success in terms of higher incomes or accumulation of capital—the more successful the individual, the steeper the tax progression becomes. On the other hand, it should be remembered that direct taxes are by no means always progressive. While this is the case with the income and property taxes of the state, the income taxes levied by regional and local bodies are proportionate above a certain minimum level. And the latter constitute roughly one-half of the direct tax revenue. When societies have become as egalitarian as in Scandinavia, even progressive taxes, moreover, do not have the same equalizing effect as they did previously. There are a few individuals who pay much more than the average in direct taxes, but their number is so small that their contribution is almost negligible. A somewhat larger number, but still comparatively few, pay less than the average. By far the largest part of the revenue from direct taxes, and of course from indirect taxes as well, is paid by the great majority of the people. This applies not only to proportionate but also to progressive taxes.

In the Socialist countries of Eastern Europe, indirect taxes are the main source of revenue. Their relative importance is rising in non-Socialist industrialized countries as well, and they have always formed the most important element in the public finances of the countries that are not yet industrialized. The Scandinavian countries for a long time resisted this trend but ultimately had to follow it to some extent. Clearly, indirect taxes are rarely as "equitable" as progressive or even proportionate direct taxes. They tend to put the major burden on people with large families and other groups with a high proportion of indispensable consumption. From the standpoint of egalitarian ambitions, they are usually counterproductive.

Another dilemma confronting the tax system of export-oriented welfare states is whether taxes should be primarily levied on individuals or on companies and other corporate bodies. On the one hand, individual wage earners are politically sensitive objects of taxation, and it is easy to argue that it is most desirable to make big corporations (and small entrepreneurs) carry the main burden of public expenditures. But under further analysis, this sort of argument proves altogether too facile. Taxes on export industries become a part of their cost of production. Even when the enterprises in question earn profits, an increase in costs at least limits their capacity for investments. Consequently heavy tax burdens make their products less competitive in the international market. This is particularly obvious in the case of taxes that are proportionate to production or to profits. But taxes that are instead related to the number of employees encourage investment in labor-saving devices which might reduce employment opportunities. And, finally, since major export industries tend to become multinational, a heavy tax burden could make them transfer production to other countries where taxes are lower, perhaps because social benefits are less generous. Actually, industries producing for the home market are confronted with many of the same problems insofar as they are exposed to foreign competition. Taxes have to be paid out of the price of their produce. And the price level determines whether they will be able to compete with goods imported from other countries. Home market industries and export industries are virtually in the same position.

To some extent, this type of problem exists everywhere, since in practically all countries the public sector has been growing with rising prosperity. But in so-called welfare states, aiming at an egalitarian social system together with political democracy, it is particularly difficult to pursue policies primarily directed toward maximum economic growth. In their immediate consequences—as distinct from what might result in the long run—such policies are rarely if ever compatible with an increase in equality. On the other hand, welfare states more than others need an economic basis, which can be created only if the economy as a whole is prosperous; and in the conditions of to-day it can remain prosperous only if it proves competitive in an international market where countries with other socioeconomic traditions and aims also attempt to achieve a growing share.

It is sometimes maintained that the free trade policies pursued thus far by the Scandinavian countries ought to be abandoned or at least modified in the light of this kind of competition. Perhaps special customs duties should be levied or quantitative restrictions placed on goods coming from countries where, for instance, the wage level is appreciably lower than in Scandinavia. Such suggestions, however, have always been countered by the argument that countries with small domestic markets, whose products therefore need a wide international market, cannot afford to take action that would almost undoubtedly lead to countermeasures endangering the very foundations of their prosperity.

Domestic resistance to heavy taxes appears in many forms. Perhaps the most obvious type of resistance, affecting both direct and indirect taxes on individuals, is the demand for compensatory wages, which can be brought forward with great emphasis owing to the strength of employees' organizations. Where such demands come from employees in the public sector, the effect of acceding to them is obviously to increase public expenditure and thus has to be balanced against the revenue from taxation. Where it is a question of employees in export industries, whether privately or publicly owned, compensatory wages increase the cost of production and make industry less competitive; the consequences may be reduced employment and indirectly also a reduction in tax revenue. Where production for the home market is concerned, reduced capacity for competition will increase imports, or raise the cost of living, or both. In any case, rising wages have inflationary effects, both on the cost side and on the demand side, while in the present circumstances rarely providing any appreciably stimulus to the economy. They are an element of the stagflation spiral.

Tax resistance is also a political fact of life. Especially since the majority of Scandinavian peoples—in contrast to less favored minorities—at present believe that they have reached definite or at least temporary saturation where social welfare is concerned, they are highly unwilling to allow any further increase in direct taxes. It is more or less generally accepted that such increases are virtually out of the question during normal times. In fact, it even appears that most people have become somewhat suspicious of certain elements of the welfare system, both transfers and collective consumption, when they have come to realize their consequences for the level of taxation.

And, finally, in daily life tax resistance appears in different and more unacceptable forms. Both enterprises and private individuals tend to organize their lives with regard to consequences in the field of taxation. Investments, for instance, are judged not only, sometimes not even primarily, on the basis of whether they are profitable, but rather from their effect on the tax level. Sometimes it appears more favorable, from this point of view, to borrow money for investments and even for expenditures, rather than to provide the necessary funds from increased earnings. Tax evasion, in the sense of using all available loopholes in the tax laws without actually breaking the law, is probably even more widespread in Scandinavia than elsewhere. In any case it is much more generally accepted than it used to be.

Such activities, while clearly undesirable, at least remain within the boundaries of the law. But illegal activities have also become increasingly common. The "gray market," where goods and services are exchanged directly, without payment, and consequently without being reported to the tax authorities, has been increasing by leaps and bounds and today is probably large enough to represent a real burden on the public economy. Even frankly fraudulent tax evasion is becoming more common and is almost accepted by the ordinary public. One of the architects of the welfare state in Sweden, Gunnar Myrdal, recently said that the Swedes are becoming a people of tax dodgers. The gap between legal and moral concepts is growing: tax dodging is undoubtedly illegal, but many Scandinavians refuse to regard it as immoral. It is difficult to see how it is possible to prevent the spread of such attitudes without drastically lowering the tax level—that is, without drastically reducing either transfers or collective consumption, or both. They threaten the very basis of the welfare state, particularly to the extent that the welfare of disfavored minorities has to be taken increasingly into consideration. The problem may not be insoluble—for instance, the majority may prove willing to pay directly for some of the benefits they receive—but so far no real solution has been put into effect.

Clearly, all this affects public finance. Local and even regional self-government is very much a part of the Scandinavian tradition.

Consequently it is by no means central, national government alone that has to finance the welfare system. On the contrary, to an extent that varies in each of the four countries and is probably greatest in Sweden, local and regional bodies have considerable responsibilities not only in adminsitering the welfare state, but equally in financing it. In the early days this caused problems especially in Norway, where it proved necessary to limit the fiscal autonomy of local bodies. In Denmark local autonomy had never been as strongly developed as in the other three countries, while both in Finland and in Sweden the parsimonious traditions of agricultural society remained long after industrialization and urbanization had taken place.

During the decades immediately following World War II the fiscal problems just mentioned did not appear unsurmountable in any of the four countries, neither for the national government nor for regional and local bodies. Budgets grew, and taxes rose at all levels, but the remarkable economic expansion that took place all over Scandinavia allowed budgets to expand more than tax rates, and with real incomes on the rise, taxpayers could be persuaded to let the public authorities take part of the increase in order to pay for transfers and collective consumption. They grumbled, but even in the higher income brackets the grumbling did not take on a revolutionary character, and the majority were too conscious of the improvement in their overall condition to react very violently to the fact that taxes rose steeply even for those belonging to "normal" income groups. In those days public authorities assumed obligations toward the citizens which were valid for the future and which in fact became increasingly costly as time went on. One reason for this was the changing population structure, with an increasing number of old people entitled to pensions and a smaller proportion of people in the wage-earning age groups. But what with the rationalization of production methods and an apparently permanently high economic growth, these problems did not seem very formidable. The public sector received greater resources.

In the 1970s the situation changed. The rate of economic growth fell, sometimes to zero or below zero, and the prospect of future high growth disappeared not only in the Scandinavian countries, but in the whole industrialized world, which was to provide the market for their products. In the new situation, it became more and more of a problem to finance the budget expansion caused by hard and fast obligations incurred during the fat years, let alone to provide further "reforms" involving improvement of social benefits.

In many respects, the problem is particularly serious at the local and regional levels. National legislatures, at least in theory, are in a position to go back on past promises. But local and regional bodies are bound by national legislation, which they have no power to amend. It is true that they also receive very considerable subsidies from the central government, but it is a moot point whether these subsidies are really sufficient to correspond to the responsibilities that the local and regional bodies are supposed to fulfill. On the other hand, they are exposed to strong pressures from local public opinion, not only at election time but perpetually. In this respect they are much more vulnerable than the central government. In Sweden, where the local bodies enjoy almost total fiscal autonomy and have always resisted any suggestion of change in this respect, the situation is becoming very difficult indeed, especially because of the tax resistance referred to earlier in this chapter.

Of course, the obvious answer to these questions should be higher productivity and efficiency, making industry more competitive and allowing the Scandinavian countries continued high economic growth regardless of what might happen to less efficient industrialized countries. With increasing shares of the world market they would obviously be better off than the others. The question remains whether the development of welfare states in Scandinavia favors such an increase of efficiency or on the contrary makes it more difficult to achieve.

One of the traditional arguments against the welfare state is that it supposedly reduced incentives to efficiency and productivity. Why, it is asked, should people go on working efficiently if they are certain of having enough to get by in any case? Surely it is in human nature to be as lazy as possible. People will work, or at least work efficiently, only if they really have to do so, the alternative being stark poverty. The Scandinavian experience does not bear out any such simple arguments. On the contrary, the decades following the social reforms of the 1930s, when social security was firmly established and further developed, coincide with what was probably the period of greatest efficiency in Scandinavian economic history. It is true that there is perhaps a difference in devotion to work, or at least in carefulness, between the older and the younger generation. But it does on the whole seem farfetched to blame social security or the welfare state for this. The tendency is universal and most probably related to the decrease in craftsmanship attending automation and other character-istics of modern industrialism. In fact, the Scandinavian labor move-ment has traditionally insisted on efficiency in production. When "solidarity in wage policies" was first introduced, the new approach was actually intended to increase efficiency in the long run. Those enterprises that were unable to pay higher wages, or even those branches of production in which the average wage level was very low, it was argued, must be regarded as inefficient and ought to disappear, their employees transferring to other, more profitable because more efficient productive units. This attitude was characteristic especially of the 1950s in Scandinavia. Thirty years later, when the tendency to unemployment has become stronger, it is less in evidence. But even now Scandinavian unions' approach to rationalized production methods differs from that of the British labor unions, partly because the latter continue to organize labor in trade unions according to the type of work performed, while in Scandinavia we have seen that there are nowadays practically only industrial unions and that wage negoti-ations are carried out on an industry-wide or even on a nationwide basis, not separately for each enterprise or group of enterprises.

This doe not mean, however, that there are no problems or that those that appear have no relation to the establishment of welfare states. As noted earlier, it is extremely difficult to assess efficiency and productivity in the service sector, whether private or public, and the number of people employed in services, as distinct from produc-tion, is continually growing. This, again, is a universal phenomenon, but at least in the public sector it is not independent of welfare. And where efficiency and productivity cannot be ascertained with any degree of objectivity, it is possible that they will deteriorate. Many observers of the Scandinavian scene contend that this has happened, at least where public services are concerned. Their contention cannot be objectively proved, but neither can it be disproved, and general impressions are not entirely without importance.

With regard to actual production, the welfare state has an approach that differs from what was accepted in more "capitalist" societies. In the latter, productivity and efficiency were measured separately for each individual enterprise, and the criteria were the quantity and quality of the product of that enterprise. It is now beginning to be accepted that such an approach is too limited. It is necessary to take into account the effects on society as a whole, on the well-being and health of employees, on the general and regional employment situation, on other enterprises in the same field and in other fields, as well as on the environment. Furthermore, it is not enough to reckon with the cost of production within the enterprise. The cost to society as a whole of maintaining related public services, for instance, roads and other means of transport and communications, has to be considered as well. If the enterprise reduces its labor force in order to become more profitable, the result may be unemployment, and taking care of the unemployed is a matter for "society," that is, for the taxpayers. The recognition of concepts such as "social cost" and "social productivity" necessitates a new approach to the whole problem. At the same time it can hardly be denied that widening the horizon makes it much more difficult to measure, and therefore to maintain, the efficiency of the individual unit of production.

As a matter of fact, few attempts at calculating the economy of social cost and social productivity are made either by management or by public authorities. The latter are simply squeezed between different pressure groups, representing the interests of maximum direct productivity on the one hand and maximum social considerations on the other, and in consequence their attitudes are rarely consistent and frequently not even rational. The arguments coming from management are on the face of it entirely rational, but since the vision of managers is restricted by blinders allowing a view only of their own enterprise or enterprises, its or their problems and interests, the conclusions presented can hardly be taken at face value.

While the labor unions have never denied the need for efficiency in production, at the same time they have at least in recent decades been totally unwilling to admit that employees should identify themselves with the enterprise where they are working, or even with the particular public service employing them. The idea that a particular enterprise or public service enjoys community of interest with its own employees apparently runs counter to both the ideology and the practice of the unions. As a result, while accepting the principle of maximum efficiency and productivity, the unions tend to make it more and more of an abstraction, relating to the national economy as a whole rather than to particular employers and employees. One should not, however, overestimate the importance of labor organizations in this respect. Where management is able to win the confidence of employees, identification takes place regardless of union attitudes, and its absence is perhaps due primarily to the "economy of scale" that obstructs human relations within industrial enterprises.

At one time it was assumed that cooperatives, especially consumers' coops, were going to play a very important, if not dominating role in the economic life of welfare states. One of those who believed this was Marquis Childs, as evidenced by his book *Sweden: The Middle Way*. In retrospect it appears quite obvious that their importance has never been much more than marginal, and that they are now stagnating. In the Scandinavian countries, consumers' cooperatives made it a rule to operate on commercial principles. They competed successfully with minor private enterprises in the retail trade, acquiring about 20 to 25 percent of the market, drove some of them out of business, and compelled the others to keep price levels down and to rationalize their system of distribution. They also went into production, but mainly in commodities they were selling in their retail shops, and only when this was warranted by the conditions of competition with private retailers. In production for exports, cooperatives have never been of any major importance, and even in the home market they ceased to expand when private enterprises had learned their lesson and became more efficient. Housing cooperatives were of great importance just before World War II but have since been largely superseded by housing projects directly managed by city authorities. Producers' cooperatives enjoy virtual monopolies in agriculture, but this is due to government policies, which they partly administer, rather than to their own independent strength and action. In the field of forestry, producers' cooperatives in Sweden expanded greatly during the 1950s and 1960s but found themselves in great difficulties during the recession of the 1970s and had to call on the government for help. In processing industries, producers' cooperatives in which enterprises are owned by the employees themselves have appeared but rarely and usually with scant success.

With respect to the general business structure, the Scandinavian countries have thus not departed very much from the general trends of the industrialized world. Scandinavian industry has done its best to develop economy of scale as well as automation. Many industrial units have become multinational in order to compete successfully in the international market. This is true especially of some Swedish Corporations, such as L. M. Ericsson (telecommunications), SKF (ball bearings), ASEA (heavy electrics), Volvo (motor vehicles). In proportion to its population, and possibly also in relation to its GNP, Sweden probably has more multinational corporations than any other industrialized country, not excepting the United States of America.

Just like the other industrialized countries, those in Scandinavia benefited from the low cost of energy (oil) in the decades following World War II. Both in Norway and in Sweden, hydroelectric power became relatively less important. Earlier it seemed to make up for the lack of mineral fuel, but by the 1930s it had already largely exhausted its potential, and when oil prices rose rapidly in the 1970s Denmark, Finland and Sweden did, as has been already emphasized, feel the effect very strongly, since their industries were based on high consumption of energy. Norway, which is oil-producing in the North Sea, was not affected to the same extent, although it will take considerable time before its oil resources can act as a real stimulus to the economy. Finland and Sweden have begun to make use of nuclear energy, although this is highly controversial in Sweden and it has so far proved neither economically nor politically possible to exploit Swedish deposits of uranium.

All this is just background. It has nothing to do with the development of welfare states, and as has already been pointed out even the relative growth of the service sector in the economy is but part of a worldwide tendency. It might be added that one particular aspect of the business structure could have been affected by the exigencies of the welfare states. Owing to the strength of labor unions and the rigidity of the wage system, small enterprises have to maintain at least the same wage level as larger ones. Moreover, in egalitarian societies with high taxes such as those of Scandinavia, it is not easy to profit from the use of owners' and operators' capital. Consequently it could be argued that the universal tendency toward concentration in producing industries, as well as in the service sector, has been further accentuated by Scandinavian conditions and policies. The difference, however, is probably marginal.

The Nordic countries combine high ambitions as welfare states with an increasing dependence on foreign trade. Exports correspond to nearly 50 percent of the GNP in oil-producing Norway, about 35 percent in Denmark and Finland, and 30 percent in Sweden. Without foreign trade, these countries could not maintain anything like their present standards of living, since their home market is small and their supply of raw materials is limited. Even taken together they cannot compete in these respects with, for instance, the European Economic Communities.

At one time there were plans for a Nordic economic community (Nordek), but these plans did not materialize, for political rather than for economic reasons. Denmark later decided to join the EEC, while a similar proposal was defeated in a referendum in Norway. In Sweden there was considerable debate on the subject, but the ultimate decision was to stay aloof on the plea of neutrality. In Finland, no proposal of membership was even broached. But the three countries who remained outside the EEC all negotiated treaties of extensive economic cooperation with that organization, and it is clear that they, no less than Denmark, are part of the Western European economy. This includes Finland, whose economic ties with the Soviet Union were very strong right after the war but have lost much of their importance as the Finnish economy has developed and become modernized. Today Finland's trade with the Comecon countries is less than 20 percent of its total trade volume. In the other Nordic countries economic relations with the Socialist countries of Eastern Europe never had more than marginal importance. In fact Nordic economic cooperation has been growing even without Nordek, under the umbrella of Denmark's membership and the other Nordic countries' treaties with EEC.

In these circumstances, and with their unavoidable policies of free trade, the economies of the Nordic countries are largely dependent on economic developments in other industrialized countries, above all in Western Europe but also in the United States and Japan. As a consequence, the scope for steering their economies by government action is increasingly limited. And this is a problem also where egalitarian ambitions are concerned. A good example is policies on interest rates. Traditionally the Nordic countries attempted already before 1939, and even more definitely after 1945, to keep the rate of interest down. This was held to favor both farmers, who had mortgaged their farms and also had to finance sizable temporary loans, and the broad strata of the urban population, since the rate of interest has of course a very considerable and direct impact on the cost of housing. Throughout the 1950s and into the 1960s these policies were pursued, and indeed the ambition to pursue them is still present. But it has proved impossible to do so in the face of rising interest rates in the major industrialized countries. Considerable, if not completely free capital movements are essential to any economy based on foreign trade, and if the relative rate of interest of one country, say Sweden, is very low, the result is an outflow of capital which rapidly threatens the economy. The smaller members of the club of industrialized countries actually need an *inflow* of capital in order to keep pace with their stronger brethren in the club, and this is possible only if the rate of interest is not much lower than elsewhere. Thus dependence on international economic relations acts contrary to domestic egalitarian policies, while the latter can be successful and raise the standard of living of broad strata of the population only if international relations flourish.

Perhaps the greatest economic problems of egalitarian welfare states such as those in Scandinavia are related to capital formation. This is only natural. Distribution of incomes has been equalized by means of progressive taxes on individuals and of transfers. But capital distribution still remains unequal. This is unsatisfactory from the egalitarian point of view. At the same time, modern industry requires a great supply of capital in order to be competitive. And since the Scandinavian countries have mixed and not socialized economic systems, most of their capital somehow remains in private hands. This is the dilemma: having great lumps of capital in private hands conflicts with egalitarian principles, but without great lumps of capital, industry, which is supposed to remain in private hands, would be unable to function.

Capital formation by individuals is based on savings. Modern industrial society therefore must encourage saving. But in the welfare state some of the traditional incentives have disappeared. Because of inflation, which apparently has come to stay, it is difficult to calculate whether saving is a profitable activity. Moreover, the immediate reasons for saving are not the same as before. People used to save for a rainy day, but now they are legally entitled to an umbrella in the form of diverse social benefits. This security does not, as we have seen, keep them from working, in part because they are after all better off earning wages than living on the dole. But saving is different: why not use the earnings at once, to brighten their otherwise dreary life? The same argument applies with regard to another traditional reason for saving: providing an education for one's children. Education is free, and supplemented by students' benefits. People also used to save in order to collect capital which should be inherited by their children. But this appears less necessary than it did formerly, and any major capital collected for such purposes is subject to heavy, sometimes almost confiscatory inheritance taxes. The justification for such taxation lies in the concept of social justice: those who inherit tend to be no better qualified than those for whom no inheritance is available. But it can hardly be denied that saving, that is, capital formation, becomes less attractive when owners lose all or some of their capacity to decide what will happen to their capital in the next generation. Obviously it is reasonable to save at a given time in order to be able to acquire, at a later date, a house, a better car, or some other substantial capital goods. This, of course, still goes on, but here too the incentive is being reduced. On the one hand, inflation consumes savings, at least in their simple forms such as bank balances. On the other hand, the tax system together with inflation favors those who decide not to have any savings but acquire what they want at once, on borrowed funds which are later paid back in devalued money.

Household savings are reduced by the equitable distribution of incomes. Spending must, of course, consume a larger part of low incomes, since most of those go to acquire the necessities or near-necessities of life. And what the "necessities" are cannot be objectively determined. The word refers to standards that rise with the average income level. With a higher income than the average, it is more natural to save at least part of it, especially in a society where ostentatious spending is frowned upon. Important here are obviously real incomes after taxes have been paid and subsidies received. Again, the greater the equality, the smaller the chance of savings.

This, however, is all theory. In fact there is little indication that the savings rate went down in any of the Scandinavian countries following their transformation into welfare states, beginning in the 1930s. Not only aggregate savings, but also the proportion of savings to earnings has remained at a level that is acceptable in comparison with that of other Western European countries, without of course coming anywhere near that of Japan.

The comparison with Japan is interesting also from another point of view. When inflation was rampant in Japan in the early 1970s, reaching a peak of more than 30 percent over a twelve-month period, the rate of interest on deposits in banks was very far from compensating for the loss in value of money. Notwithstanding, the Japanese continued their high savings rate and deposited their savings in banks, although on the face of it this was manifestly unreasonable. By the same token, Scandinavians continue to save to about the same extent in spite of reduced incentives.

Different explanations can be found for this phenomenon, apparently showing that neither Scandinavians nor Japanese are "economic men" in the sense of acting to maximize their economic advantage. One possible explanation is the force of tradition. This is probably correct in the case of Japan, where the "negative rate of interest" on savings was in effect only for a very brief period. It is less plausible in the case of Scandinavia, where the background changed gradually over several decades. Another explanation could be that even in the circumstances of the welfare state individuals retain a certain feeling of insecurity, or that they are simply not in the habit of calculating their long-range economic advantages and disadvantages. Moreover, during certain periods credit restrictions have been applied, making it difficult for ordinary individuals to borrow from banks or otherwise in the open market, or encouraging savings for instance by tax allowances or by making them a precondition of certain loans. All this is speculation; but the maintenance of a reasonably high level of household savings by individuals remains a fact.

This does not mean that the problem of capital formation has been resolved for the Nordic countries. It still presents great difficulties, since the combination of their dependence on industrial exports and the very limited size of their home markets actually calls for a rather steeply *increasing* level of capital investment if they are to remain competitive in the world market today. And such investment cannot easily be financed from the stagnating savings of individuals, as were the less extensive investments required some decades ago.

Thus far, we have dealt with savings by individuals. This of course includes also the capital in the hands of the banks, since it is savings by individuals which makes up bank accounts. Insurance companies are different, and their capital actually plays a very considerable role in the Scandinavian economies, notwithstanding the fact that the welfare system provides a considerable part of the security which elsewhere can be found only in private insurance policies. On the other hand, both banks and insurance companies are subject to strict limitations on their investments. This is done in order to safeguard depositors and policy holders, but it also means that their capital is not always available where it would make the greatest contribution to economic development.

Up to a point successful enterprises are able to provide their own capital by "plowing down" their profits in investment for further development. This is also favored by the tax system, which only to a minor extent touches capital that is reinvested in the company, while coming down heavily on dividends paid to shareholders. It was characteristic of Scandinavian enterprises in the first decades after 1945 that they relied largely on this type of capital formation, in fact to such a degree that the government sometimes worried about being deprived of its power to steer industrial development. On the other hand, while such capital can be used to some extent for extending the activities of the enterprise, it is more favorable for existing units than for new ventures. And it provides only very limited resources which can be carried over from a boom tinto a subsequent recession of any length.

Another factor in the capital market of Sweden, but not of the other three Nordic countries, is the very large funds established in connection with the system of general old age pensions (ATP). Actually, controversy over the new system in the 1950s and 1960s was related less to the pensions—which were generally regarded as necessary or at least highly desirable—than to these funds. They were criticized as a Socialist device reducing the freedom of capital investment. In order to meet such criticisms, it was initially stipulated that the funds could not be employed for the acquisition of stock or for similar long-term capital investment in enterprises. Later the rules were modified, and one of the four pensions funds is now available for such purposes. On the other hand, the governing boards of the four funds enjoy such independence that the state is unable to use the funds for steering the economy. Moreover, investments have been made very cautiously and have not included acquisition of decisive influence in any industrial or commercial enterprise. Still, there is little doubt that the pensions funds have both directly and even more indirectly contributed to the possibilities for remunerative investment in productive enterprises.

Recently a new proposal has come under consideration both in Sweden and in Denmark. Labor unions, it is argued, could be persuaded to restrict their wage demands if private enterprises were compelled to invest a considerable part of their profits in special, regional cooperative funds, which should be invested according to policies acceptable to the unions. The scheme is labeled "employee funds" in Sweden, where it was hotly debated during the election campaign in 1982. The specific plans for the funds were, however, never made very clear. Thus it is by no means decided whether they should be governed, at least indirectly, by the unions or by boards designated in general popular elections. In Denmark the term "economic democracy" is applied to similar ideas, but these are not of the same immediate interest as is the case in Sweden. And in both countries it is argued that this is just another technique for introducing Socialism and destroying the free market economy. In fact many of its proponents would probably admit that the ultimate aim is to liquidate or at least drastically curtail private ownership of the means of production, while the diversity of channels of public influence should preserve some of the competition that was characteristic of the "capitalist" system.

In this respect it appears probable that the Yugoslavian system of decentralized Socialist economy has at least in part served as a model for Scandinavian Socialists. More important, however, is another argument that has been repeated over and over again in the debate. The pattern of "solidarity in wage policies" prevents the employees of successful enterprises from reaping major benefits of their employers' successes by means of wage and salary negotiations, since they have to consider also the situation in less successful enterprises in the same branch of industry, or even of less successful branches of industry. This situation favors shareholders in the successful companies. In order to obviate such offenses against "social justice," these shareholders should be forced to forgo some of their advantages by means of fees levied on company profits above the average as well as by being compelled to issue additional stock, to be subscribed presumably by "employee funds" outside their control. It is maintained also that this plan would favor capital formation and investments in productive industries at the expense of short-term consumption and investment in nonproductive, purely financial enterprises. It could also be used in order to facilitate the development of backward regions of the countries. However, the fundamental aim is probably to strengthen and stabilize the power of labor in relation to that of private capital and to provide the labor movement with a citadel of power that could withstand reverses in parliamentary elections.

The proposal has been actively opposed, partly on ideological grounds but also from the standpoint of its practical consequences. It is characteristic of the atmosphere of debate in the Nordic countries that the latter type of counterargument has been the most prominent. "Capital," "capitalist," and "capitalism" being bad words in Scandinavian public language, it is doubtful whether public opinion can be influenced to any major extent by proving that "employee funds" or "economic democracy" injures the legitimate rights of ownership. The public is not quite convinced that there are any "legitimate interests" in the case of capital owners. Still, the new ideas have by no means taken hold with the public. Powerful organizations like the labor unions are also objects of suspicion, if one degree less so than "capitalists," and not everybody is convinced that they would continue to watch over the interests of wage and salary earners if the unions were directly or indirectly involved as owners of enterprises. Furthermore, even many of those who were originally very critical of capitalism have come to think that it would be difficult to maintain a pluralist system of democracy if economic power were to be concentrated in the hands of politically elected authorities together with labor unions who would often be their allies. Finally, strong practical arguments are advanced as well. There seems to be a serious risk that the governing boards of funds of the proposed type would be unable to resist pressures from those interests that would require them to use their investment capacity in order to "save" enterprises in difficulties and thus contain or postpone local unemployment. There appears to be but little confidence in their capacity to hold rigorously to investments in successful and potentially expansive industries.

Already at present the unions have accumulated considerable quantities of capital. This was done in order to provide the necessary resources for use in the case of strikes, lockouts, and similar events. In view of the long periods of labor peace especially in Sweden, but also in the three other countries, the unions have been forced to use their resources in labor conflicts only to a very limited extent. They have therefore often put their money in more permanent investments, but only rarely in industrial or commercial undertakings. Instead they have acquired real estate or similar permanent capital goods.

Another policy for capital formation was put into effect in the 1950s and 1960s, when there still was a margin for possible tax increases. At that time, the idea was to have the public sector, both state and local units, finance all its investments out of annual revenue, leaving the domestic capital market free for loans to be floated by industrial and commercial enterprises. In reality this would mean "saving" by the public authorities through revenue financing of lasting real capital investments. The policy was successful for a while, when times were good, and was on the face of it in agreement with anticyclical economic theory as far as it went. Also, it is true that industry in the Nordic countries was at that time able to make useful investments at relatively moderate cost. The system was, however, also utilized for expansion of the public sector by increasing public revenues and expenditures during periods when according to the accepted theory public investments ought to have contracted; the long-range effects were consequently not what had been envisaged. Actually, the state and local bodies acquired little or no remunerative property. On the contrary, as has been pointed out earlier, the expansion of the public sector involved considerable commitments for the future, which had to be fulfilled regardless of general economic trends.

The "managerial revolution" in Scandinavia, as in other industrialized countries, has transferred power from shareholders into the hands of highly skilled technocrats and administrators, employed by them but habitually not following their wishes. To this extent, "capitalism" nowhere functions as it did in the nineteenth century. But what is specific to the Nordic countries is a determined policy enforced particularly through the tax system and aimed at reducing the economic yield to individual shareholders. Not only is the company taxed (at a proportionate rate) for its declared net profit. In addition, individual shareholders have to pay state taxes at a progressive rate for the capital they hold as stock, and both state and local taxes for their income from dividends. Thus shareholders enjoy neither power nor any appreciable profits from their capital. The advantage to them lies exclusively in the rising value of stock when times are good; but if and when they want to realize their capital by selling, the profit may be subject to income tax. It is likely that those who invest in company shares have more of the characteristics of "economic man" than do other individuals. In any case, investment of this type has proved attractive only in times of relatively high rates of inflation, and even then it has proved less attractive than investment for instance in real estate. There is no doubt that it is increasingly difficult for enterprises wanting to embark on new and slightly hazardous ventures to get access to necessary capital.

What is characteristic of the societies described here is that they attempt, in highly industrialized and sophisticated countries, dependent on constant exchange of goods and services with the rest of the world, to establish economic and social equality while maintaining effective political democracy. Not content with equality of opportunities in a competitive setup, they intend to realize equality of results, at least to a relatively great extent, and to restrict the scope for competition among individuals. Redistribution of incomes has been largely effected by means of collective consumption as well as by transfers through taxes and subsidies. While capital distribution is still unequal, both the power and the profits of capital have been drastically reduced, although not completely abolished.

In such societies, traditional economic incentives have become largely meaningless. The presumed reactions of "economic man" consequently do not operate along traditional lines, or perhaps not at all. This applies in a number of different fields: work, savings, investments. By far the largest part of the net national product goes to the broad groups of consumers, most of whom are wage earners employed either in corporate private enterprises or by public authorities. Profits or other net incomes out of the ordinary are regarded with suspicion and sometimes held to be downright immoral. In any case they can be acquired almost only by chance, for instance by winning a prize in a lottery, or by illegal or immoral means such as evading taxes.

It is no exaggeration to say that this is a new economic order—based on the same principles as what is being called by that name in international relations, but different in being at least in great parts a reality and not just a dream. It should be added that Scandinavia is far from unique in having realized something of the sort. In fact, to a larger or smaller extent the same new economic order is found all over Western Europe and even on the other side of the Atlantic Ocean, as well as in Australia, New Zealand, and Japan. The interest in studying the welfare states of Scandinavia lies in their having acquired a relatively long experience of what can be achieved by the system and what problems it involves.

One of the prerequisites for success is that the economy must remain internationally competitive and consequently that productivity should be maintained at a high level. In the welfare state, where traditional incentives are no longer efficient, and competition among individuals is frowned upon, this calls for a sort of unselfishness, or high moral standards among ordinary wage earners, managers, and entrepreneurs. To this extent, it is basically "Socialist." Its most fundamental principle is solidarity, not individualism. Not individual gain or competitive success, but solidarity with one's fellowmen, is supposed to act as an incentive for efficient production.

As we have seen, both the labor movement and other mass organizations have for a long time emphasized the need for solidarity. This began when they felt that they were fighting other groups ("classes") or individuals. Solidarity was motivated by the need to unite against common adversaries. But with the advent of the welfare state it became increasingly difficult for the majority of the population to maintain class consciousness in the sense of feeling oppressed. What became necessary at that stage was to create solidarity with society as a whole, not negatively, on the basis of nationalism and chauvinism, but as an incentive for positive action directed toward the well-being of all fellow-creatures.

It is extremely difficult to determine the extent to which such solidarity has been achieved. Traditional fears that with social security people might stop working, saving, and investing have so far not proved realistic, but there are no certain indications whether this is because of genuine solidarity, because of the economic climate, or simply because old habits are apt to continue even when their original justifications have disappeared. In corporate enterprises the profit motive still operates, but in somewhat new ways. Calculations based on the effects of the tax system create as much interest as those relating directly to productivity, since the capacity to remain competitive depends largely on the former. And in the export-oriented economies of Scandinavia this must be the most important concern, even from the standpoint of solidarity with society as a whole. "Common men" (and women) are in a different situation. For them, the conflict between individualism and solidarity cannot be avoided. Since it is only by illegal or immoral means (or by sheer fluke) that they can increase their incomes appreciably above the average, the temptation to use such means is correspondingly greater. There are indications that both prostitution and crimes against property have also become more common, since they provide sources of income out of reach of fiscal authorities.

The appearance of such phenomena does indeed involve serious problems for the further development and maintenance of welfare states in the Nordic countries. Economics is after all a matter of social psychology. If the negative tendencies become more widespread, or even if they continue to appear on the same scale as in the recent past, this indicates that it has been impossible to establish such lasting feelings of solidarity as can compensate for the disappearance or decreasing importance of traditional economic incentives. It is doubtful whether anything can be changed by instituting harsher legal penalties for the infraction of rules established to safeguard the strength and growth of resources for the public sector. Legislation running counter to widespread opinions about what is permissible has rarely proved effective. And if nothing can be done to change attitudes in this respect, the basis of both transfers and collective consumption is faltering.

The development of a new economic order in the Nordic countries after the Second World War coincided with spectatcular economic growth in the industrialized world as a whole. During the least part of this period the Nordic countries even improved their economic position relative to other prosperous countries. It thus seems obvious that their egalitarian policies did not impair their competitive capacities, in any case not to any alarming extent. The pessimistic predictions of some critics apparently came to nought. Some other observers even argued that the shoe was on the other foot. The "economy of high wages" should be conducive to efficiency and productivity, and with increased feelings of security, higher standards of living and greater equality, the people would devote themselves more wholeheartedly to pursuits benefiting society as a whole.

But the relation of cause and effect may have been entirely different. Granted that egalitarianism did not prevent economic growth, it is equally possible that it was only thanks to economic growth that social and economic differences could be leveled. As long as there was economic improvement for everybody, reapportionment of material benefits in favor of groups that were less well-off could take place without too much difficulty. With stagnating or even diminishing resources, competition might reappear and "social justice" become less attractive, especially when the latter had to be applied in favor of minority groups.

Experiences of the late 1970s and early 1980s indicate that the second interpretation might be the correct one. On the other hand, it is possible that the aforesaid tendencies are characteristic only of a transitory phase and result from difficulties in adapting to new conditions of life and work in postindustrial or "postmaterialistic" society. In that case, there is no direct threat to the existence and further development of the new economic order, but rather a very definite need to analyze how it can be made to function in an international environment where the countries in question must exchange goods and services with those whose economic policies still work along more traditional lines.

This need has become more important because of another development that has become evident in recent decades, namely, the growth of multinational elements in economic life. So far, multinational enterprises have remained national to a considerable extent, but it would be overly optimistic to believe that they could in the long run be prevailed upon to allow idealism or national solidarity to determine their field of operation. National legislation affects them very little in that respect. If they want to transfer from countries where their ambitions for expansion and profit seem to be frustrated into others where they are more appreciated, it is difficult if not downright impossible to prevent them from doing so.

To the layman following the current debate on economic policy, it appears that all participants are arguing on the basis of national societies where the economic self-interest, at best enlightened, of groups and individuals still determines their actions and reactions. This was of course true of classical economists such as Adam Smith and David Ricardo, but it applies almost equally to John Maynard Keynes, whose ideas were so important for the growth of welfare states both in Scandinavia and elsewhere. And Marxism, for all its bitter denunciation of capitalist society, starts from the same assumptions, and its doctrine provides only the most sketchy picture of what could be the alternative in terms of a working economic system. Syndicalism and utopian Socialism both appear to be irrelevant to an internationalized economy. The practical experiments with Socialism in Eastern Europe and elsewhere provide no guidance to societies like those of Scandinavia. Regardless of whether or not such regimes have been successful in securing satisfactory economic growth and reasonably high standards of living for the common people—and most outside observers would say that they have failed in this respect—it is incontestable that in the process they have dispensed with most of the requirements of individual and social freedom as well as of political democracy. All indications seem to suggest that this is because they have not had confidence in the capacity of moral principles, such as that of solidarity, to replace traditional incentives as the mainspring of economic development.

Should this prove to be different in welfare states such as those of Scandinavia, it is hardly too much to say that the sociological or social-psychological basis underlying economic theory has changed and that consequently the theory itself will have to be reconsidered in its entirety. The effect of such a reconsideration on economic policies must be very considerable, to say the least, in Scandinavia as elsewhere in a world where national economic measures have to be adapted at every point to a changing international environment. Enthusiastic moralists maintain that this is what is going to happen. In their opinion it is no longer necessary to rely on self-interest, not even on enlightened self-interest, as the basis of economic relations. Its place can be taken by solidarity: class solidarity, national solidarity, or even international solidarity.

Economists persist in arguing on the basis of traditional psychological assumptions. But contrary to what was the case in the 1930s, there is no wall-to-wall carpet of economic theory on which to stand while dealing with what is essentially a new situation. Neo-Keynesians concentrate on measures for overcoming unemployment, supply-side economists on actions that appear to give hope of reducing inflation. It may well be that the followers of one of these groups, or the supporters of both, can achieve a modicum of success in regard to their specific objectives. Unemployment may go down temporarily at the price of rising inflation; inflation may be reduced at the price of growing or permanently high unemployment. But the combined phenomenon of stagflation is hardly even analyzed by the economists, and no recommendations are brought forward which could enable bewildered politicians to reduce unemployment without danger of creating higher inflation, or to overcome inflation while achieving the goal of something like full employment.

Governing the Welfare State

The Scandinavian welfare states are the offspring of political democracy. There was considerable welfare of a paternalistic type before the advent of democracy, and civil rights were comparatively well protected long before popular government was established. But the characteristic elements of welfare states were established as a result of popular pressure exercised through the accepted channels of democratic systems, and not from benevolent forces above the heads of the common people. In fact much or perhaps even most of the movement toward democracy was motivated by the wish to create political mechanisms suitable for improving the living standard of the working classes.

Consequently an understanding of the political framework is indisputably necessary for an analysis of these welfare states. Among other things it explains the haphazard and illogical form in which welfare arrangements appeared, at least in the beginning. The founding fathers did not consistently set out to realize systematically conceived ideas of the good society, but were content to solve immediate problems, as indeed all democratic governments are apt to do.

But it is equally important to consider the administrative system. This, also, is a product of historical developments, most of which took place long before the welfare state was even thought of. Just as much as constitutional principles, administrative practices are conditioned by national culture. They differ fundamentally from one country to another. It is a serious mistake to regard them as just technical gadgets which from time to time can be adapted to the needs of the moment. No administrative order can be made to work efficiently if it is not understood by the people, and popular comprehension of innovations develops as slowly in this respect as in others.

It should be noted that in all four Nordic countries democracy has been taken for granted for a long time—in fact ever since the First World War. In Scandinavia the world was apparently made "safe for democracy." Fascist tendencies appeared for a short while in Finland at the beginning of the 1930s, but they never became predominant, and in the other countries they were negligible, at least if one excepts the quislings in Norway and Denmark during the German occupation. Communism nowadays appears in the form called "Eurocommunist" and has thus more or less completely abandoned the doctrine of the dictatorship of the proletariat. In fact political democracy is being regarded as self-evident to such a degree that it is no longer debated or even analyzed. Hardly anyone is willing to entertain the idea that it may not be safe forever and that an effort is needed in order to maintain it. On the contrary, the word "democracy," being universally regarded as honorific, is used to cover a number of other ideas: for instance, democratic education means education in freedom, and economic democracy signifies egalitarianism or alternatively the power of wage earners over management in industry. Once the term is accepted, it would appear to be invidious to oppose the idea. On the whole, most people know what political democracy means. They may not be able to define it, but they easily recognize its presence or absence, and they undoubtedly want it.

The establishment of a "new economic order" in the Nordic countries has affected their constitutional and political life and even more the working of their public administration. Considerable changes have taken place in these respects, although in accordance with tradition they have been gradual rather than sudden, almost imperceptible rather than spectacular. It would be a mistake to pass over them lightly, but they are not always easily identified. The extent to which they have been caused by the establishment of welfare states and not by other contemporary developments often remains in doubt. Such things as the vastly increased power of the mass media also affect both politics and administration, and they are but distantly related to the new economic order. Moreover, in many cases, perhaps in most of them, what has happened is not specific to Scandinavia. Similar changes and tendencies to change appear in other industrialized countries and even those outside that category. The Nordic countries are often no more than examples of what is happening throughout the world.

If we look back into the past, we shall find that constitutional developments were rather different. Sweden's constitution of 1809 was influenced by earlier constitutions and practices, as well as by general European ideas during the Enlightenment and the French Revolution. Parliamentary reform came in 1865. Subsequently the franchise was gradually widened, and universal suffrage for men and women was finally achieved right after the First World War. Responsible Cabinet government also was established gradually over a period of almost one hundred years while the power of the monarchy diminished throughout the nineteenth century, and since 1914 it was never exercised independently, although the terms of the constitution still presumed its existence. In 1973 a new constitution replaced the patchwork that remained from 1809, the idea (possibly unrealistic!) being to express constitutional realities in the document.

Norway, which had been a part of Denmark until 1814, adopted a new constitution—which still remains in force—in 1814, a few months before the country was united with Sweden in a dynastic union, that is, under a joint king but with two separate Parliaments. Eventually the Norwegian legislature became supreme and in 1905 achieved dissolution of the union with Sweden without repealing the constitution. On the whole, similar constitutional developments appeared a little earlier in Norway than in the neighboring country.

In Denmark kings retained supreme and virtually unlimited personal power a few decades longer than on the Scandinavian peninsula. A new constitution was adopted in 1848, however, and since then developments have been parallel to those of Sweden and Norway, although they were complicated by problems of nationalism connected with the duchies of Slesvig and Holstein.

As long as Finland was part of Sweden it had no constitution of its own but was ruled in accordance with Swedish constitutional law. The relevant constitutional documents of 1772 and 1789 remained in force in Finland when in 1809 the country was transferred as a "Grand Duchy" to the Russian realm, and since they gave preeminent power to the Crown they could be accepted by the czars, though not without occasional conflict. On becoming independent in 1918, Finland adopted a new constitution, and after some hesitation it was decided that the country should become a republic, not a monarchy. In most respects, however, the constitutional structure became similar to those of the other Nordic countries.

Thus, while the chronology differs, and while there are innumerable differences in detail—some of them not without practical importance—the framework is now of the same type in all the countries: political democracy, exercised through parliamentary Cabinet government. All four have written constitutions, and their practices conform more or less faithfully to the enacted rules. It can also be said that all four countries are moderately legalistic in their approaches: more so than Britain, but less so than France and Germany. The legal system is of the usual continental type, embodied in written legal codes. Historically speaking, these can, however, be said to represent codified common law, and the influence from Roman law and from the Napoleonic codes, while clearly noticeable in the case of Denmark, is negligible in the three other countries. Courts of law are independent of both the executive and the legislature, although a judicial career frequently involves periods of service in administrative office and very few judges have ever served as attorneys.

One of the strongest traditions of Liberalism (in the European rather than in the American sense of the word) has always been insistence on the rule of law, the supremacy of legal precepts over considerations of expediency. This has also been part of the Nordic tradition, and it played a particularly important role in Finland during the period when that country was ruled by the czars. In principle it is still universally accepted. But with the growing belief that public authority should be used in an "equitable" manner and so as to further "social justice," rather than to uphold the letter of the law, this tradition may be losing its importance.

In trying to understand this process, it is important to note a difference between the situation in Britain and the United States, on the one hand, and continental Europe including Scandinavia on the other. In the traditional system of the two countries first mentioned, the rule of law almost invariably meant power for the general courts of judiciary. On the European continent no such power was vested in the ordinary courts. The corrective against abuse of power by officials was a recognized system of appeals to higher authority and ultimately to the Crown. Later, appeals of this type were transferred to special administrative courts (the most well-known example is the French Conseil d'Etat), which gradually acquired practically the same independence as other courts although specializing in administrative appeals and employing other, usually less complicated procedures. Scandinavia is no exception to this rule, and it should be remembered that there, as well as elsewhere on the European continent, the traditional status and authority of the official bureaucracy was very high.

Thus judicial review of administrative acts, let alone of legislation, was relatively unusual, though not unknown, and held no great importance. This was one reason for establishing in Sweden the office of "ombudsman," an institution that has acquired worldwide recognition but whose original functions are not always well understood. In Swedish law a private citizen traditionally had no recourse in the courts against misconduct or malfeasance in office by civil servants. Only the Crown and its representative, the "chancellor of justice," could prosecute in such cases. In the eighteenth century, during which a system of parliamentary government obtained in Sweden for about fifty years, this official came to be elected by Parliament. Toward the end of the century the appointment reverted to the Crown. But the new constitution of 1809, while still maintaining the position of chancellor of justice as the chief law officer of the Crown, established alongside it the office of "ombudsman of justice." The ombudsman was to be elected by Parliament and report to it, and to watch over the interests of citizens in their relations with holders of public office. Concurrently with the chancellor, the ombudsman was entitled to prosecute in cases of misconduct or malfeasance in office, and it became increasingly common for citizens to complain to him even when no legal issues were involved. This practice had not been foreseen, however, and for a long time it was criticized as improper.

Legislation establishing safeguards for the liberty and independence of individuals often has to be applied by administrative authorities and not only by the courts. This tendency has been further emphasized owing to the general distrust of courts and lawyers on the part of social reformers and of interest groups such as the labor unions, as well as to some extent by the mass media. There are obvious historical reasons for this distrust. Courts undoubtedly used to act as a conservative element in society, and thus were regarded with suspicion by the advocates of change. This was clearly seen in labor market cases during the latter decades of the nineteenth and at the beginning of the twentieth century. In addition, there is a Marxist or semi-Marxist argument: members of the legal profession belong to the upper middle class and are therefore supposed to be out of sympathy with the aspirations of the working classes. Administrative agencies should be different. They are subject to more direct political control and could be made amenable to new, "democratic" tendencies in society. It should also be remembered that in the Nordic countries lawyers have not been very active in political life, while elsewhere they have often formed the vanguard of radical political parties.

The constitutional protection of human rights requires special comment. The Swedish constitution of 1809, which as noted earlier remained in force until 1973, guaranteed no other freedoms than freedom of the press, although admonishing the king in general terms to respect civil rights. The Norwegian, the Danish, and the Finnish constitutions, on the other hand, contain more or less extensive provisions about such rights, and so does the new Swedish constitution. In this respect, as well as in regard to prescribed procedures, courts are entitled to review administrative acts and even legislation. In reality, the right is very seldom exercised. Moreover, it is characteristic of all four countries that the protection of civil rights is a matter of personal civil liberties and freedom of discussion rather than of private property. In fact the chapter on civil rights that was included in the Swedish constitution after the reform of 1973 hardly refers to private property, and in Norway and Denmark, where the situation is different, courts have still been most unwilling to invoke constitutional guarantees even against measures involving considerable economic restrictions. It goes without saying that this has been most important for the development of welfare states. Nothing like the judicial action taken against the New Deal in the United States would ever have been possible in Scandinavia.

In accordance with European Liberal traditions, the protection of civil rights has been regarded as a matter of protecting individuals against the power of the state and its organs. It has been a question of protecting legal freedoms and not of guaranteeing positive intervention by public authorities. The function of protecting such freedoms rests not only with the courts but also with the administration, which in Scandinavia as well as in other Western European countries is bound by rules similar to those applying to courts.

New attitudes toward relations between society and individuals have influenced the concept of civil rights. None of the Nordic countries tried, as did Ireland, for example, to enact "positive social rights" in their constitutions, but the insistence on individual freedoms became more controversial. This insistence had in Scandinavia, as elsewhere, arisen out of dissatisfaction with paternalistic interventions. Now dissatisfaction with *laissez faire* emerged, and constitutional protection of individual freedoms, especially those relating to private property, became suspect. In fact, while private property including private control over the means of production is by no means abolished, it is no longer unanimously respected as a fundamental individual right. Its maintenance in the field of economic production is mostly regarded as a matter of expediency. There is widespread agreement that productivity and economic growth are favored by the continued existence of a comparatively large private sector. But even leading representatives of management within this sector accept the idea that they have definite social responsibilities. Private enterprise is expected not only to justify its existence by satisfactory economic results but also to consider other values. Managers must see to the welfare of both employees and consumers, and they should follow accepted public policy, for instance, in limiting their involvement with certain foreign countries such as South Africa. If management fails to follow such principles, legislation is enacted to compel them to do so. Regulations of this type are often controversial, but this is because of their substance and not because they are held to go beyond the reasonable functions of the state.

Another problem is that of respect for private life in an interventionist society. It is a trite observation that modern techniques lend themselves to excessive control of the life of individuals. To some extent the Nordic countries provide examples of this, especially in the economic field, but on the whole public opinion has been very watchful. There are, for instance, few countries in the world where legislation against dangerous effects of computerization has gone further than in Scandinavia. To cite one example, different public authorities are not entitled to examine and compare the data in their respective computerized registers without receiving special permission. Such permission is sometimes withheld even when demanded on the plea that comparison would be a useful means of preventing frauds.

The four countries practice parliamentary Cabinet government, and in theory at least it follows the British model. There is no division of power in the constitutional system, only division of functions. The basic idea is best expressed in the new Swedish constitution (Instrument of Government): "All public power in Sweden derives from the people. . . . The Government governs the country. It is responsible to Parliament." The only exception to the supremacy of Parliament over the executive is the right of the Government to appeal to the people by dissolving Parliament and calling for new elections. (It should be noted that in this book I follow the European practice of employing the word *Government*, with a capital *G*, to signify the executive branch—usually the Cabinet and associated Ministries.) This power does not exist in Norway, and in Sweden it is used but sparingly. In Denmark it is, however, exercised very frequently and in Finland, where it is held by the president and not by the Cabinet, it is a threat continually held over the heads of political parties when they prove unwilling to make the compromises necessary in order to establish and maintain coalition Governments.

In reality Governments are politically dependent on parliamentary majorities, but Parliaments depend on Governments in their day-to-day work. Cabinets are formed on the basis of the parliamentary situation, and all or at least most of their members are drawn from Parliament. It is the monarch in Denmark and Norway and the Speaker in Sweden who conduct the negotiations prior to the appointment of a Cabinet, but this is mostly a matter of form, except perhaps when there is no clear majority for any party or group of parties. The president has the same function in Finland, and he is sometimes more actively involved in the process, but there too the choice of solutions and above all the choice of ministers rest with the parliamentary parties.

Legislation as well as budgeting is introduced through Government bills. Even when there are minority Governments, in the absence of any definite parliamentary majority, private members and even parliamentary parties can rarely achieve more than modifications in Government proposals, requests for legislative or budget proposals addressed to the Government, or expressions of more or less generally formulated wishes by Parliament. Foreign policy remains almost entirely in the hands of the Government, although there are provisions for consultation or debate in Parliament or with its representatives. Also, the power of Governments to issue executive ordinances supplementing legislation is rather broad and can be exercised with little or no parliamentary control.

Democracy in the Nordic countries is essentially representative in its application. It is possible to call for a referendum, but this is consultative and can take place only after a majority decision in Parliament. In Denmark and Sweden there are exceptions to this rule, but only for amendments to the constitution, where a referendum can be decisive. Otherwise Parliaments are free to make their own decisions even after a popular vote has taken place. Normally they will of course abide by the popular resolution, as did the Norwegian Storting in the question of Norway's relations to the European Economic Communities. But since the referendum is not legally binding, its result may eventually be overturned after the lapse of a decent period of time. Shortly after the Second World War the Swedish people voted (although with a low voter turnout) to continue to drive on the left-hand side of the road, but less than two decades later Parliament on the initiative of the Government decided by an overwhelming majority to change this traffic rule—and the people hardly complained when the new rule was put into effect.

All the legislatures are unicameral, with certain provisions for dividing the single chamber in Norway (and to a certain degree in Finland also). Denmark and Sweden had bicameral legislatures until comparatively recent dates, 1953 in Denmark and 1969 in Sweden. During the establishment of their welfare states both countries thus worked within a bicameral system, a fact which contributed to the need for political compromise, although the upper houses had already ceased to be the "conservative element in the constitution" which was held to be desirable in the nineteenth century.

The electoral system is one of proportional representation. There are modifications, not only to provide for the sufficient representation of even sparsely populated areas but also involving certain guarantees against the emergence of excessively small political parties. However, on the whole all shades of political opinion are reasonably well represented. This means that there may often be no clear-cut parliamentary majority, and minority Governments may be unavoidable. The substance of political decisions is of course influenced by such circumstances. Both legislation and budgeting are frequently the result of compromise rather than of consistent policies. Certain decisions require qualified majorities in the Parliaments, of two-thirds or even five-sixths of the votes cast. In Finland this practice is frequently applied, although in theory the special rules refer only to temporary departures from constitutional provisions. In Sweden it is quite recent and refers only to certain procedural questions.

Notwithstanding Cabinet government, the Nordic legislatures work through parliamentary committees (utskott, udvalg), which usually take several months or at least weeks before reporting on proposals before them, whether these are Government bills or private members' motions. Committees do not hold public hearings but frequently hear experts *in camera* or demand statements from administrative agencies, organized interest groups, and/or other organizations. In the past they enjoyed great authority and often amended Government bills out of all recognition, but today this practice occurs infrequently, even when there are minority Governments in office. And Cabinets enjoying comfortable parliamentary majorities are usually able to keep their parties together. Under such circumstances committee members can rarely do more than achieve minor modifications in proposals or else register their objections in minority reports.

Denmark, Norway, and Sweden are all monarchies, and it can hardly be said that there has ever been any republican movement of importance, although some doctrinaire democrats in Sweden were rather vociferous in the late sixties and early seventies. On the other hand, since the First World War the monarchs have never exercised any real power, regardless of the letter of the constitutions. Their position is purely symbolic and ceremonial. Nevertheless, the institution is very popular as long as no attempt is made to extend its influence beyond the limits set by rigid constitutional practice. During the German occupation of Denmark and Norway during the Second World War, the kings of these two countries served as symbols of national freedom and unity, although still without exercising political power, and to some extent this can be said to have been the case in neutral Sweden as well. Whether the monarchy represents a reserve of national strength which could gain importance again in the event of an especially severe crisis, is open to question.

The presidency of Finland is a different matter. The president is chosen by electors specifically elected for this purpose and not by Parliament, although the electors offer themselves on tickets presented by the ordinary political parties. He is by no means a figurehead only. Foreign policy is his special domain, and there he is to a great extent independent of the Cabinet. The minister for foreign affairs in fact works more closely with the president than with his Cabinet colleagues. Also, the president takes an active part in the formation of the Cabinet and often acts as a mediator between the political parties participating in a coalition Government—and practically all Finnish Governments are based on coalitions. On occasion he has refused to accept the resignation of a Cabinet and has ordered it to carry on, and in some cases where the formation of a politically representative Cabinet appeared to be impossible he has appointed caretaker Cabinets under prime ministers selected by himself. All this has been possible and indeed has occurred from time to time ever since Finland gained its independence, but Presidents Mannerheim, Paasikivi, and Kekkonen, who held office after 1945, enjoyed an even more powerful position than did their earlier colleagues. This was largely because they were more or less personally responsible for handling the ticklish relations of Finland with the Soviet Union. The substance of domestic policies, however, has always been regarded as the business of the prime minister and his Cabinet, and not of the president.

There are some characteristics of the democratic process in Scandinavia which differ from what obtains in most other Western countries. They pertain not only to legislative but to some extent also to administrative procedures.

Not only in Sweden but throughout Scandinavia important legislation is usually prepared by reports from committees appointed *ad hoc* by the Cabinet. These are similar to the Royal Commissions in Great Britain, and in order to avoid confusion with the committees of Parliament the British term will be used for the Scandinavian phenomenon also. It should be noted, however, that commissions are much more common in Scandinavia than in Britain. In earlier days most of the Royal Commissions were composed of experts, recruited chiefly from the civil service, and indeed bodies of this type are still appointed from time to time. But commissions dealing with matters that are politically important or controversial or otherwise call for decisions in Parliament frequently comprise members of all or most political parties including the opposition, as well as of labor unions, cooperatives, employers' organizations, and so on. Even Communists are nowadays sometimes appointed to membership. Commissions are given considerable time for their deliberations, often several years. They are provided with their own secretariats. They usually attempt to reach at least partial agreement. Their members, especially those who also have seats in Parliament, tend to maintain contact with the leadership of their respective political parties, so that compromises reached in the course of discussions indicate similar agreement by parliamentary parties. Commissions work mostly *in camera*, and public hearings do not take place as a rule. On the other hand, minorities in commissions have every opportunity to present their own reports in cases where no agreement has been reached, and the secretariat is supposed to assist them as well as the majority.

It is obvious that this practice tends to reduce the scope of political controversy. Even when a commission presents separate majority and minority reports, there is often agreement on a number of important points, although not on all of them. And in the attempts to reach unanimity, at least on part of a question, members tend to dilute their ideological differences and by the same token to prefer vague but universally acceptable solutions to those that are clearly defined and therefore also more controversial. Political parties usually feel bound by the stand taken by their representatives on commissions, since they were consulted about the appointments, and will consequently be unable to take up extreme positions at later stages.

Appointment of a Royal Commission may be a means to shelve a question which it appears inexpedient to resolve at the time, but this is usually not the main reason for its existence. Regardless of temporary exigencies, it is generally accepted that careful study by a commission should take place before important matters are placed before Parliament. And reports are usually printed for the convenience of the public, thus providing opportunities for discussion in the media.

Even when based on long and careful deliberations, commission reports are usually not directly translated into proposals to the legislatures. The next stage, also specifically Scandinavian, is what has been called administrative consultation ("remiss"). This means that the published report—or occasionally, when no commission has studied the subject, a memorandum prepared within the relevant ministry—is referred to a few dozen government agencies, interest groups, etc., which are usually given a month or two to prepare comments on the report. These comments are also available to the media. Thus, in preparing legislative proposals the Government has access not only to a considered study by people with different political opinions, but also to the views of interested parties and of administrative experts. Once the Government has decided to act, this information can be used by the opposition as well.

There is little room for surprise initiatives in this system. In fact the machinery sometimes appears to work at an excruciatingly slow pace. Yet the crux of the matter is whether the media find that a report or other proposal, or the comments on it, are worthy of the attention of the public. Whenever they do, they have every opportunity to take action and create suitable awareness of the situation. If they do not, the public may remain in more or less complete ignorance of what is about to happen. An interesting example was the adoption of Sweden's new constitution in 1973. For some reason constitutional questions were out of fashion in the late 1960s and early 1970s. Consequently the proposed total revision of the constitution was given only perfunctory attention in the media, and up to a very late stage it can hardly be said that the public realized that it was happening. Toward the end, there was an unexpected spate of public interest, largely critical of the new constitution. By then it was too late. Both the Government and the political parties had taken up definite positions which they would or could not modify, and the criticisms were entirely ineffective. In fact a considerable part of the discussion took place only after the new constitution had been finally adopted.

Moreover, all these time-consuming procedures, interpolated as they are with comments by the mass media and by agencies and organizations during administrative and legislative consultation, have a restraining effect on parliamentary debate. Before a question of any importance is even introduced in the legislature, practically all interested parties have determined what their position is to be, all possible arguments have been thrashed out over and over again, and there is little opportunity of discovering any new angles. Also, by that time party discipline is often applied. On the one hand, this means that lobbying in the American sense can rarely be very effective, but on the other hand, there is also very little scope for individual legislators or their constituencies to influence developments. Individual voters are usually unable to reach their representatives until the decision has already become virtually unalterable.

An important effect of the new economic order has been a change in the character and extent of legislation. The traditional Liberal concept was that laws should on the whole provide a framework within which individuals should be free to pursue their interests. With the new interventionist policies, this principle could no longer be maintained. Legislation became one aspect, together with several others, of policy-making, sometimes of a vague and diffuse character, especially when it meant that public authorities should embark on new activities. The quantity of legislation grew astronomically, and under the parliamentary system of government, proposals emanating from the executive branch perforce must form the main basis of legislative activity.

Naturally, the attitude of the public also changed in these new circumstances. It is interesting to make a comparison with the "managerial revolution" in industry. Just as the owners of private enterprises, the shareholders, often became unable to judge the policies of "their" enterprise except by its immediate economic results, so even highly educated voters are unable to follow the activities of their representatives in the legislature. When results appeared to be unsatisfactory or unpleasant, the people started to blame not only the ruling party or parties, but "politicians" in general. Such populist tendencies are by no means particularly characteristic of Scandinavia. Indeed one proof of the strength of Scandinavian democracy is that they have not yet endangered the constitutional structure. But the fact that they exist can hardly be explained otherwise than as a consequence of interventionism.

Another effect of the interventionism inherent in the welfare state is "collective bribery" in politics and administration. There is comparatively little real graft in Scandinavia. Neither politicians nor administrators are habitually for sale. On the other hand, as in all other countries, whether democracies or dictatorships, there is an obvious tendency for those who wield political power to use it for the benefit of particular groups that are important in the electorate. Powerful interest groups can expect more favors than groups and individuals who are unable to exercise political pressure. This universal tendency grows more important, however, as more power is put into the hands of political and administrative authorities. The members of politically unimportant groups are given less and less opportunity to further their interests.

Similar influences appear in public administration as well. Under the new economic order, one of the basic functions of the state and its agencies is to control the private sector, not only in order to maintain a suitable framework of rules, but so as to steer it in directions that are desirable from the standpoint of accepted public policies. Not one of the four Nordic countries has moved beyond mixed economies to outright state socialism, but if anything this makes the steering function even more important. In addition, the traditional interplay of supply and demand is not held to give sufficient protection to consumers. Marketing and advertising are regulated at many points, not only in order to provide sufficient consumer information, but also for other purposes, such as to prohibit advertisement of alcoholic beverages. There may be a clash between the interests of consumers and those of employees, for example, in regard to the hours and days when shops are permitted to be open. Which of the conflicting interests is to prevail becomes a matter of political decision. But all the decisions just referred to must be implemented by administrative authorities. And finally, powerful organized interest groups intervene and make their influence strongly felt.

In the structure of their central administration, three of the four countries differ from the usual pattern. In Sweden, Finland, and Norway ministries do little actual administration. This is left mostly to more or less independent agencies under the Government, whose administrative decisions are not dependent on the minister or officials directly subordinate to him. Consequently administrative procedures are not subject to direct political influence. And while the Government may find ways and means to keep the agencies under its thumb, the legislative branch is given little or no opportunity to influence their activities.

In all four countries, there are integrated regional—"county"— agencies representing central government and subject to little or no immediate democratic influence at their own level. These agencies correspond rather closely to the offices of the Prefects in France. But

Denmark, Norway, and Sweden also have elected regional councils with their own functions and their own administrative services, separate from those of the agencies of the central government. In Sweden, but not in Denmark or Norway, the regional councils have recently been given a certain amount of influence over the composition and therefore the operation of the parallel agencies as well, while the functions of the two branches still remain separate.

At the local level, there is generally speaking no separate administration representing central or regional government. Elected councils and their services are responsible for the administration as a whole. Indeed, Scandinavia has a very long tradition of local self-government. This is particularly so in Sweden and Finland, but to a considerable extent in Denmark as well. And in Norway it was the introduction of local self-government in the nineteenth century that marked the beginning of democratization. The basis of self-government in all four countries was that the geographical units in question, usually the same for Church and secular purposes, were relatively small, comprising only a few hundred up to a couple of thousand inhabitants. Consequently decisions could be made by representatives who were familiar with practically all details of the problems involved, even at a time when privilege rather than democracy was the basis of government. When regional self-government was introduced, which happened much later, it was handled by representatives who almost invariably had experience from the field of local government and brought such experience to bear on their new functions. Further, both at the local and at the regional level, taxation and budgeting were on the whole independent of any controls—but also of any subsidies—from the central government. As a result, both the level of ambition and the choice of solutions to problems varied considerably from one place to another. Undeniably, there was no equality or justice in the distribution of benefits among the inhabitants of different regions and localities. Some were favored, usually because tax incomes were greater in their home units; others were subject to what must have been felt as negative discrimination.

In the twentieth century circumstances gradually changed. The administration of local and regional self-government became or at least appeared to become more successful with the growth of political democracy. Parliamentarians, as always, were largely recruited among persons with considerable experience of local and regional administration. As a result, they found it natural to make use of this administration for the purpose of implementing reforms initiated at the central level. At the same time there was growing unwillingness to accept the fact of discrimination between different regions and local units.

New legislation especially in the field of social security and welfare therefore provided not only for administration by local and regional units, but also for considerable subsidies from the central budget for these units, and for uniform standards of implementation. Local and regional authorities, although elected and technically "self-governing," were beginning to act in one case after another as agents of the central government, at the expense of the central government rather than on the basis of their own taxes, and in accordance with rules and regulations issued from the central administration. While the local bodies, which have their own budgets and in principle the power of levying taxes themselves, used to exercise corresponding power over their choice of functions as well, they have now largely become the agents of central government. Their duties are in most cases determined by nationwide legislation, leaving them only a certain and not always very large freedom in deciding what ambitions to maintain in the execution of such laws. The regional councils, in whose administration health and hospital care are the dominant elements, enjoy greater liberty, but even this is far from complete.

At all levels, central as well as regional and local, the welfare state has brought about a great increase in administrative functions and ambitions, but also in administrative powers. It is becoming increasingly difficult to distinguish between policy and administration. Especially central administrative agencies are more and more frequently making semi-political decisions, and subject to no immediate control by political, democratically elected officers. And this is not necessarily because they are themselves hungry for power, but because legislation and executive ordinances often lay down the principles to be followed only in very general terms, leaving even a number of politically important decisions to be made by the administrative agencies who must implement them. At the same time, both the legislature and ministers have to deal with an increasing number of intricate problems, about which they cannot be expected to have the necessary expert knowledge. This makes them dependent on advice from the experts of administrative agencies. Consequently, these agencies exert considerable influence over the frankly political decisions made by the legislature, the Cabinet, and individual ministers.

Like the courts, the administrative agencies traditionally were supposed to be concerned chiefly with applying legal rules issuing from the legislature and the executive. The reason for their independent position was precisely this: they should not be subject to day-to-day influence from organs of a political character, but only to the general principles embodied in permanent and publicly announced rules and regulations. This, it was assumed, would be in the interests of the public, giving legal security to individual citizens. In the welfare state, it is held that "common sense" rather than legal rules should guide administrative practice. What common sense means is, of course, subject to different interpretations, much more so than expressly formulated rules and regulations. Moreover, administrative agencies may decide it is within their power to give advice to citizens about what is best for them, although they may not understand it themselves. "The National Board of Health and Social Welfare (Socialstyrelsen) wishes you to eat six to eight open-face sandwiches a day" was the text of a poster widely distributed in Sweden a few years ago. The public's reaction to the poster was definitely negative, although most people probably ate at least six to eight open-face sandwiches daily of their own volition. But the fact that such a statement ever appeared is nonetheless significant.

In some fields similar administrative guidance becomes almost unavoidable. To the extent that collective consumption, paid for wholly or partly out of public funds, takes the place of individual consumption, paid for entirely out of the pockets of individuals, it is obvious that administrative agencies must assume the right to control spending. This is largely the situation in regard to subsidized housing, daycare centers, and so on. In some cases, moreover, technically complicated issues are involved, calling for expertise available to the bureaucracy but not to ordinary people. This is true, for instance, with regard to building techniques, energy conservation, and similar functions that are directly relevant to the individual.

At the same time, concepts such as "social justice" and "equitable distribution" also have to be applied by the administration. It is often held that "rationing by the pocketbook" is unacceptable in an equitable society. This, of course, means that people should not be given an opportunity to pay for what they want, since some are better able to pay than others. And to "rationing by the pocketbook," there is no alternative but rationing by administrative action, as long as scarcity obtains. In fact, this is a logical effect of collective consumption.

In addition to that, administrative agencies everywhere (and not only in the welfare state) are compulsive empire builders, constantly widening their ambitions. This is particularly true of local self-governing agencies, which for obvious reasons want the citizens of their own locality to enjoy advantages at least equal to those of other parts of the country. Such ambitions inevitably result in growing budgets and rising local taxes.

All of this, in the aggregate, means that the establishment of a new economic order, involving the welfare state, collective consumption, equitable distribution of incomes and benefits, etc., unavoidably gives increasing power to administrative agencies. It should be noted that it is the administration, and not politically elected or appointed organs or the courts, that acquires this power, and that it tends to become much more discretionary than in the individualistic societies based on competition. Not even special administrative courts have the opportunity to exercise the kind of control that was habitual in the past. And the stronger the insistence on "social justice," as distinct from the "technicalities" of legal security, the more pronounced this tendency becomes. A notable example is the efforts to counter tendencies to tax evasion, efforts which of necessity appear to an increasing extent when taxes rise and tax resistance—as discussed elsewhere in this book—becomes increasingly widespread in the welfare state. Consequent demands on the integrity, loyalty, and unselfishness of bureaucractic personnel are also a characteristic of the changing social order.

A special factor contributing to the increase in power of the bureaucracy is, of course, computerization. In traditional authoritarian societies, the power of the authorities was necessarily tempered by inefficiency. They were simply unable to exercise the control over citizens to which they were legally entitled. This is no longer the case; and indeed computerization is a necessary element in the establishment of social justice. Distribution of social benefits, admission to educational and other institutions, assessment of taxes—all have to be trusted to the computer if impersonal justice is to be achieved. The computer alone is wholly impartial. At the same time, the registration of clients/citizens necessary for such purposes also provides means of control entirely different from those previously available. As has already been mentioned, legislation in the Nordic countries is comparatively strict in limiting the use of computerized data. But this is a matter of legislation; and legislation can be amended. To the extent that automatic data processing is *used* in administration, it can also be *abused*; although this may not have happened to date.

Thus, the situation of the individual citizen has been radically changed. He or she enjoys greater material security, more justice in the distribution of material benefits, greater equality, increased opportunities for education and enjoyment, and more spare time in which to enjoy these advantages. At the same time, the individual is subject to greater administrative control, real or potential. And although the administration is watched over by organized interest groups, these groups themselves have become more bureaucratic by virtue of their new functions, and thus their leadership becomes less and less subject to democratic control. The interests of individual citizens, and of the general public, are supposed to be sovereign in democratic welfare states. But individuals may sometimes find that this is true in the abstract rather than in practical application—not because of ill will or malpractices on the part of those who govern, but because the latter unavoidably find themselves in a position rather distant from that of the governed, and because this fact becomes increasingly important the more an interventionist social system strives to benefit citizens by providing in detail for their common needs without being able to take individual and special cases into account.

Criticism of the growing role and power of administrative agencies and administrative personnel often refers to "bureaucracy" in the abstract as one of the evils of modern society. What exactly is meant by this term is not always very clear. Without a doubt, however, ordinary citizens are increasingly irritated by something that they call by this name. This is by no means more characteristic of Scandinavia than of other parts of the industrialized world. There should have been reason to believe, however, that the reaction ought to have been milder in these countries than elsewhere. Administrators—"bureaucrats"—have traditionally enjoyed high status, and as has just been emphasized they are normally very honest and reliable. Moreover, in all Nordic countries but Denmark, they have always been more independent of those holding political power than is the case elsewhere; this was both before and after the establishment of political democracy. In Sweden, Parliament was expressly prohibited by a clause in the old constitution from interfering with or even discussing administrative decisions. Citizens ought therefore to have been well conditioned to accept the growing role of the bureaucracy.

In fact, resentment is caused chiefly by some specific aspects of the bureaucratic system. One of these is bureaucratic procedures: excessive formalities, unintelligible terminologies, delays in making decisions—all the things that come under the heading of "red tape." It would be unjust to deny that this is at least to some extent the result of most honorable intentions on the part of bureaucrats. In their anxiety to reach just and equitable decisions, they find it necessary to acquire a wealth of information both in general and in regard to particular cases. When wielding the powers necessitated by collective consumption, avoiding "rationing by the pocketbook," and so on, they must weigh a number of different considerations, and all this takes time. Procedures become "bureaucratic" because they aim at perfectionist social justice. And this becomes increasingly irritating to ordinary people as the field of bureaucratic activity widens and it impinges more and more on the normal life of the citizen.

This, of course, is not the only explanation. Bureaucrats are often happy to show how powerful they are, and procedural delay is a well-known instrument for this purpose. They are fearful of consequences to themselves if they make mistakes, and the only safe method of avoiding mistakes is to avoid decisions. They are the prisoners of traditional practices and constitutionally unwilling or even unable to change them. This has always been true, but of course it is more apparent with the increasing functions of the administrative authorities. At the same time, freedom of debate and democratic consciousness bring criticism into the open.

The second aspect of "bureaucracy" has already been referred to: it is the power of administrative officials, even those of relatively low rank, in relation to ordinary citizens. This also is by no means a new phenomenon; it existed in authoritarian systems before political democracy was even considered a practical possibility in Western society. But at the same time it causes great resentment. It had been assumed that the establishment of democratic government would put an end to it, but with the growth of an interventionist, "welfare" state it is coming back again. And it appears to be unavoidable.

Collective consumption, after all, must be administered, and who else but the bureaucrats can fulfill this function? At one time it was assumed that it could be done by democratically elected representatives of the people, but this was when things were relatively simple. Complicated administrative functions require experts, and experts become bureaucrats whoever originally appointed them to their offices.

This phenomenon also is a counterpart of the "managerial revolution" that has taken place in the private sector. Neither voters nor their representatives in Parliaments or Cabinets really administer the public sector. They can only lay down certain rules, which have to be applied and interpreted by the bureaucrats. And the more complicated and wide-ranging the problems, the less detailed the rules can be. Consequently political democracy in the literal sense becomes less real the more interventionist the society becomes. This is not because of any conspiracy between elected representatives and bureaucrats, but results simply from the circumstances. And since the Nordic states provide an example of highly ambitious interventionist societies, the element of direct democracy is weakened, and even representative democracy tends to give way to increasing bureaucratic power.

The problem of controls is a traditional issue in the public sector. In any democratic system, controlling the use of public power—whether political or administrative—is of primary importance. In fact this was recognized as a necessity long before the emergence of democracy in the modern sense of the word or the establishment of any "welfare state." But control of administrative authorities became both more difficult and more important with the founding of the new economic order. This phenomenon is not specifically Scandinavian. It was discussed as early as the 1920s by an eminent if controversial British judge (Lord Hewart), who called his book on the subject *The New Despotism.* But for various reasons the problem of control should be seen in the light of new relationships between citizens and public authority which are more characteristic of the Nordic countries than of most others.

As we have seen, increasing interventionism cannot but alter the character of legislation. Laws have to be more vague and leave more discretion to administrative authorities the more the state tries to interfere actively and in some detail with the behavior of citizens. An example is the problem of tax evasion, as distinct from tax frauds.

And who could deny that this is a perennial problem of the welfare state? Social legislation also must work with concepts such as "equitable" which are not easily defined and applied by the courts, whether administrative or others.

Not only because control is increasingly difficult, but also because of the greater scope given to public authorities, the welfare state demands great integrity and honesty from its civil service and its politicians. Whatever is being said by their critics, it can in fact hardly be maintained that public servants in the Nordic countries have been short on honesty or loyalty. By international standards, both Scandinavian politicans and their civil servants are on the whole very reliable in these respects. It remains to be seen whether this is a result of traditional concepts, established in an earlier social structure and likely to disappear in the new circumstances. So far there are few indications—if any—of deterioration in public morality of the executors of the new economic order.

A corrective to the increasing power of the bureaucracy was at one time thought to be the role of organized interest groups, which consequently were given a greater say in administrative decisions. But this has not solved the problem. For obvious reasons those representatives of interest groups who take part in such decisions are unable to consult their members in individual cases, and as time goes on they find themselves less and less able—or willing—even to guess what the attitudes and reactions of their members are likely to be. This is one aspect of the bureaucratization referred to earlier. As a matter of fact, since they rarely can take part in day-to-day administration, they may even know less than the professionals about the reactions of ordinary people.

Another recent development that has further complicated the problems of bureaucracy is the increased emphasis on personnel questions within the public services themselves. The number of public employees grows in proportion to the emphasis on public functions, or probably—if we are to believe Professor Parkinson—beyond, perhaps far beyond such proportions. At the same time one of the most important principles of the welfare state consists in safeguarding the interests of employees in relation to employers. This originally applied to "capitalist" employers in the private sector. But from the employees' point of view, it is of course equally valid for those who happen to work in the public sector. As a matter of fact, it is often maintained that public authorities ought to be "model employers," pointing the way to private enterprises who are unwilling to listen to employees' demands.

This in itself is enough to make an important pressure group out of the personnel of the state and local administrations. But in addition, it should be kept in mind that in the Nordic countries, as distinct from Great Britain, for example, public employment has never been incompatible with the exercise of full political rights. Both in their Parliaments and in regional and local councils there have always been elected members who are at the same time in the employ of the corresponding public bodies. In recent years this tendency has increased. A large proportion of members of Parliament, for instance, are public employees at different levels, and nowadays usually not at a very high level. It is obvious that this gives them considerable leverage as a group. In fact, the interests of bureaucrats, as employees, are increasingly taken into consideration. Political parties are very much afraid of offending either them or their organizations. At the same time, public employees regardless of their own political opinions and ideologies take care not to offend any political party whose attitudes may influence their interests.

A special problem is that of "administrative democracy," corresponding to "industrial democracy." The tendency is for employees in the private sector, or rather their organizations, to claim successfully the right to participate in decisions in the enterprise where they work, at least to the extent that such decisions directly or indirectly influence their employment opportunities and working conditions. Especially in Sweden their right to do so has been granted in law and is extensively interpreted. Corresponding claims arise for those working in the public sector. Here, however, their negotiating counterparts are not horrible capitalists, but democratically elected representatives of the people. The risk of conflict between "administrative democracy" and political democracy as a whole cannot be neglected. And for the working of the administration, this is of considerable importance. Already, at least in Sweden, the comfort and well-being of public employees is officially recognized as a criterion of administrative efficiency.

Does all this mean that the interests of the general public are correspondingly disregarded? The argument on the other side is that employees work better and more efficiently if they are kept happy and know that their interests are taken into proper consideration. This is undoubtedly true. At the same time, it cannot be denied that public interest and group interest may conflict, for instance with regard to such simple and mundane things as office hours in public agencies. In addition, employees' organizations have a vested interest in resisting reductions in the number of staff employed, and sometimes even the introduction of new and more efficient procedures. It has been found everywhere that efforts at administrative rationalization do not always enjoy favorable consideration by employees' organizations; and this is equally true in the public and in the private sector.

The developments discussed above are relevant at all levels of public administration: central, regional, and local. But perhaps the greatest changes have been taking place at the regional and local levels. The centrally directed elements of local and regional administration have become proportionately more and more important. This is largely a result of their having been given new functions connected with the working of the welfare state. The insistence on "equitable distribution of benefits" between regions and localities gives further emphasis to this tendency, and this is perfectly logical: uniformity is by definition opposed to independence.

Another consequence is that both regional and local government has become increasingly professionalized, and that on the plea of efficiency and equity the size of local units has been increased by mergers. If local administration is to consist chiefly of the application of rules and regulations issued from the center, specialized knowledge is required in order to interpret these rules and regulations; if it has to be uniform both over comparatively large local units and for the country as a whole, familiarity with local conditions and needs, or with the personalities of citizens involved, loses most of its importance. Moreover, local administration becomes a full-time job, no longer acceptable to citizens elected as representatives of the people but dependent for their living on private occupations. Although elected councils and committees continue to exist, they have to limit themselves to such functions as budgeting and control, while professional administrators—local and regional civil servants—take over the administrative functions. The role and the problems of bureaucracy are the same at the local and regional levels as in central government. This, of course, is contrary to tradition. But it is a logical consequence of the new circumstances existing in the interventionist system of the new economic order.

It follows from all that has been said that the role of public administration, and of professional administrative personnel, has increased very considerably with the establishment of the welfare state. As a consequence, it should be assumed, administrative efficiency has acquired greatly increased importance in the public sector. On the face of it the success or failure of the new economic order would seem to depend largely on the degree of efficiency that can be achieved. We may thus feel compelled to ask ourselves whether the model of the Nordic countries actually shows an increase or a reduction of administrative efficiency.

But it is impossible to answer this question, because efficiency criteria have grown increasingly difficult to define. When the functions of public administration were few and easily identified, it could be determined, both for individual agencies and for public administration as a whole, whether these functions were on balance efficient or inefficient, that is, whether they were able to achieve expected results. If this is more difficult, not to say impossible today, it is precisely because in an interventionist society public administration, and even its constituent parts, are given so many different functions that efficiency can no longer be related to any single one of them.

Moreover, the very concept of efficiency has come to include several incompatible elements. It can be held to mean the capability of reaching or even exceeding accepted levels of ambition, regardless of the financial outlay and quantity of staff employed. It might also be interpreted as productivity, that is, the most economical use of available resources of funds and personnel. Or it could mean—as is often the case when financing is a problem—keeping expenditure and employment of staff at a low level without catastrophic results for the quality of service provided. At different times and in different fields all these interpretations are used. Substantive agencies themselves think in terms of the first, rationalizing agencies in terms of the second, and ministries of finance usually in terms of the third. The general public, of course, want it both ways: service should be perfect, but it must not be costly.

Even apart from this, and assuming that efficiency could be defined in the abstract, there remains the question of priorities. Within practically every field of administration distinctly different goals have to be pursued, and efficient results with regard to one of them may be achieved only at the cost of sacrifice in other respects. The American economist, political scientist, and Nobel Prize winner Herbert Simon cites the example of environmental protection. This may well be an extreme case, but it is difficult to find any administration today that could afford to be single-minded. As a result, they can all be justifiably accused of inefficiency by those who have different priorities.

Administrative traditions in Scandinavia used to put great emphasis on legal security. Most senior civil servants had legal training, and they used to be proud to say that they protected the rights of individual citizens equally with the courts of law. The choice between administrative efficiency and the careful observation of legal rules was regarded as the most recurrent and also the most difficult one facing administrators. Today much less is said about legal security. This does not mean that civil servants have become careless with the rights of citizens. On the contrary, they are probably as honest and as conscientious as they have ever been. The difference does not lie in their morals but in what is expected of them. And not infrequently the choice these days is rather one between administrative efficiency and the interests of public employees, as safeguarded and protected by their powerful organizations. Sound arguments can be advanced in favor of this attitude. But it certainly does make a difference from the point of view of private citizens not employed by public authorities, or at least not by the public authority they are dealing with.

It has already been emphasized that public administration in Scandinavia is very honest, in the sense that there is much less graft, bribery, and other types of outright corruption than in most other countries. But to what extent are officials in the habit of discriminating in favor of prominent, influential individuals, and what is the attitude of public opinion in this respect? Two cases can be cited as illuminating: those of Mogens Glistrup in Denmark and of Ingmar Bergman in Sweden. Both deal with the sensitive field of tax administration.

Glistrup is a successful lawyer and a prominent politician, whose political creed is almost exclusively concerned with what he regards as the excessively high tax level in Denmark. He has been prosecuted by the authorities for having fraudulently evaded taxes. He maintains that he has been acting within the letter if not within the spirit of the law, but he has been found guilty in courts of both the first and the second instance. He has appealed, and pending the result of the appeal remains a member of the Danish Parliament—reelected after both the first and the second conviction.

Ingmar Bergman is an internationally known Swedish film producer with financial interests outside the country as well. The tax authorities, maintaining that he had been using his outside interests for the purpose of fraudulently avoiding Swedish taxes, took drastic action against him, including temporary arrest and search of his property. Ultimately, courts found him innocent of any fraud, although the tax assessment was changed in the direction of what the authorities had claimed, and although it was obvious that he had been far from helpful to them during the investigation.

Two conclusions can be drawn from these experiences. One is that the authorities did not hesitate to take action, although the persons in question were in positions of power or eminence. It is true that the Bergman case may have made Swedish tax inspectors and prosecutors more circumspect thereafter, but this is only an assumption for which no proof has been adduced. On the whole, the two cases can be said to indicate that the integrity of public officials remains reliable insofar as personal considerations go. But equally interesting, and more disturbing, is the reaction of public opinion. The political position of Glistrup in the electorate has not been damaged by the prosecution and so far not even by the conviction. It remains to be seen what will happen if it remains valid on appeal and if as a consequence he is expelled from Parliament. In the case of Ingmar Bergman, sympathies have invariably proved to be on his side, although it is unlikely that the authorities would have found themselves in any particular trouble if they had taken similar action against an unknown taxpayer. The idea that the public favors "the underdog" and feels righteous satisfaction when the mighty have fallen is not supported by these cases. On the contrary, it appears that the average taxpayer feels a sort of vicarious satisfaction when tax officials lose their case against any individual, whether in a high or in a low position. But this, of course, may mean that administrators as representatives of the state are seen as extraneous by citizens, political democracy notwithstanding.

To sum up: the "welfare state" is by definition interventionist in nature. The welfare of citizens can be guaranteed only if the state and its organs take action in a number of matters formerly left to individuals themselves. At the same time, it must be kept in mind that the establishment of welfare states at least in the Nordic countries followed the advent of political democracy. It was the majority of citizens themselves who wanted their material welfare to be guaranteed, even at the cost of interventionism. They voted for it in no uncertain terms. The responsibility was their own.

The working of an interventionist society involves a great number of detailed decisions. Only principles can be formulated by the legislature or other political bodies. And the rules thus formulated must of necessity be somewhat general. When concepts like "socially just" and "equitable" grow in importance, legislation that embodies traditional legal ideas and that is basically individualistic, or at least tending to emphasize the protection of private as against public interests, has to be modified. The more perfectionist the attitude in this respect, the more details have to be regulated by public agencies – not by the courts, which after all mainly apply the law, but by experts. Interventionism in detail calls for expertise, and expertise is to be found chiefly among administrators. Thus, consistent interventionism increases the role of public administration. Administrative agencies have to be given more and more power in matters of direct importance to individual citizens. And they have to be staffed by experts, not by laymen elected as representatives of the people. Democratically elected bodies can lay down principles and exercise a certain amount of control, but they are unable to run the adminstration themselves.

This has become quite obvious in the Nordic countries, perhaps especially at the local level, where the administrative function has been transferred from the traditional elected bodies and officers to professional civil servants. It should be emphasized that the honesty of the civil service has not suffered in the process. On the whole, the Scandinavian civil service at the central, regional, and local levels remains one of the most honest and conscientious in the Western world as far as individual administrators are concerned.

Another problem has arisen, however. One of the characteristics of the welfare state is to reduce the power traditionally held by employers over employees, the objective being to reduce the role of private capitalists and private capital. But employees in the public sector, whose number has been growing rapidly under the new economic order, naturally insist on the same protection, the same rights, and the same privileges as their colleagues in the private sector. Thus, while retaining in their individual capacity whatever unselfishness used to be characteristic of public servants, in their collective capacity and through their unions they insist that their interests should be considered important, regardless of whether or not this is also in the interests of the "clientele," that is, of the general body of people not employed in the public sector.

These changes have not failed to affect public opinion. It was undoubtedly the wish of the majority of the people to establish welfare states, accepting interventionism with their eyes open. That was how democracy worked. But it is also a democratic privilege of the people to react to new and unexpected developments regardless of their causes. The reaction has been to view the powerful administrative agencies necessitated by the establishment of the welfare state as extraneous, partly because actual administration no longer is in the hands of elected representatives, partly because those representatives are not as accessible as before in matters of direct importance to the individual citizen. Populism is a growing tendency in welfare states, but it has not yet led to any practical results, at least not in Scandinavia.

Serpents in Paradise

Critics of the welfare state are only too happy to blame all the social ills of Scandinavian and similar societies on their new approach to relations between society and individuals. This is understandable in view of the fact that original expectations were very high. Abolition of existing injustices was supposed to solve all social problems within a very limited period of time. Improvement of the material conditions of the broad strata of "common people" was hailed as the one thing that was really needful. Disenchantment naturally followed when it was discovered that no new heaven and earth had been created and that serious social problems can still be identified in such prosperous societies as those of Denmark, Finland, Norway, and Sweden. It was strengthened by the fact that younger generations without experience of the ills that had been abolished underestimate the progress that has taken place.

Such reasoning is unjustified and iniquitous, however. Abuse of alcohol has been traditional for centuries in the Nordic countries, perhaps especially in Finland and Sweden. Its modern and more frightening counterpart, drug abuse, is by no means limited to welfare states, nor is its prevalence proportionate to the degree of welfare. The same applies to crime, which is becoming increasingly widespread throughout the world. There is all over the industrialized world today a decline in the strength of religious and other traditional values. It would be highly unjust to blame such developments on "welfare or "social security." Moreover, there are some who deny that there is any blame to apportion: after all, they say, a new moralism is emerging, based on different standards but no less rigorous than its predecessor. In criticizing the welfare state, what should be identified first are the problems specifically relevant to the new economic order, directly or indirectly. Second—but only second—it is desirable to estimate the limits to what can be achieved by the creation of welfare states.

At the outset, some general observations should be made, however trite they may be, because they are too often forgotten. When one group of social problems have been solved, other problems automatically come to the surface. The latter may not be new problems but may have been forgotten in the past because attention was focused on others. Also, practically all solutions to problems create new problems, less serious, one would hope, than the previous problems, but very real nonetheless. The objectives of the welfare state were originally limited to establishing basic material security and a higher standard of living for the majority of the people. Eventually ambitions increased: what should also be established was greater, perhaps almost complete equality in regard to material standards and benefits. Finally, the idea of greater permissiveness, or perhaps different types of restrictions, may also have been present.

A great number of today's social problems are related to a general increase in material prosperity rather than to changes in the distribution of its results—to the affluent society rather than to the welfare state. Contrary to some expectations, a prosperous society invariably appears to be a stressful society. This observation can be made almost everywhere, regardless of whether the distribution of material benefits is equitable or not, the reason presumably being that prosperity calls for high productivity and stress is the price that has to be paid for high productivity. International mobility of goods, persons, and even of ideas has all sorts of effects, most of them probably beneficial but others most definitely harmful. Drug abuse in most countries is possible because of international traffic in drugs, which in turn is facilitated by international travel. Urbanization cannot by any stretch of the imagination be called a consequence of the establishment of welfare states. It is a consequence of industrialization in the widest sense of the word. But it is obvious that an urbanized society has social problems quite different from those of agricultural societies. They may even be greater and more serious, although this is a moot question. Generation gaps and conflicts between older and younger generations have appeared from the beginning of human intellectual exercises. In any case they were obvious in the Greek city-states of antiquity, as seen from the works of Plato and others. They became more acute and disturbing with the decline of traditional values just referred to. And these, again, are consequences mainly of industrialization, urbanization, and prosperity and certainly not of social security. "Subcultures" are an equally ancient phenomenon, which previously appeared in the guise of religious sects. Such sects are not unknown today, but subcultures of a purely secular nature also appear, due to the general tendency to secularization.

Some social problems existing before the advent of the welfare state are still present in Scandinavia, contrary to optimistic expectations. Economic equality and equality in civil rights have not always guaranteed equality of status between different occupational and other social groups. In many fields, such as that of housing, it has proved impossible to prevent "rationing by the pocketbook" of scarce and highly desirable commodities. Some critics may ask what pocketbooks are for, if not to permit a certain amount of "rationing," but this is beside the point, since the objective was to abolish such phenomena. Segregation, for instance through separate housing areas, is still in existence, and movement between social groups has not risen to expected levels, whether or not these groups can still be called classes.

It would, however, be useless to deny that some other social problems are more directly relevant to the measures taken in order to establish an egalitarian society. In the first place, egalitarianism and welfare are expensive commodities, thus calling for rising prosperity and productivity. While there is no reason to believe that the problems just mentioned as consequent on prosperity would have been easier to solve in a less egalitarian society, the combination of egalitarian ambitions and the call for high productivity involves at least a psychological and probably also a practical dilemma.

Equality has always been seen in terms of equality between groups and classes; to this extent Marxist thought early influenced the Nordic countries. As a consequence, individual needs and desires must take second place. The dominant role of organizations such as unions and cooperatives is a characteristic of Scandinavian society, and in these large and powerful organizations individual members are not given much freedom of action. A typical example is found in the housing field, where individual tenants, or tenants of individual housing units, are sometimes unsuccessful in fighting their own organization for the right to negotiate separately with their landlords.

One of the slogans of the advocates of the welfare state has been that "society is to blame," for poverty, delinquency, and many other ills. In the long run such attitudes have eroded individual responsibility, despite the warnings against such developments that were issued by some of the pioneers of the welfare state in Scandinavia. The opposition to "charity" has had similar effects: suffering and need "should" be dealt with by the state and local authorities at the expense of the entirety of taxpayers, and as a consequence individual citizens/ taxpayers believe that they are under no obligation to act. This often applies to the children of aged parents. Voluntary social work is frowned upon and has virtually disappeared, with some exceptions in the case of religious organizations, but the vacuum has not always been filled.

A considerable part of the rise and equalization in standards of living has taken the form of more leisure for everybody. And increased leisure has usually not had any adverse effect on productivity. Shorter working hours have usually been compensated by automation and other rationalization of working procedures, as well as probably to some extent by greater assiduity, more intense application to work. But further developments have not always given the lie to the old proverb that "idleness is the parent of vices," and in fact occupying one's spare time has come to be an accepted social problem which for obvious reasons was unheard of a hundred or even fifty years ago.

But this is not all. Growing prosperity together with urbanization and increased emphasis on the equitable distribution of goods and services characteristic of the welfare state have created a type of society differing not only from that which was known to the reformers of the 1920s and 1930s, but also from what they visualized and hoped for. Like all social structures, it involves problems, some of which are new or imply an aggravation of what was experienced before. The changes are apparent in a great number of different orbits: demographic structure, attitudes toward society held by the older and younger generations, the situation in the labor market, relations between men and women, private and public morals, crime and delinquency, the family structure, housing, education, ecology, and the status of underprivileged minority groups. Each of these has to be considered by itself before we can evaluate the achievements of the welfare states.

Demographic developments in Scandinavia have on the whole been similar to those of other industrialized countries, and the differences that do appear can at least in part be explained by different experiences during the two world wars. The accompanying tabulation shows birthrates and death rates since the beginning of the twentieth century.

	Live Births per Thousand Inhabitants				*Deaths per Thousand Inhabitants*			
	Denmark	*Finland*	*Norway*	*Sweden*	*Denmark*	*Finland*	*Norway*	*Sweden*
1901-10	28.6	32.5	24.5	25.8	14.2	14.3	18.7	14.9
1911-20	24.9	27.0	24.8	22.1	13.0	13.8	18.9	14.3
1921-30	20.8	23.6	20.1	17.5	11.2	11.3	15.0	12.1
1931-40	17.9	19.7	15.3	14.5	10.7	10.4	14.0	11.7
1941-50	21.0	24.2	19.6	18.5	9.7	9.8	13.6	10.4
1951-60	17.1	20.8	18.3	14.7	9.1	8.7	9.3	9.7
1961-70	16.6	16.8	17.5	14.8	9.8	9.7	9.6	10.1

There are clear differences between the four countries, reflecting the pace and characteristics of their economic development, but also different experiences especially during the Second World War. The end results, however, are similar although not entirely identical, as appears from the following figures for the percentage of their population belonging to different age groups:

Age	*Denmark* *(1978)*	*Finland* *(1977)*	*Norway* *(1977)*	*Sweden* *(1978)*
0-4	6.7	7.4	6.9	6.1
5-9	7.2	8.3	8.1	6.7
10-14	8.2	8.6	8.0	7.3
15-19	7.8	9.1	7.6	6.5
20-24	8.1	9.7	7.6	6.7
25-29	7.6	7.2	7.5	7.3
30-34	6.1	6.3	7.5	8.2
35-39	5.6	6.0	5.4	6.7
40-44	5.6	6.4	4.7	5.5
45-49	6.0	6.1	5.2	5.4
50-54	5.8	5.2	5.7	5.7
55-59	5.7	5.4	6.1	6.3
60-64	5.3	5.1	5.5	5.6
65-69	4.9	3.8	4.8	5.4
70-74	3.8	2.7	3.8	4.4
75-79	2.6	1.6	2.9	3.2
80-84	1.7	0.8	1.7	1.9
85-89	0.8	0.3	0.7	0.8
90-	0.3	0.0	0.3	0.3

Falling birthrates are typical of all prosperous countries; so are falling death rates and increased life-spans. It might be assumed that the tendency to low birthrates should be particularly marked in Scandinavia, where there is practically no Roman Catholic population and birth control is consequently not inhibited by religious considerations. It is difficult, however, to identify any such differences. Scandinavian birthrates, it is true, are lower than those of Italy, for instance, but higher than those of Austria. The conclusion seems to be that neither religion nor the emergence of the welfare state has had any serious impact in this respect.

On the other hand, at certain times there has been discussion about the changing proportion of different age groups. As has been mentioned in another context, Alva and Gunnar Myrdal initiated a debate on the problem in Sweden in the 1930s. They demonstrated that in the long run the low birthrate would lead to a diminution of the working population, in proportion to the old and the very young, and they argued that this would involve serious consequences for the prosperity of the people. The Myrdals therefore advocated conscious population policies. But in their opinion these should take the form of general rather than specific actions. They argued that the reason for the fall in birthrates was that families with children were confronted with an unsatisfactory economic situation. With efficient birth control, people would therefore choose to have no children at all or comparatively few children as long as their economic situation did not improve significantly. The answer was to introduce economic benefits, such as child subventions, and to provide better social services to both children and mothers.

There is no denying that the impact of this argument on the development of social security and welfare was powerful indeed. It was one of the causes of increases in both transfers and collective consumption. The impact on the birthrates, on the other hand, was not very great. It may well be that the debate initiated by the Myrdals did for a limited time make Swedes and other Scandinavians conscious of the existence of the problem and may have contributed, together with other causes, to a temporary increase in birthrates. But no lasting effects could be established.

Recently another type of debate has arisen. It is related to the decline in the institution of marriage and the increase in the number of married women that are gainfully employed outside the home. It is maintained that these developments call for increased social services to families, especially more daycare centers. Women will refuse to bear children, so the argument goes, unless society relieves them at least partly of the practical burdens of parenthood. But it is difficult to believe that action of this type will have more impact on birthrates than did the increase in social services for families fifty years ago. There could be other good reasons for providing better public services to families with children; this is not the place to discuss such problems. But from the standpoint of demographic developments, its effects are likely to be negligible. As can be seen from comparisons with other industrialized countries, there is no connection between improved social services for families and rising birthrates.

Death rates are a different matter. Unquestionably, improvement of healthcare services sharply affects the life-span. The stationary or perhaps even rising death rate at present obtaining in the Scandinavian countries is unavoidable: even with the best possible healthcare, the death rate remains proportionate to the relative size of higher age groups.

The changing demographic structure has brought a new set of problems, those related to the care of the aged. The decline of the institution of the family in Scandinavia, as in other industrialized societies, means that sons and daughters are both less willing and less able than before to take care of aged parents. In accordance with the general principles of the welfare state, this duty falls to the organs of society. Old age pensions were the immediate consequence of such attitudes. In addition, from the 1930s on Scandinavia has maintained relatively high standards of institutionalized care for the elderly, at least in the outward appearance of homes for the aged. A later development has been the recognition that there are serious problems besides those that can be solved by old age pensions and beautiful homes for the aged. Some of these are to be found in the medical field, and recently—but only very recently—there has developed an increased interest in geriatrics. However, the scientific study of medical problems associated with old age has not resulted in entirely satisfactory care for the elderly, and it is more difficult to recruit doctors and paramedical personnel for geriatric service than for other areas of medical care. In addition, the existing systems of geriatric care are criticized as impersonal and therefore not acceptable from a humanitarian standpoint. It is increasingly maintained that the welfare state

tends to "buy off" its senior citizens with pensions and institutionalized treatment, without considering their own wishes and ambitions,
and that the lack of a meaningful occupation during retirement creates serious psychological problems.

It is not easy to weigh the importance of criticisms such as these.
Obviously, with people past retirement age forming a numerically
greater part of the population their difficulties are coming into focus.
Also obvious is that the ambitions of senior citizens are colored by
their own experiences and hopes during earlier periods of their lives,
when the habits and attitudes of the people and society were different
from what they are today. Circumstances of this type tend to magni-
fy the problem unrealistically. But even with such reservations, it can
hardly be said that the welfare states in Scandinavia have lived up to
their ambitions in relation to older generations. Fifty years ago, Gustav
Möller used to refer to his old mother in debate after debate on social reform. If she were alive today, she would undoubtedly be much
better off in economic terms. But it is not quite certain that she would
be happier than she was in the 1930s.

The changing demographic structure is also important in its effect
on public opinion. The attitudes of youth have traditionally been regarded as the attitudes of the future; and at certain times, for instance
in the 1960s, it was almost taken for granted that they were the only
ones that counted. In a political democracy, however, what counts
are the attitudes of the majority of the people, as apparent at election time. In Scandinavia every effort is made to enable even the very
old to cast their votes. The minimum age for voting is eighteen years.
Participation in elections is very high, but somewhat lower in the
youngest age groups. With about 13 percent of the population above
retirement age and about 15 percent between the ages of twenty and
thirty, voters are still predominantly middle aged, but despite the
percentages, the young do not dominate over the retired. And the
political importance of the latter is bound to increase over the next
decade or decades. This will undeniably have a significant effect on
public opinion and public policies.

Those belonging to older age groups still remember what their
countries were like before the introduction of the welfare state. To
them the word "poverty" retains its original significance of actual
material need and even outright destitution. On the other hand, they
also remember times when it was regarded as a disgrace to "live on

welfare." This attitude is disappearing, and indeed one of the objectives of the welfare reforms of the 1930s and 1950s was to abolish it. Basing social welfare on solidarity and not on charity should make it universally acceptable. But to say that the negative attitude is disappearing also means that it has not yet disappeared completely. In the older generation, there is still an unwillingness to request welfare benefits and a certain contempt for those, especially those younger people, who are demanding or accepting help from the organs of society. In fact, among people of the older generation, two contradictory attitudes are held. On the one hand, they are proud of the welfare state which has grown up during their lifetime, and they believe that they have contributed to it at least by their votes in general elections. Their hope was that their children would be better off than they had been themselves. And undoubtedly such hopes have been realized. On the other hand, their remembrance of past hardships works the other way as well. One often hears that "we had to make a real effort; but they . . ." There is a tendency among those who remember the years before 1939 to resent anything that in their opinion means an excessive attempt to make everything easy, too easy, for those who grew up in the 1960s or later.

So much for the older generation. The younger ones—the dividing line should probably be drawn between those who grew up before 1950 and those who do not really remember the Second World War—tends to take the present prosperity and material well-being of their compatriots for granted. They can hardly imagine what things could have been like before the advent of the welfare state, neither the problems of those days nor the efforts that went into their resolution. As a consequence they may disparage the importance of economic benefits and of social welfare. Their support for the continued existence of the welfare state is consequently far from assured.

Envy is supposed to be a typically Swedish trait, hence the phrase "the Royal Swedish Envy." It is debatable whether it is more Swedish than Scandinavian and whether it is more characteristic of Scandinavians than of other peoples. But there can be no question about its importance in regard to the welfare state. It played an important role at the time when the welfare state was being established. The poor were jealous of the easy life of the rich. The idea of social justice takes root most easily when it refers to those injustices to which you yourself are exposed. As a driving force behind the social reforms following in the wake of political democracy in Scandinavia, envy played as great a part as solidarity.

But in the long run, once the welfare states were established, its role changed. The equitable distribution of social benefits is jealously —enviously—guarded over by the public, and not in Sweden alone. We have already seen this in the attitude of the older generation: "we had to - - -; but they - - -." And in all age groups people wonder: "why should we pay in order that they may be lazy?" There is, for instance, a widespread belief, whether well founded or not, that health insurance benefits are abused by those who find it expedient to take an unscheduled holiday now and then. The new type of envy is no longer directed against the rich alone, but also, and perhaps principally, against the indigent. Humanitarian attitudes toward criminals and delinquents are exposed to similar if not the same criticisms: "we make a real effort to remain, at least on the whole, within the boundaries of the law; why should they be permitted to break it with complete or almost complete impunity?" And finally the fairness of the whole system is questioned: are social benefits really distributed in accordance with inflexible legal rules and without favoritism by those who are supposed to "take care of" people in need of help?

One fundamental difference between the generations appears, or at least used to appear, in the attitude toward work. There was a time when most people considered work to be the central point of life. It could be tiring, boring, and outright unpleasant, but still it was the most important thing in the world. Personal life, including family life, had to take second place. Unemployment was to be feared above all other misfortunes. To a considerable extent, middle-aged Scandinavians have retained those attitudes. On the other hand, the younger generation has had little experience of unemployment, let alone of its consequences with respect to material need. This generation expects work to be "meaningful," not only in the sense of being useful or even indispensable to society and to other citizens, but also from the standpoint of workers themselves. Otherwise even unemployment may be preferable. And even when employed in jobs that are satisfactory in these respects, individuals may hold the sphere of personal relations outside the place of work to be the more important. There have always been those who "live only for their leisure time," but undoubtedly their number is growing. Nor can it be denied that this change of attitude is closely related to the development of social security and welfare.

There is, especially among the younger generation, a rather negative attitude toward traditional types of industrial employment. In a Swedish television program in 1979, a young woman stated, "None of us who went to school in the late sixties expected that we should ever have to work in a factory." Yet most of the employment opportunities available are to be found in factories or in work that is even less "meaningful."

All this may be changing again, however. All over Scandinavia unemployment is rearing its ugly head after so many years of "full employment." And for various reasons, the first people to be fired today when the labor force has to be reduced are the young and not the old. Even more frequently reduction is effected by employing no new—young—people. With fresh experience of unemployment for themselves of their contemporaries, those belonging to the younger generation may experience a change of heart, finding once more that work is valuable in itself, whether "meaningful" or not, and not just as a source of income. In the television program just referred to, the woman in question was shown to make her living sweeping railway cars.

Another change of attitude results from the perceived change in character of the clientele of the welfare system. As long as the public believed that this clientele consisted mainly of "normal people," who differed from the majority of the population only by virtue of age, illness, or other obviously unavoidable circumstances, only a limited strain was placed on solidarity. In fact the situation is still the same, but to the general public it appears to have changed. It is maintained, if inaccurately, that a considerable number of "welfare cases," possibly a majority, consist of habitual drunkards, drug abusers, ex-criminals, and juvenile delinquents. Most people refuse to identify with such individuals and tend to think that these have themselves to blame for their misfortunes. There is also a widespread belief that refugees and other immigrants constitute a burden on the welfare system, although as a matter of fact they tend to call for public assistance much more rarely than the indigenous population.

Finally, the general acceptance of the welfare state as a guarantee that certain minimum requirements should be available for everybody, whatever may happen to them, does not necessarily imply an equally positive attitude toward the progressive realization of an egalitarian society. Outwardly it appears that Scandinavian societies have realized the principle that all men (and women) are equal, at least as far as equality of opportunities is concerned. Differences in status still exist, but they relate to occupations and positions rather than to social origins and actual incomes. Moreover, these differences frequently come under attack, and those who make use of their benefits tend to be shamefaced about it. But it is doubtful whether equality of results, rather than equality of opportunities, really enjoys much popular support—even within the labor movement, as we shall see when we come to the problems of the labor market.

It should be emphasized that the observations made in the previous paragraph refer to the state of public opinion as it can be identified at the present time. Maybe the resistance to equality of results is only a transitional phenomenon and public attitudes will adapt themselves to the new ideas of an egalitarian society—just as about a thousand years ago they were supposed to adapt themselves to the ethical doctrines of Christianity. In such matters it would be rash to hazard any prophesies.

The labor market in Scandinavian postindustrial societies differs in many respects from what was characteristic of the period before 1939. But it has to be noted that the establishment of welfare states in the Nordic countries has by no means succeeded in abolishing unemployment. This would probably have disappointed the founding fathers more than anything else. In the experience of the 1930s they thought they had found firm reasons to believe that at least mass unemployment would come to be classified with plague and smallpox as scourges of the unenlightened past and would no longer be a threat to progressive societies. In fact it has proved possible to provide even rather generously for the material economic needs of the unemployed, but quite impossible to abolish the origin of their plight.

In an earlier chapter some of the causes of this shortcoming have been explained. A few of them are found in purely economic facts, mostly related to the dependence on international economic developments. Some others are the growth of the potential labor force, diminishing social mobility, and changing attitudes toward work characteristic of welfare states, especially among the younger generation.

But whatever the causes, unemployment remains a major social problem, most of all since such a great proportion of the unemployed are young people.

None of the Scandinavian countries have accepted outright the idea that work, or opportunities for work, should be regarded as a civil right. (Although the new Swedish constitution obliges "the public" to safeguard the rights of work, housing, and education, this precept is only a generality and not legally binding.) This is largely for practical reasons. As long as a free labor market exists, it is impossible to define such a right in an intelligible and practical manner. It is undoubtedly regarded as one of the duties of society to do as much as possible in order to provide job opportunities anc contain unemployment through suitable economic and social measures. This principle is intrinsic to the welfare state. It has been largely, although not completely implemented in the Nordic countries. But there is still no agreement as to its significance with regard to the quality of the employment opportunities that should be offered or their apportionment between the private and the public sectors of their economies.

Moreover, the effect of well-meaning measures may not always be such as was intended. Sweden in 1974 enacted legislation to protect employees from dismissal. It is maintained—although not conclusively proved—that this legislation has made employers unwilling to recruit inexperienced personnel, since they are obliged to keep them on the payroll even when they prove unsatisfactory. This attitude may have aggravated the problem of unemployment among the young.

The quantity of opportunities for gainful employment is finite at any given time and at any given wage level. No society can afford to keep people employed in either the private or the public sector unless they perform functions that are economically viable. And here problems related to automation come into the picture. The value of human labor has to be measured against the value and cost of employing machinery. Pessimists maintain that increased use of computers and industrial robots will drastically reduce the number of jobs available for human beings. Optimists, on the other hand, argue that all new technical devices have in the long run provided more jobs than they have abolished. But regardless of whether we take the pessimistic or the optimistic view, it can hardly be denied that the character of jobs will change, as it did with the emergence of other technical devices in the past. This will call for greater mobility and adaptability on the part of the labor force—at a time when there is a clear tendency for mobility and adaptability to diminish rather than increase. To this extent it seems that the needs of modern technology and the attitudes created by the welfare state in the labor market may find themselves running afoul of each other.

Another tendency appearing in the labor market today is the increase in part-time employment. This involves special problems. One of the minor ones, which must, however, be mentioned, is that it distorts income statistics. The statistically "lowest income groups" consist largely of individuals who are of their own free will working part time and not full time, and who consequently earn a lower annual income. A more significant fact is that a majority of those working part time are women and particularly married women who retain the chief responsibility for running the household while still finding it necessary to earn an individual income. The tax system also encourages women not to work full time, attitudes toward the respective roles of men and women being what they are. Consequently the tendency to part-time employment is highly unpopular among those who regard equality between men and women as a supremely important element of the egalitarian welfare state. It is equally unpopular among labor union leaders, but for different reasons. Employees working part time are less loyal to unions than their colleagues working full time. A considerable proportion do not bother to join any union at all. In addition, this type of employment creates difficulties in wage negotiations applying the principle of solidarity in wage policies. Are those employed part time to be regarded as "low wage groups" or not? In fact they often take less interest than others in wage levels, which of course also explains their passive attitude toward the unions.

As pointed out earlier, the welfare state has to be paid for out of the total social product. Consequently, in order to fulfill its ambitions it calls for high productivity in the whole of the economy and particularly in industry, since in Scandinavia as elsewhere the welfare state is based on a highly sophisticated industrial society. But it is not always easy to reconcile the call for high productivity with such ambitions of the welfare state as equalization of incomes, the influence of employees and especially of their nationwide unions on the management of individual enterprises, and the claim of individuals to be employed in jobs of their choice. This type of clash is becoming increasingly apparent in Scandinavia.

In regard to labor relations, labor conflicts, and agreements, it has be be emphasized that in all four countries both employees and employers are widely organized. Their organizations are industry-wide and nationwide, and negotiations take place at that level, leaving only the details to be worked out for each particular enterprise. There is no legislation prohibiting either strikes or lockouts. The general principles of labor relations apply not only in the private sector but also to public employees. In other respects, the countries present rather different pictures. Both in Denmark and in Finland strikes have continued to occur with a certain frequency. Norway and Sweden, on the other hand, have a relatively good record of peace in the labor market. The system traditionally applied in Sweden and sometimes called "the Swedish model" is particularly interesting. It has meant that both Parliament and Government on the face of it remained aloof from wage and salary negotiations. The only exceptions were a few (but by no means all) cases involving public employees, where they passed or threatened to pass legislation prohibiting strikes. Otherwise both strikes and lockouts were legally permitted on the expiry of collective contracts. And employers' and employees' organizations were left to negotiate for such contracts either directly or with the help of mediators appointed by the government. It should be noted that the mediators would only make suggestions to the parties and had no power to pass binding awards. Occasionally, when the Government came to the conclusion that an agreement reached in this way had implications that were dangerous to the national economy, it later "corrected" the agreement by making such changes in taxation as raising the level of value-added tax. This system worked quite well for nearly fifty years, from the late 1930s on. During the Second World War and right after it the unions severely restricted their demands. Later, there was a continuous rise in the real wage and salary level, accepted by employers with little or no resistance. As a consequence, open conflicts rarely occurred.

Opinions vary as to the causes of the success of the "Swedish model." One explanation is that the Social Democratic Governments in power from 1945 to 1976 cooperated closely with the labor unions and thus presented the employers with an irresistible united front, at the same time successfully moderating union demands. Another one is that given the spectacular economic growth during this period, private enterprises had every reason to accede to the demands of unions as long as they were not obviously excessive, rather than to risk open conflicts, and that the unions on their side had a strongly centralized leadership with a good understanding of economic realities.

An open conflict of some weeks' duration in the spring of 1980 affected major parts of both the private and the public sectors, causing considerable inconvenience to citizens and great losses to industry. It was resolved mainly to the advantage of the unions and through the traditional mediation system, but in spite of this many voices were heard saying that this was the end of the "Swedish model." It is of course much too early to draw sweeping conclusions like that. After all, the system worked, if not without difficulties, and in the subsequent year all major conflicts were avoided. What the experience of 1980 shows, however, is that regardless of which party holds political power, the unions are more powerful than the representatives of capital, at least in the absence of a really serious slump.

Finland in 1906 was the first country in Europe to give women the vote. Norway followed in 1907, Denmark in 1915, and Sweden in 1921. Other measures, chiefly concerned with the legal position of women in society and their access to higher education and public service, had been adopted in all four countries successively since the latter half of the nineteenth century. These reforms were particularly important in their indirect effects. It is no exaggeration to say that the fundamental principle of equality between men and women is more widely accepted in Scandinavia than in most other countries of the world; this is seen in legislation, in the apparent attitudes of the public, and in actual practice. In fact the position of women has changed drastically, and there has been a corresponding impact on society as a whole. The most important element of change has been the growing role of women, both married and unmarried, in the labor market. As has just been mentioned, this trend has added considerable numbers to the total labor force, and it is characteristic that today no one ventures to say, as was frequently said fifty years ago, that at the threat of unemployment married women should be the first to be fired. Some of the industrial welfare legislation introduced supposedly for the protection of women in the nineteenth century and prohibiting for instance their employment as miners has been repealed as

contrary to the principle of equality. It is no longer possible for employers to pay lower wages to women than to men working in the
same jobs, although it is still true that wages tend to be lower in jobs
where most of the employees are women.

The proportion of women in high political and administrative office
has grown considerably. Parity between men and women is far away,
but the demand for it is sometimes broached. As a result of the latest
elections (in 1981, 1979, 1981, and 1982, respectively), there are 42
women out of 175 members of the Danish legislature, 52 out of 200
in that of Finland, 40 out of 155 in that of Norway, and 90 out of
349 in that of Sweden. In each case this comes to about one-fourth
of the total membership. And although Iceland is outside the range of
this book, it is worth mentioning that in 1980 Vigdis Finnbogadottir
of Reykjavik became the first woman to be elected president of a
democratically governed state.

Equality between men and women is one of the fields where the
impact of egalitarianism is as strong as ever. In fact it is much stronger
today than it was at the time when women were definitely discriminated against — a not unusual phenomenon of social perfectionism.

An extremely important factor contributing to the changing relationships between the sexes is birth control, which is very widely,
almost universally practiced in Scandinavia. With contraceptives in
general use and abortions being practically free, childbirth becomes
almost entirely a matter of the woman's own choice. Many women
decide that it is more important for them to remain in their jobs
without interruption than to bear children. And a few professional
women come to the conclusion that they would prefer to adopt a
child rather than bear it themselves.

At least in theory equality between men and women can be
achieved in two ways. Society can accept the fact that men and
women are performing different roles, while seeing to it that the roles
usually assumed by women are given both a sufficiently high status
and equal economic remuneration. The other alternative is to try to
abolish differences in roles completely or almost completely. In the
Scandinavian countries it is the latter alternative alone that is regarded
as acceptable. This approach does, however, involve difficulties that
are becoming increasingly obvious. It runs counter to traditions existing from time immemorial. In concentrating on the access of women,
including married women and mothers, to the general labor market,

it calls for equal division within a family or a couple of the "ground service" such as care for children and other household work. And it appears that while employers can be cured of the habit of discriminating against women, if necessary by means of legislation, it is much more difficult to cure husbands of the habit of leaving household work to their wives. Ironically, old attitudes remain particularly strong among the "working classes," while the "upper class" families and especially intellectuals are more amenable to new ideas. But general insistence on a classless, nonhierarchical society tends to keep the former groups from being influenced by the habits of what formerly used to be called "their betters."

At various times it has been fashionable to criticize Scandinavian welfare states, and particularly Sweden, for the prevalence of suicides, "immoral practices," "free sex," and so on. There is no doubt that such criticisms were grossly exaggerated. In fact a considerable number of tourists from presumably more "moral" parts of the world have found themselves most disappointed by visits to the Nordic countries. Still it can hardly be denied that these are permissive societies, probably among the most permissive in the industrialized world.

Permissiveness, of course, is neither good nor bad in itself. It all depends on what is permitted, and how this is judged by those expressing their opinions. Like beauty, permissiveness is largely in the eyes of the beholder. It is in fact only another word for tolerance, and over the centuries opinions have been changing throughout the Western world as to what should and should not be tolerated: religious heresies, political opposition, long hair, unusual dress (or undress), heterosexual and homosexual relations, drunkenness, use of drugs, violence to children and violence by children.

In most Western and particularly most Protestant societies the influence of religion has diminished during recent centuries. As a result, there is increasing uncertainty about moral standards, since these used to be drawn from religious sources and to a considerable extent enforced by representatives of religion. Legal rules of course remain and have even been proliferating, but they are no longer reinforced and supplemented by the same accepted moral standards.

Since the beginning of the twentieth century, hypocrisy has been more vigorously attacked in Scandinavia than in most other parts of the world. It is hardly an exaggeration to say that the molders of public opinion have tended to regard it as an unforgivable sin, perhaps nearly the worst of all. This has made for great and to some foreign observers deceptive openness. Few Scandinavians are anything but proud of this characteristic of their societies. At the same time it has to be remembered that hypocrisy is the tribute of vice to virtue and that its disappearance may therefore not always be exclusively to the good.

Subcultures of different types, which adopt their own moral standards after rejecting a number of those traditionally existing, have been growing in importance all over the Western world since the Second World War. Scandinavia is no exception, nor is the tendency more visible there than elsewhere. Danish society is particularly susceptible to this development, while Finland and Norway have seen less of it, with Sweden somewhere in between. This does not mean that Denmark and Sweden are more "immoral" than the other Nordic countries, nor that the difference need be permanent. It may be that it can be accounted for by purely geographical reasons. Finland and Norway are less exposed to foreign influence, and experience shows that in due time the same tendencies are apt to reach all Nordic countries.

In the present context, the main question to be answered by observing Scandinavia is whether there is any logical and actual connection between permissiveness and the emergence of welfare states. Are such states likely to show more permissiveness than others; and if so, for what reasons? It is difficult to see how the establishment of social security and welfare could have any effect in this respect. Only if one assumes that fear of poverty and unemployment tend to keep people, and especially young people, within the boundaries set up by conventional moral rules could the abolishment of such fears be regarded as a cause of permissiveness. On the other hand, a general emphasis on individual liberties and on rationalism and the disestablishment of social hierarchies undoubtedly has such an effect. A rigid collectivist society can never be permissive. It is unable to tolerate such deviations from normal behavior and attitudes as are in principle and almost by definition acceptable in open societies, however inconvenient they may be to rulers and political and social majorities.

There could be a connection between certain other characteristics of the welfare state and the change in moral standards. The emphasis on leisure rather than work is one of them: because conventional morals used to be strongly work-oriented in Scandinavian society, because a satisfying use of leisure may seem to call for expensive activities requiring funds not easily acquired by permissible means, and because the attitude toward the human environment changes with an increase of leisure time. The tendency to regard crime and delinquency as "the fault of society" rather than of the individual and thus to erode the idea of personal responsibility could also lead individuals to follow their own inclinations rather than the rules set up by conventional morals. Such arguments must not be stretched too far, however. In most societies today, even those that are the most rigid in principle, crime and delinquency are increasing.

In the Nordic countries, as elsewhere, it appears that the attitudes of the common people are far more rigid than those of social reformers. The latter, who attempt to delve deeper than just to the symptoms of misbehavior—or deviant behavior—and try to identify its causes, are more likely to sympathize with delinquents and insist that they be allowed a certain amount of freedom. In both Denmark and Sweden the question of narcotics exemplifies such differences. So-called pot Liberals, who refuse to treat the use of for instance cannabis as a serious offense, meet with little sympathy from the man or woman in the street. On the other hand, it is unclear whether it is the hardliners or the pot Liberals who have been more effective in dealing with the social problems involved.

And finally a sort of new moralism is growing up in the Scandinavian welfare states. It is directed against commercialism, competition, and individual egotism. Its basic principle is solidarity, not only as enforced by legal regulations, but as an independent moral principle. It could be argued that the "permissiveness" of societies such as the Scandinavian ones is not so much a loosening of morals as a change from one moral system to another. The so called free sex in Scandinavia is a case in point. The institution of marriage is widely questioned and largely replaced by less permanent relationships. Such relationships are usually monogamous, so that it seems inaccurate to call them immoral, whether one regards them as acceptable or not. On the other hand, the hope that greater sexual freedom should put an end to prostitution has not been fulfilled.

The new moral attitudes do not mean that problems of crime and delinquency can be taken lightly or that they are taken lightly by either public opinion or public authorities in Scandinavia. On the contrary, they are widely publicized and occupy a great deal of interest, both among those who call for more law and order and among those who emphasize the personal problems and difficulties of delinquents and criminals.

Statistics indicate that crime, as a whole, is on the increase. This applies both to crimes against property and to crimes of violence. Both assault and battery and "muggings" have recently become much more common in Scandinavian cities. An increasing number of cases of rape is also reported. At the same time, so-called economic crimes —tax frauds and environmental destruction, but also large-scale trade in narcotics, fraudulent advertising, profiteering, and usury—are also apparently more prevalent than before. But it is not easy to draw conclusions from such statistics, which for obvious reasons can refer only to offenses known to the police. Since it is well known that police resources are insufficient for the investigation of all reported crimes, a number of "minor" crimes and misdemeanors are never reported by the victims. And the accuracy of statistics may vary from one year to the other. All that can be said is that there is an increase, not how great it is.

Another disquieting tendency is that juvenile delinquency and crime, even serious crime, seem to be increasing at a faster rate than crimes committed by adults. Statistics may be a bit misleading since some of the objectionable activities now reported to the authorities may a generation ago have been dealt with privately and summarily, especially by authoritarian parents. Nevertheless, abuse of alcohol and drugs by children has undoubtedly been increasing in recent decades, and there is no doubt that this has had serious effects on the incidence of crime.

The victims of burglary, robbery, and other crimes of violence complain that society does not afford them sufficient protection. To what extent this is correct, or rather to what extent it represents a change from earlier circumstances, is as usual difficult to ascertain. What is quite obvious from the statistics, on the other hand, is that comparatively few perpetrators of crimes of this type are actually apprehended and brought to justice; and this may always have been so. But whatever the actual truth of the matter, there is no denying the existence of widespread suspicion and dissatisfaction in regard to law enforcement, with a consequent lack of trust in the state.

It is sometimes affirmed that these evils can be blamed on the welfare state. Crime is increasing, it is maintained, because individual responsibility has eroded; because parents no longer have to be responsible for their children but can transfer this responsibility to anonymous agents of "society"; because people, especially young people, have too much leisure; because criminals and delinquents are treated with excessive leniency; and because it is no longer necessary to "behave" in order to keep a job. Many theoretical arguments can be adduced in support of such statements, as well as against them. In reality, problems of this kind are no more serious in Scandinavian or other welfare states than anywhere else.

But it is equally necessary to emphasize that the establishment of welfare states does not appear to have had the opposite effect either. At one time it was fashionable to maintain that crime and delinquency were largely caused by poverty and that the situation could be set right by raising the standard of living of the poorer elements in society and achieving a more equitable distribution of incomes. Such expectations have not been justified. In some individual cases it is possible to relate criminal tendencies to depressing personal experiences, such as poverty, lack of educational opportunities, conflicts with parents or an otherwise unsatisfactory family life. But there is no indication that general improvement of the social environment has made people more law-abiding. In this respect, the establishment of welfare states appears to have had neither positive nor negative effects.

One of many popular ideas about Scandinavian welfare states is that they have exceptionally high suicide rates. The following figures showing the number of suicides per 100,000 inhabitants in some selected countries should indicate the real situation.

Hungary (1975)	38.4	United States (1970)	12.7
Finland (1974)	25.1	Poland (1975)	11.4
Austria (1975)	24.7	Iceland (1975)	10.1
Denmark (1973)	23.8	Norway (1975)	9.9
Czechoslovakia (1973)	22.4	Netherlands (1974)	9.2
West Germany (1974)	21.0	Great Britain (1974)	7.9
Sweden (1974)	20.0	Italy (1972)	5.8
Japan (1975)	18.1	Spain (1974)	4.0
France (1970)	15.4		

It is obviously more than difficult to find any relationship between the social system and the frequency of suicides. Hungary, a

Communist country, has by far the highest suicide rate, more than three times as high as Poland, another country from the same category. Finland comes next on the list, rather closely followed by Denmark. In Norway, on the other hand, the suicide rate is less than half of what it is in Sweden, which appears seventh on the list. Austria, a mainly Catholic country, has the third-highest rate, whereas Italy and Spain, which are also primarily Catholic, appear at the bottom of the list. The most likely conclusion is that suicide statistics are unreliable. In some countries suicides are outlawed either by law or by religious and social stigma. As a consequence, another cause of death is reported when a suicide has taken place. In other countries, such as the Nordic nations as well as Japan, there is no such stigma, and suicides are reported honestly. In any case, it is obvious that there is absolutely no correlation between suicides and welfare states. Norway is no less of a welfare state than Finland.

A more real problem, and one more definitely connected with social developments in Scandinavia, is the decline of the family. During the last decade, the number of marriages decreased consistently. By international standards it is low, as is apparent from the following figures giving the number of contracted marriages per 1,000 inhabitants in sixteen selected countries:

United States (1976)	9.9	Netherlands (1977)	6.7
Czechoslovakia (1977)	9.1	Finland (1977)	6.5
Hungary (1977)	9.1	Denmark (1977)	6.3
Japan (1976)	7.8	Italy (1977)	6.1
Great Britain (1976)	7.7	Austria (1977)	6.0
Iceland (1977)	7.1	Norway (1977)	5.9
Spain (1976)	7.1	West Germany (1977)	5.8
France (1977)	6.9	Sweden (1977)	4.9

The low figures for Scandinavia may mean only that the practice of having a family within the confines of a marriage has been to some extent discarded in favor of a family structure based on other permanent relationships, which also may have certain economic advantages because of the tax system. It should be remembered that the United States, which tops the list for contracted marriages, also has a very high divorce rate. It is of course impossible to determine the permanence of family relationships not taking the form of marriages, but they are generally assumed to be more easily dissolved. Another general assumption is that the decline of the family in its traditional form is largely caused by the tendency of women to remain gainfully employed after they have borne children.

The strongest impact of these developments is to be found in the position of children. Much of their education—and this applies even to very young children—is being gradually transferred from the "nuclear family" to larger units such as schools and daycare centers. Experiments have also been made with "collective households," comprising several couples with their children. The idea of these establishments is not sexual promiscuity, as some people apparently believe, but joint education of the children of several couples. It should be added, however, that such collectives are by no means common; nor are their numbers on the rise. They originated with young intellectuals, and to the extent that they exist, they are populated by the same types of people.

A consequence of the decline of the "nuclear family" is that parents no longer feel the same responsibility for their children. This is often deplored, not least in discussions about juvenile delinquency. "Society," the critics say, can never take the place of parents, and children who see but little of their mothers and fathers are likely to suffer psychologically from lack of affection and tenderness. In the counterargument, it is emphasized that affection and tenderness by no means always characterized the "nuclear family" and that children in the older system often suffered from authoritarian and outright cruel treatment by their parents. It is still too early to say whether either of the two arguments will prove to be right. What is clear, however, is that the new situation requires fundamentally new approaches, that it is neither universally accepted nor even understood, and that the position of children in the new type of society definitely poses social problems. These may be no greater than preexisting ones; but they undoubtedly *appear* to be greater because they are unfamiliar.

Housing is another perennial problem. There are few fields of social development where so much has been done in Scandinavia. Since the 1930s public authorities, state as well as municipal, have been directly involved in housing construction and have also provided housing subsidies. Scandinavian architects have come to concentrate more and more on housing projects and less on monumental buildings. In all four countries, satellites to big cities have given opportunities for new ventures and experiments in the construction of family dwellings. Tapiola outside Helsinki and Vällingby outside Stockholm are well-known and more or less successful examples.

And yet there is widespread discontent. One reason for this is that with the rise in general standard of living, combined with rent subsidies, demand has grown much more quickly than supply. Not only young families, but also single young men and women from the age when they leave school (around sixteen and seventeen) take it for granted that they should have dwellings of their own and no longer stay with their parents. At the same time the movement of population from rural into urban areas and between different urban areas has automatically increased demand.

Housing standards have also been going up. Not only is there much more space per individual, but there are also more conveniences such as central heating, bath and shower facilities, and household appliances of various types. The Swedish study of living conditions in 1975, referred to in a previous chapter, gives clear indications of what is regarded as normal or even indispensable today. As a result, much of the older stock of housing facilities in the cities is outmoded and no longer regarded as acceptable — except by certain environmentalists and other groups of mostly young intellectuals.

Construction and modernization of houses are becoming increasingly expensive because of the aforementioned rise in standard requirements, because of higher wage levels, and because of general inflationary tendencies. This has a considerable impact on the rent level, which is the more noticeable since the housing policies largely concentrated on general subsidies which were intended to keep rents down. The burden on public finances for such subsidies grows very quickly with increasing costs of house-building. At the same time tenants and their organizations complain that an increasing percentage of their available income is tied up in rents.

In Scandinavian cities, not only the majority of families in the lower income groups but also most of those belonging to the middle classes traditionally lived as tenants in apartments. In the 1930s, there was a considerable growth of housing cooperatives, and municipally owned corporations ultimately took over most of the responsibility for constructing new blocks of apartments. Here again, rising standards of living created new demands. Detached and semidetached houses became increasingly popular, partly because they provided more privacy and access to gardens, partly because owning one's own

house became an important element of security, a profitable investment, and perhaps also a status symbol. Not only salary earners but
also families belonging to the so-called working classes tried to change
their housing habits. However, housing a given number of families in
separate houses rather than in apartments obviously required more
land—which became a problem with the growth of cities—and more
investments in streets, roads, water pipes, sewers, electricity, etc., all
of which under Scandinavian traditions fell within the orbit of collective rather than individual consumption. The consequent rise in local
taxes, which applied to all citizens of the community whether they
were living in houses or in apartments, created widespread resentment.

In summary it can be said that the Scandinavian welfare states
have been very successful in raising housing standards but have not
been able to build enough housing facilities in the cities to keep pace
with demand. To a considerable extent the two are related: it is
largely because of the insistence on high standards that demand and
supply have failed to balance.

One of the things the pioneer generation of the Scandinavian welfare
states valued most highly was education. And what should be the
purpose of education? Since few of the pioneers had themselves obtained a higher education, they did not quite know what it was, except that it was something valuable. The educated should be able to
lead a better life. Education should help the representatives of the
working class to hold their own in the democratic system. But at the
back of the reformers' minds was probably also the traditional idea
that those who managed to get a better education would rise out of
the working class and get better, more interesting and sophisticated
jobs, carrying greater prestige and influence in society.

The original idea was that basic education should be prolonged
and at the same time that attendance at public, as against private
schools should be compulsory for everybody, including those who
were going to continue beyond the required minimum. The high
schools (gymnasier) and universities should remain more or less as
they had always been, or at least be modified no more than was required by the development of learning in the world. But as time went
on, further educational concepts appeared, chiefly among intellectual
reformers.

One of them was that as much as possible of the educational system should become universal, if not compulsory, and that differentiation should disappear as far as possible, since it led to discrimination against the less gifted youths. The quantity of educational facilities should increase but it was no longer regarded as necessary to emphasize the need for quality in the traditional sense. Second, in a democracy, it was argued, schools should no longer be hierarchical even where relations between teachers and students were concerned, but formed in accordance with democratic images. And third, among the students "elitism" was frowned upon: competition should not be encouraged. There is no doubt about it that these ideas, and even the practical conclusions drawn from them, were largely the result of American influence. It appeared in the theories: many Scandinavian educationalists studied in the United States and came back to their own countries with a very critical attitude toward traditional European education. And it appeared also in pedagogical methods and psychological approaches. Malicious critics used to say that educational reform in Scandinavia often meant taking over concepts and methods that had been the vogue in the United States twenty years earlier and had since been discarded in the country of their origin.

Among other things the American influence ran counter to the traditional continental European, and perhaps especially Scandinavian idea that the purpose of education, both higher and lower, was to prepare for particular professions or vocations. Consequently more time than previously was given in schools to general "theoretical" education, which should be useful for everybody, and less to specific vocational or professional training calling for differentiation. It was even maintained—again in accordance with certain American traditions—that the most important purpose of schools was character formation, not actual teaching of knowledge and skills, although the latter had unfortunately tended to stand in the way of the former in the traditional school system.

All this must also be related to the changing position of the family. With both parents working full time outside the home, their offspring became "key children," with the keys to their homes on strings around their necks, who had no contact with their parents until several hours after school was over for the day. Parents therefore were anxious that schools should take care of students as long as possible, even longer than was actually required for teaching purposes. They—but of course not the educationalists—often subconsciously came to regard school as a place where their children could be stored until parents came home. Consequently there could be no opposition to prolonged attendance in school every day. On the contrary, great interest arose in facilities to keep the children occupied and under control after the normal school day was over.

The changing situation in the labor market has made it increasingly difficult to land a good job on the basis of the compulsory minimum of education alone. Also, since this minimum offers less specialized training than before, it is less useful from the standpoint of preparation for work. Increasing emphasis has therefore again begun to be put on vocational schools, and these are being integrated into the normal school system.

In the realization of all these tendencies, Sweden has been more extreme than the three other Nordic countries. In Sweden there are very few private schools. Practically all children of school age are educated at schools operated by the municipalities in accordance with more or less standardized modern methods. In Finland more of the traditional school system remains; Denmark has many more private schools; and in Norway the attitude toward the ideas prevailing in Sweden is rather critical.

Unavoidably, universities and similar institutions of higher learning have been affected by the new approach to scholastic problems. Here also there is controversy about their very purpose. To what extent are institutions of higher learning to be concerned primarily with research and training of researchers, or with professional training, or with general education beyond the school level? Again American influences have been at work reducing the traditional emphasis on professional training and research. The effect has been less definite, however, than at lower levels of the educational system. Especially young students themselves insist that their degrees should lead them more or less directly to jobs in their chosen professions and are highly disappointed when such jobs are not available — as is now often the case because of the spectacular growth of the student population.

It should be remembered, finally, that universities in Scandinavia, while highly respected by the people, represent no independent force in society. In this respect they are less important than those of France, Italy, and many other continental European countries or even of the United States. Even in 1968, when "student unrest" spread from the United States and France to Northern Europe, no really revolutionary movements grew out of Scandinavian universities.

On the whole, education presents a typical dilemma. The old educational system was authoritarian and elitist. It was not a suitable medium for the dissemination of egalitarian ideas. Thus, it was unacceptable from the point of view of the new order. At the same time, as far as the elite was concerned it was effective. Those who managed to survive its rigors—and it was basically a question of elimination on the basis of intellectual qualities, the social selection beng indirect only—managed to obtain high standards. By international comparison intellectual culture in Scandinavia had reached a very high level, perhaps particularly manifest in the field of scientific research. Education outside the traditional school system, especially in the folk high schools, was in many respects also elitist; at least it resulted in the creation of a new type of elite.

Not only was the new educational system more egalitarian, it was also uniform. By enlarging educational opportunities, it was no longer possible to cater to intellectual elites. It was argued that those who had exceptional intellectual capacities would always be able to hold their own in any system. As far as their personal well-being was concerned, this was probably true. It is much more doubtful whether they will in the future be equally able, or indeed willing, to make an exceptional effort and produce exceptional results. Another aspect is that of discipline, corresponding to "law and order" in society as a whole. Today's parents grew up in a system that was authoritarian, both in families and in schools. From the point of view of latter-day reformers, this was completely unacceptable, and new attitudes are being propagated, culminating in the recent Swedish legislation prohibiting parents from using corporal or other humiliating punishment on their children (although without any sanctions for infringement of the prohibition). At present, parents and teachers are blaming one another for the disorderly conduct of children, and tend to unite in blaming the new, "lawless" attitudes toward discipline. It is probably impossible to establish with any degree of certainty whether children are on an average more "lawless" today than they used to be. Most probably, changes have taken place in the directions of both more and less "lawlessness." It is equally difficult to establish to what extent the changes have been brought about by more permissive attitudes of society and not by the disruption of the traditional family system, or simply by the strain and stress of urban industrial society.

But whatever the truth may be, there is no denying that public opinion is at least for the time being often reacting negatively to permissiveness toward children. To quote an old maxim in social psychology, "When men believe things to be real, they are real in their consequences."

In Scandinavia, as in most industrialized countries, problems of ecology are causing great concern among the public, especially among the younger generation. Most of the relevant problems are caused by industrialization and have little or nothing to do with the creation of welfare states. There can be no doubt that material prosperity in general is an expensive commodity, not least for the natural environment, but on the whole this has no real relation to how prosperity is distributed among the different groups and individuals in society. It is equally clear that a more equal distribution does nothing to *remedy* the environmental difficulties. These consequently present an example of problems that have recently captured the attention of the public and that are neither resolved nor created by the new economic order.

In one respect, however, they are made more acute by the equal distribution of prosperity. Many Scandinavians take part of the rise in their standard of living in the form of shorter working hours and longer vacations, using their leisure to leave the urban areas and live an outdoor life in the mountains, in the forests, on the seashore, or in the vast archipelagoes of Finland and Sweden. They build summer houses, go camping and hiking, and ride around in motor cars, motorboats, and sailboats. It stands to reason that "unspoiled nature" is affected by such an exodus, even if the vacationers are very careful— and it is by no means likely that they will be. It is equally obvious that the amount of wear and tear nature will suffer is almost directly proportionate to the number of people who make use of it. Attempts have been made to establish environmental protection by appropriate legislation, but so far with very limited success.

The progressive ecological destruction is causing great disappointment in environmentalist ("green") movements, which are supported above all by young people with all sorts of social backgrounds. The environmentalist argument, which in Scandinavia as elsewhere is mainly directed at the destruction caused by industrial activities, is that modern society is excessively materialistic in its approach to development and welfare. This runs counter to the traditional ideas of the welfare state, which assumed that social problems could be solved by material progress. While the general attitudes of environmentalists are radical, and while they are ready to accept drastically increased interventionism in the pursuit of their goals, they thus also question the traditional policies of welfare reformists. The welfare state is an effective instrument for the equitable distribution of material benefits, but it provides no solution to the problem of what should be done when material goods are given only secondary importance.

The establishment of the welfare state was founded on the assumption that the majority of the people were comparatively poor, a "proletariat," and that the objective should be to take, for their benefit, some undeserved prosperity away from the privileged minority. Such a "Robin Hood policy" was held to be social justice. In the present Scandinavian welfare states the majority of the people are far from a "proletariat," and the favored minority are no longer as favored as they used to be, materially speaking. But this does not mean that there no longer are any underprivileged groups. The main difference is that these groups constitute minorities and no longer the majority. From the standpoint of social justice this is a great improvement indeed, but it does not mean that life is rosy for everybody.

In the first place, economic equality does not necessarily mean equality in social status. This applies to relations between the majority of the people and traditionally privileged minorities, which while living under roughly the same material conditions still enjoy higher status. And it is particularly important in regard to certain disfavored minorities. Foremost among these are the immigrants. Since the Second World War, the Scandinavian peoples have become less homogeneous than they were traditionally. Already just before and during the war a not inconsiderable number of refugees from Central Europe and from the Baltic states (especially Estonia and Latvia) found their way to Scandinavia. In recent decades there has been an even larger influx of refugees, for instance from Hungary and Czechoslovakia, and even more from Latin America, South Eastern Europe (Christians from Turkey), and even from Africa. In addition, the boom in the 1960s and early 1970s attracted "guest workers" not only from one Scandinavian country to another, but also from farther away, especially from

Yugoslavia and Turkey. All this has been mentioned in connection with problems of a demographical character.

Few of these immigrants have returned to the countries of their birth. It is not easy to find reliable figures on the number of immigrants, since many of them have already acquired citizenship in one or other of the Nordic countries and official statistics do not distinguish between citizens on the basis of their ethnic origins. But it is quite clear that their numbers are sufficiently high to create a new situation. Some traditional North American and British problems have thus come to be experienced even in Scandinavia.

In terms of income (both wages and salaries), the immigrants can hardly be called underprivileged. With few exceptions they belong to the same labor unions as native people and earn their incomes on the basis of the same collective contracts. It is true that many of them find employment in jobs that are unattractive to the natives, but this appears to be a transient phenomenon. On the other hand, housing presents a problem. They are not welcomed by all landlords, nor by all neighbors, and as a result they often tend to be segregated in certain urban areas where the real estate is owned by the municipalities or by municipally controlled housing corporations, or else relegated to less desirable premises. One of the most important difficulties relates to the education of their children. In some schools half or more than half of the pupils come from immigrant families—but the families have not all immigrated from the same countries. Language and cultural differences present serious problems.

The clash between the cultural traditions of the immigrants and that of their new environment is becoming obvious. There have even been some rather serious riots springing from the animosity of native Scandinavians toward their new neighbors. Some of this originates directly from the difference in social *mores*. It is not unusual to see blonde Scandinavian girls in the company of "blackheads," as male immigrants are sometimes contemptuously called, but it is rare indeed to see blonde Scandinavian boys in the company of "blackheaded" girls—presumably because immigrant families permit greater freedom to young males than to their young females. In this respect, as in others, the clash appears at different age levels and not least between schoolmates and between teachers and parents. And in regard to *mores*, to language, and to other elements of national culture, it is a controversial question to what extent immigrant groups should preserve and maintain their own traditions and to what extent they should simply be expected to assimilate to the conditions of their new environment.

Another ethnic group confronted with the same set of problems, although they are the very opposite of recent immigrants, are the Lapps living in the northernmost parts of Finland, Norway, and Sweden. They complain that they are about to lose their national heritage, that their traditional nomadic existence is no longer possible, and that their natural habitat is being destroyed. And finally there are the gypsies. Traditionally they kept very much to themselves, at the same time being treated almost as pariahs by the rest of the population. From the point of view of modern Scandinavian ideas, this attitude is no longer acceptable. But it is far from easy to change common attitudes. A further complication is that some gypsies are also immigrants, for instance from Finland into Sweden.

In the Scandinavian countries, as elsewhere, there is a certain proportion of disabled or otherwise seriously handicapped individuals. In a society of the traditional type they were to some extent taken care of by their families, or otherwise left to the mercies of private charity. Today, families are on the whole neither as willing nor as able to assume such duties as before, private charity is frowned upon, and the responsibility is transferred to society as a whole. Partly for this reason, and partly because of new attitudes toward this type of human suffering, attempts are made to integrate the disabled as much as possible with the rest of society, especially by finding employment for them in normal occupations and places of work, and at the usual wages and salaries. This is the avowed objective, but to date it is very far from being universally attained.

At the bottom of the list are the minorities consisting of "social outcasts"—persons burdened with a criminal past, alcoholics, drug addicts, and others who refuse to conform to generally accepted social standards or are frankly unable to do so. This is from many points of view the most difficult problem of all. At least in principle most Scandinavians would grudgingly agree that immigrants, Lapps, gypsies, and disabled people should after all have the same rights and privileges as they themselves enjoy and that some of them, such as the disabled and the refugees, may even be entitled to a certain amount of special sympathy. In the case of the "social outcasts" no such sympathies can be expected. On the contrary, the common attitude is that "they have only themselves to blame" and should certainly not be treated too softly. At the same time, at least some of the younger people belonging to these categories are apt to establish subcultures, based on modern permissive ideas, and thus further emphasize their repudiation of accepted habits, conventions, and morals. A case in point is the "Christiania" district in Copenhagen, a haven particularly for drug addicts, which Danish authorities have willingly or unwillingly tolerated for over a decade. Like most other problems mentioned here, this one is by no means specifically Scandinavian, but it is impossible to deny that the welfare state and the permissive society have thus far been completely unable to solve it.

How should one judge the Scandinavian welfare states from the standpoint of "social problems," in the more limited sense of the word? It can hardly be denied that they were definitely successful in solving those problems that they set out to solve from the beginning. They established material security for their peoples to an extent that nobody had ever dreamed of. Poverty, in the traditional sense of the word, was abolished even for the most underprivileged groups in society. Unemployment, while by no means abolished, no longer meant the same kind of catastrophe for individuals and families. As far as material conditions are concerned — and that is what the pioneers were thinking about fifty years ago — the achievements are impressive indeed. If they are not regarded as wholly satisfactory, it is because expectations are higher today than they were at the outset. This is particularly obvious in the field of housing.

Most of the serious social problems that are now apparent did not exist, or were not seriously considered, fifty years ago. And moreover, in regard to for instance crime, narcotics, alcoholism, or environmental destruction, there is no indication that any other industrialized societies are better off than the welfare states of Scandinavia.

Perhaps because the reformers were to some extent influenced by the ideas of Karl Marx, they considered social problems from the point of view of classes rather than of individuals. They were strongly opposed to the idea of charity, which they regarded as degrading for recipients. As a consequence, they always preferred general measures to the selective ones, and public authorities to voluntary organizations or to any voluntary work. They did not admit that there could be social problems that cannot be solved by any type of legislation but require dedicated and selfless work by individuals. This is not difficult to understand, since the most important social problems in their days related to large groups of persons or even to whole strata of society. But the situation is different today.

Another aspect of the same problem is the erosion of individual responsibility. If "society," or "the social order," or "the economic system," is to be blamed for everything that goes wrong, then criminals, alcoholics, drug users, etc., are themselves blameless. Indeed, one of the most common arguments in this connection is that they should be "liberated from feelings of guilt." To a great extent, such liberation has really taken place. This being so, do they still have the same ambition or incentive to make an effort to change their ways? At least in theory, this decline of individual responsibility could be the fault if not of the welfare state, then at least of the permissive society. And as has been pointed out before, both loom very large in Scandinavia.

Politics and Issues

In an earlier chapter I briefly described the constitutional structure of the Nordic countries. There can be no doubt that this structure had become not only much more democratic but also more conducive to compromise at about the time when the welfare state was emerging in Denmark, Finland, Norway, and Sweden. This was hardly a matter of pure chance. For various reasons, it was difficult for popular majorities to realize their wishes immediately in the face of vigorous minority opposition. As a result, compromise was frequently necessary. The welfare state was not initiated by universal consent, but it was undoubtedly established through what Danckwart Rustow, in the case of Sweden, has called "the politics of compromise." The machinery of compromise, therefore, can be regarded as part of the political framework of the Scandinavian welfare states.

Of course changes in the economic and social structure have in turn had their effects on the political situation. For instance, the development of democracy and the increase in public activities led to changes in the social structure of political bodies. It used to be characteristic of the Nordic countries that there were comparatively few lawyers in politics and that politicians were "ordinary" citizens, pursuing their lawful activities in private life simultaneously with their political functions. There were not only many journalists but also many farmers, other small entrepreneurs, and manual laborers in politics.

When not reelected, these could go back to working fulltime in their other occupations. To cite an authentic case: a skilled mechanic who had held a high office in his labor union and subsequently been elected to Parliament on a not entirely safe seat used to go back to the lathe in the summertime so as not to lose his skills.

It is still true that there are few lawyers in politics, but otherwise recruitment is changing. Politics are becoming a full-time profession, and an increasing number of politicians have been working at nothing else since their student days. The majority are still recruited from outside politics, but chiefly among public servants. Not only in Parliaments, but also in local and regional councils and other political bodies, blue-collar workers, farmers, and other entrepreneurs are becoming more and more scarce. Even Communist parties, which like to maintain that they are the real representatives of the interests of the "working classes," are increasingly being transformed into parties of disgruntled intellectuals in the public services.

There can hardly be any doubt that such changes influence the character of political life. The farmers and blue-collar workers who dominated it fifty years ago had an extremely pragmatic approach. They were personally familiar with the practical problems of the broad strata of the population and wanted to improve their lot as quickly as possible, even if that meant sacrificing favorite utopian schemes. The new type of politician has proved more *doctrinaire*, hoping to establish an ideal type of society where all problems are solved and nobody gets less than they are morally entitled to get—or more, for that matter.

Political parties were the most important factor in the establishment of the welfare state. They were formed on the basis of relatively well-defined ideologies, and on the whole they have retained this character, in contrast to parties in the United States. However, there is no denying that not only workers' unions and cooperatives but also employers' organizations, free religious communities, and the temperance movements played an important part in the creation of the welfare state. Sometimes these various elements were closely connected. Liberal parties were not only supported but also strongly influenced by religious and temperance movements, and above all the Labor parties have always been very closely related to the unions and during some periods to consumers' cooperatives. At one time it was common to speak of the four branches of the "labor movement:" the Social Democratic Party, the unions, the cooperatives, and associations for adult education. Farmers' parties, which were important in all four countries especially while there was still a sizable farming population—and which remained powerful even at a later stage—used to work rather closely with producers' cooperatives in agriculture, although there never was any formal relationship.

In fact political parties and other politically and socially active organizations constitute a comparatively rigid element in the political system. Their organizational fabric is either not at all or at most only very superficially regulated by law. They are, however, officially recognized in all four countries. Their bylaws and practices differ not only from country to country but also between the various parties in the same country. On the whole, party organization tends to correspond to the administrative divisions, with locals for each of the municipalities, regional districts corresponding to provinces or counties, and a central organization for the whole country. At each level there is a general meeting, held annually except at the central level. In smaller locals this meeting is attended by members who pay dues. In larger locals as well as in regional districts and in the central organization, the general meeting is attended by directly or indirectly elected representatives of members. Thus, just as in the constitutional structure of the country, the emphasis is on a system of representative democracy.

Collective membership is important above all in the Swedish Labor party, where union locals decide by majority vote to affiliate with local party organizations. This system is often criticized both by non-Socialists and by Communists and has even been repeatedly condemned by resolutions in Parliament, although never expressly outlawed. It differs, however, from the corresponding relationship in Great Britain in that the Swedish unions exercise no formal power in the central organization. Party activities are financed through members' dues, through voluntary contributions from labor unions, cooperatives, and private enterprises, and through outright grants from the state and municipalities—in the latter case according to strict rules safeguarding proportional justice for all parties. On the whole, direct contributions from unions to the Labor parties tend to exceed, sometimes by far, the support given by private enterprise to the non-Socialist parties. The law puts no limit on the amount of money that can be contributed to political parties, but contributions are not deductible for tax purposes.

Party discipline in Parliaments, county councils, and municipal councils is usually strong. There are of course exceptional cases where individual members or groups of members decide to vote against their party on the basis of their personal convictions in an important question, but these are decidedly infrequent, and a member who has rebelled against his or her party may not be nominated for reelection. On the whole, parties can be regarded as outwardly homogeneous entities, maneuvering against each other and occasionally negotiating with one another on the assumption that it is possible for the leadership to "deliver the votes" of parliamentary, regional, or local representatives at the relevant level. On the other hand, the central leadership is rarely able to exercise any real power or even influence over what is being done in the periphery. Maneuvers and negotiations are particularly necessary when the support of one or more small parties will tip the scales in favor of one of two parties or blocs of more or less equal strength in Parliament or in regional or local councils, but they are frequently held to be necessary on other occasions as well, when it is regarded as desirable to engage more than a bare majority in important decisions.

None of the four countries have a two-party system, and Denmark and Finland have at times had nine or ten parties represented in their Parliaments. Social Democratic Labor parties exist everywhere, and normally they are the largest single party, although they rarely enjoy majorities of their own independently of all others. Conservative parties appear under different names: Conservative Peoples party in Denmark, Rallying party (Samlingspartiet, Kokomus) in Finland, The Right (Höire) in Norway, Moderate party in Sweden. In recent elections they have tended to gain more votes than any of the other non-Socialist parties, but over the years this has varied greatly; on certain occasions they were so weak as to be almost negligible. Liberal parties, also under different names, exist or until very recently have existed in all four countries, although in Finland and Norway they have for a long time been extremely small; Denmark has two parties (Venstre and Radikale Venstre) that lay claim to the name of Liberals. What used to be Farmers' parties today call themselves Center parties in Finland, Norway, and Sweden. In Denmark one of the two "Liberal" parties (Venstre) has traditionally represented farmers' interests. Christian Democratic parties are represented in the Norwegian and Finnish Parliaments.

In Finland, Norway, and especially in Denmark there exist parties "to the right of Conservatives"; they are apt to call themselves Progressives. To the left of the Social Democrats left-wing Socialist parties play a sometimes important part in Denmark and Norway. Communist parties are never outlawed today (they were not permitted in Finland before 1945), but they are extremely weak in Denmark and Norway, comparatively speaking very weak in Sweden, and really important only in Finland. In addition, there are some parties that exist in only one of the countries, such as the Swedish Peoples' party in Finland, the Center Democrats in Denmark, and so on. All told, there are at the time of this writing nine parties with seats in Parliament in Denmark, eight in Finland, seven in Norway, and five in Sweden.

On the fringe there are often one or two additional parties, which do not manage to collect the popular vote necessary for representation in Parliament but which may be more successful in elections to regional or local councils and exercise a certain influence on public debate. One of these is the Justice party in Denmark; others are the Christian Democrats and the Environment party in Sweden. On the other hand, some of the parties represented in Parliament have by common consent been left out of consideration in the formation of Governments. This applies to "Progressives" in Denmark and Norway and similar parties in Finland, to Communists in Denmark, Norway, and Sweden, and perhaps also to left-wing Socialists in Denmark and Norway. But in Finland Communists usually have some seats in every Cabinet, whereas the Conservatives have been excluded since the Second World War.

To the outside observer, the party systems may appear somewhat confusing. But in Denmark, Norway, and Sweden the Social Democratic Labor parties have traditionally been so strong that voters— and also the news media—normally think of the parties as belonging to one of two ideological blocs: Socialist or non-Socialist. Communists and left-wing Socialists are seen as willing or unwilling supporters of the Social Democrats. This division into blocs is not entirely fair since both in Denmark and in Sweden there have been coalitions, either outright coalition Cabinets or informal "understandings," between Social Democrats on the one hand and one of the non-Socialist parties on the other. Also, the non-Socialist parties have by no means always worked very well together, and they are often suspicious of one another.

To some extent, a similar situation is developing in Finland, but since World War II politicians in that country have been unwilling, largely for reasons connected with foreign policy, to act on the same assumptions as their Scandinavian colleagues, and as a result the Center party, the Social Democrats, and the Communists have for most of the time been locked together in an uneasy partnership with each other, usually with the support of one or more of the small parties. While the voter in Finland may conceivably also think in terms of Socialist and non-Socialist blocs, this is hardly ever admitted in political debate or even in the press.

The life of party organizations of course concentrates on elections, while parliamentary parties are almost equally interested both in getting themselves reelected and in influencing the constitution of Cabinets. No party has tried the method of open primaries for the selection of candidates, and this is consequently left to members of the party and their representatives at the district level. In Sweden and Norway, voters in fact usually think of themselves as voting for a party rather than for particular representatives, although there can be exceptions to this rule. In Denmark and especially in Finland, the modes of election allow voters more influence in choosing between different candidates on the party list, but even there general party policies and the actual leaders of the parties are the main consideration.

Under these circumstances, and because of the working of proportional representation, selection of candidates is often virtually in the hands of a few active party workers in each constituency. These tend to think in terms of occupational and other groups rather than of personal qualities. In order to attract the voters, the list has to comprise persons from different corners of the constituency, from different occupations traditionally supporting the party—manual workers, farmers, white-collar employees, small entrepreneurs, and others— both men and women, both older persons and a couple of youngsters, and so on. Most of the persons appearing on the list for the first time have little or no chance of being elected, but the very fact of appearing may be important for the future. A person who was put among the candidates on the list on one occasion is likely to appear again, and perhaps higher up than previously. Powerful interest groups may also wield their influence with the parties by placing their favorite candidates on the list or moving them to a position higher up than was the original intention. At nomination meetings, party members or their regional representatives listen very carefully to arguments of this kind. On the other hand, with the exception of the Communists whose parties work according to centralist principles, few local or regional party organizations are willing to take advice from the central leadership in the selection of candidates.

An extremely important role in Scandinavian political and social life is played by organized interest groups—popular movements, pressure groups, or whatever they are called by admirers and antagonists. They have developed along similar although not totally identical lines in all four countries. Most important among them are the labor unions, but many others also exercise very considerable influence: consumers' cooperatives, producers' cooperatives in agriculture, tenants' organizations, housing cooperatives, employers' associations, educational associations, and many, many others. It is no exaggeration to say that the Scandinavian countries are unique in the prolificity of organizations for all human activities. At one time it was jestingly said that the only omission was the absence of a Society for the Promotion of Sleep.

Most of these organizations originated in attempts to redress imbalances in society and create a new balance of power. This applies on all sides. Workers organized in order to balance the overwhelming power of employers; employers organized when they found themselves incapable of separately resisting union demands; while white-collar workers organized so as not to be squeezed between blue-collar workers' unions and employers' organizations. Consumers' cooperatives were formed to enable workers to hold their own against private capitalists, in this case mostly private shopkeepers, but when the cooperatives gained real power the private retail trade began to organize. Producers' cooperatives in agriculture had similar origins but became important only by virtue of state subsidies to agriculture and the regulatory system necessitated by state intervention. Examples could be cited practically without end. It should be noted, however, that few spontaneously established organizations were concerned with welfare or social security, and that voluntary welfare organizations have on the whole played a much smaller part in the Scandinavian countries than for example in Great Britain and the United States, let alone in the Roman Catholic countries of Europe.

All these organizations claim to be voluntary, and this is correct in that no one is legally bound to be a member. In fact the situation is rather different. In some cases legislation gives certain organizations power even over nonmembers. This has been true of producers' co-operatives in agriculture—not only in Scandinavia, but also in Great Britain, for example. In Sweden the same is true of tenants' organizations, even in apartment buildings where the tenants expressly ask for independence from "their" organization. But the most important problem in Scandinavia, as well as in many other countries, is to be found in the labor market, where salaries, wages, and working conditions are determined by agreements between organizations of employees and organizations of employers, even for those concerned who prefer to remain outside the organizations—and where social pressure to join, especially in the case of labor unions, is extremely strong.

The argument in favor of "solidarity" and against remaining outside the organizations is very convincing up to a point. It is thanks to the activities of the unions/employers' organizations that wages are as high/moderate as they are. Consequently those who remain outside and refuse to pay dues are profiting from the sacrifices of others, and this is usually unacceptable. But this argument is obviously a simplification, especially in present circumstances, since in a particular case it is conceivable that the employees/employer could do better, even much better, if they were allowed to arrange matters by themselves without outside intervention. Yet so far the percentage of organized employees/employers remains very high indeed, higher than in most other industrialized countries.

Taking the field of social organization as a whole, it can be said that there are many different shades from totally voluntary to more or less compulsory organizations. All four countries have Lutheran state churches, which means that in the absence of a declaration to the contrary citizens are held to be members of the church, pay taxes to it, and have the right to its services, as well as to vote in its affairs. On the other hand, there are important religious organizations outside the state church, "free churches," whose members have seceded from the state church or established themselves as separate entities without doing so and who finance their organizations by voluntary contributions, often very handsomely. Producers' cooperatives in agriculture are directly supported by state policies, but consumers' cooperatives and housing cooperatives are completely voluntary, although in some respects favored by tax legislation. The situation in the labor market has already been mentioned, but it should be added that in Sweden voluntary unemployment insurance is organized around associations that are administered by the respective labor unions, although technically independent of them. You may belong to either organization while remaining aloof from the other, but this rarely happens.

It can be said without exaggeration that all organizations are democratically governed; even the structure of state churches is democratic rather than hierarchical. But the type of democracy that they practice is mostly representative and not direct. In this respect they differ less and less from the system of state and local government than they did in the past. Whereas members, let us say of labor unions, formerly exercised a very direct influence on wage negotiations and took action for the improvement of working conditions, such participation is becoming more and more unusual. On the whole, individual members have to rely on their elected representatives, who in turn elect representatives at the next level, and so on. And participation in these elections is much lower than participation in elections to Parliament and regional and local councils, there being frequently no controversy over candidates so that the election can take place by unanimous consent. Actual election campaigns are relatively unusual, except where Social Democrats and Communists fight one another for the control of a union, and even that happens more and more rarely. By the same token, the work of the organizations, which used to be conducted by ordinary members in their spare time, is now mostly in the hands of elected officers working full time year after year, or even of employees. This is sometimes called "bureaucratization," and while the term is regarded as inadmissibly insulting by active organization leaders, it is difficult to find a more apt description of the situation. After all, bureaucrats are also respectable human beings.

A serious question is whether developments have in fact led to the establishment of a "corporative" state, or rather of a corporative society existing side by side with the state, and with powers comparable to, or even stronger than, those of its democratically elected organs.

As long ago as 1948, in an article in the periodical *Social Research*, I called the Swedish system "pluralist democracy," indicating that democratic power was exercised through several different channels, thus giving citizens an opportunity to cater to several different interests, and this was regarded as a compliment rather than a criticism. Even the term "free corporativism," which I used in Sweden about the same time, was accepted without demur, although it was probably regarded as excessively academic. Now, on the other hand, the representatives of organizations violently resent any talk of "corporativism." What has happened?

In the first place, society has become more complicated, and so has the position of organizations. Until rather recently, it was presumed that labor unions and employers' organizations should deal with wages, salaries, and working conditions, producers' cooperatives with the supply and price of their products, tenants' associations negotiate with private landlords about rents, etc. — all separately and independently of other considerations. Economic and social policies were supposed to be the business exclusively of "regular" democratically elected representatives in Parliament and in regional and local councils. It is now recognized that these things cannot be kept in watertight compartments. To take the most obvious example: economic policies cannot be independent of wage and salary agreements, which on the other hand must start from certain assumptions about taxes. Thus the state will try to exercise some influence over wage and salary agreements, but labor market organizations feel equally bound to influence tax policies.

In the second place, with power in organizations becoming more centralized and bureaucratic, members can no longer identify themselves with the leadership of the organizations to the same extent as before. Moreover, practically every citizen belongs to more than one organization, representing his or her different interests — as an employee, as a tenant, as a consumer, as the owner of a motor car, as a parent, and so on. This did not create very great problems as long as each organization was active only in its own particular field, but when they all try to determine the conduct of state economic policies, and perhaps in different directions, their members run the risk of being unable to develop enough multiple personalities to identify themselves with all of them.

This development is also relevant to political parties, which resent the fact that organizations encroach on their traditional functions. Moreover, a citizen who belongs to a political party and to a number of interest organizations, some of which practice policies conflicting with those of his or her party, may think that the organization of society does not conform to his or her right of participation in democratic decisions.

A Swedish social scientist belonging to the Social Democratic party once argued that a stable labor market could exist only with a Social Democratic Cabinet in power. It required, he maintained, identity of interest between the labor unions and the ruling political party. Obviously, this means that democratic government should be put aside in the interests of labor peace, an assumption for which he eventually found it difficult to get much support. But in any case, this identity could be established only if all or practically all union members—and not only a majority of them—belonged to the Social Democratic party. At the time when he made his claim, this had already ceased to be the case; one-fourth of the union members no longer voted that way, and most of the dissidents did not support the Communists but one of the non-Socialist parties. It goes without saying that a worker who votes Communist, Conservative, or Liberal resents the fact that the union of which he or she is a member actively supports the Social Democrat election campaign both with money and with political statements.

All this is creating a new situation. The traditional political and organizational balance of Danish, Finnish, Norwegian, and Swedish society no longer exists, and the quest for a new balance has been unsuccessful to date. Since the establishment of the welfare state was based on "the politics of compromise," and since the politics of compromise presumed balance between different forces in society and above all in politics, the change is closely related to the future of the welfare state in Scandinavia.

Up to 1919, that is, until the final establishment of political democracy, Scandinavian politics were just as ideological and there was just as much polarization as in most other Western European countries. During the years between the two World Wars there was considerable change in this respect, perhaps connected with the reduction of French and German influence and the corresponding increase of British and American influence on Scandinavian political thought and attitudes. From the 1920s on, politics in Denmark, Norway, and Sweden became increasingly pragmatic, and the same tendencies gradually developed in Finland as well.

The pragmatic and compromise-prone attitudes appeared not only in party politics, but equally in the relations between interest groups, notably in the labor market. The most characteristic example was the so-called Saltsjöbaden agreement in Sweden between the Federation of Labor (LO) and the Federation of Employers (SAF) which took place in 1938 and cleared away a number of controversial issues. But it also implied that in the future the parties should try to solve labor market problems through negotiation, avoiding state intervention as much as possible.

In parliamentary politics, and even more in the politics of regional and local councils, it also became almost the fashion to insist on "broad-based solutions" rather than prolonging controversy. This was motivated by a wish to maintain political continuity regardless of changes in the political fortunes of parties—although in fact such changes were far less striking in the Nordic countries than in most other parts of Western Europe. But there was also considerable emphasis on certain values common to all democratic parties in the years right before the Second World War, during the war, and in the years immediately following it. The threat of Fascist, National Socialist, and Communist dictatorships was a very real external force. It was also generally realized, at least among well-informed politicians of all parties, that Fascism and National Socialism in their countries of origin had arisen largely because of the failure to establish stable government and viable economic policies. As regards the latter, after the somewhat acrimonious debate that took place between economists and their followers in politics in the late 1920s and early 1930s, John Maynard Keynes had almost an apotheosis as the patron saint of democratic economies. Such attitudes obviously facilitated compromise on economic policies and not least on policies of social security. It was easy to mistake the willingness to make compromises for unanimity as to ultimate aims, and indeed this mistake was very often made.

There were many other circumstances that facilitated the growth of compromise policies and compromise-prone political relations. The Scandinavian peoples were homogeneous from the standpoint of religion, and with the exception of Finland also in regard to language.

In Finland, the conflict between the Finnish-speaking and the Swedish-speaking elements in the population was serious in the 1920s and 1930s, and it was at that time in fact perceived as a conflict of class and not only one of language. With the growth of a prosperous Finnish-speaking middle class in the cities, as well as because of the experiences of the wars with the Soviet Union in 1939-40 and 1941-44, relations between the two language groups improved considerably. There is now comparatively little trace of the old antagonism. While the Swedish-speaking element finds it increasingly difficult to maintain a strong position in society, the Swedish People's party is on the other hand an almost indispensable member of any coalition Cabinet. Moreover, although there were for long periods Social Democratic Governments in Denmark, Norway, and Sweden, the margin between Government and opposition was always narrow enough for the latter to have at least a chance of coming into power at the next election. As a consequence, Labor Governments had to be very much concerned about the opinions of those voters on the margin who might hesitate in their choice and eventually come down on the anti-Socialist side if the majority adopted legislation that appeared to be definitely Socialist in character. In fact there was a consistent tendency in elections up to the middle of the 1960s for Labor to lose votes when they tried to be openly Socialist and to gain additional support when they appeared to follow the middle of the road. It is true that politics were dominated by economic issues, where there were clear-cut ideological differences between Socialists and "bourgeois." But it is equally true that nobody ventured to propose drastic changes in the economic system, and that in the "mixed economies" practiced in all four countries even a Labor Government was compelled to give serious consideration to the needs and wishes of "capitalist" enterprises and their leaders.

As has already been indicated, compromise politics of this type favored the development of welfare states. Labor Governments might theoretically have wanted to introduce an anticapitalist economic order at one stroke, thereby presumably hoping to improve the lot of the working classes. But this was not practical politics. Specific improvements of the lot of these classes were much more widely acceptable, and one could always hope that they might finally add up to a new economic order.

Thus it can be said that while the idea of the welfare state originated in parties and organizations pledged to social change on a large scale, its actual realization was made possible through the politics of compromise. Again, compromise is not the same as unanimity, although it may give rise to unanimity and in fact created a situation where it was generally presumed that unanimity existed.

Finland had special problems. In the first place, economic development came more slowly there, partly because the country had other preoccupations than those concerned with developing a prosperous society. Second, since the Civil War in 1918 class feeling was stronger in Finland than in the three other countries, and on both sides. The result of the 1941-44 war brought new difficulties. There was some genuine resentment in the country against those who had failed to avoid open conflict with the Soviet Union, but above all the establishment of good relations with this powerful neighbor required consideration in domestic policies as well. No party was strong enough to govern on its own, and there were certain limitations in the formation of coalitions. Immediately after the war, not only Finnish Conservatives (Kokomus) but also Social Democrats were regarded with suspicion in Moscow. The attitude toward Social Democrats changed comparatively soon, but since the war Kokomus has not been part of any governing coalition, which ironically has allowed the party to gain increasing support from the voters. On the other hand, Finland is the only Nordic country where representatives of the Communist (or Popular Democrat) party have been members of the Cabinet, with the exception of a short-lived Danish Cabinet formed immediately after liberation in 1945.

Denmark, Norway, and Sweden have followed similar although as usual not identical lines, with the Social Democratic parties in power, if on some occasions only precariously, most of the time. This party has been a little weaker in Denmark than in the two other countries, and in 1976 Sweden was the last of the three to have a non-Socialist Cabinet. As a consequence, economic policies in Denmark were somewhat less egalitarian than in Norway and Sweden, although hardly more successful.

The traditional mechanics of compromise varied from country to country. In Finland, certain decisions require a two-thirds or even five-sixths majority in Parliament, so that there is even a constitutional basis for the quest for "broad-based solutions." But in contrast to the other three, Finland has a tradition of coalition Cabinets, often illustrating the adage that necessity makes strange bedfellows. The parties in the coalition have usually attempted to compromise not only on the formation of a Government but also as question after question arises in the course of its lifetime. Occasionally, when the parties failed to form a viable coalition, the president would appoint a caretaker Cabinet, but this would usually take no major political initiatives. Most decisions of any importance in Finland since 1918 have been the result of laboriously achieved compromises within coalition Governments.

In Norway, compromise solutions have usually been devised by the Cabinet. There have been few coalitions. But conscious restraint on the part of Governments without safe majorities or anxious to maintain national unity has prevented extremist tendencies from gaining importance. Denmark, on the other hand, has developed the peculiar tradition of package deals between the Government—often minority Governments—and some opposition parties. These deals, "Forlig," usually take place under the threat of resignation by the Government or of a dissolution of Parliament for a special election. In spite of the fact that elections are both expensive and hazardous for the political parties, dissolutions have become more and more frequent, and the lifetime of a Danish Parliament rarely exceeds two years. Often it has been much briefer than that.

In Sweden general agreements of this type have been less common, although they have occurred now and then. The most notable example was the so-called horsetrading (kohandel) between the Social Democrats and the Farmers' Party in 1933, which inaugurated not only more than forty years of Social Democratic ascendancy over the other parties, but also the establishment of the welfare state in Sweden. Another technique of compromise in Sweden is dependent on the political composition of Royal Commissions, whose members may be able to bind their respective parties to a compromise before even administrative consultation, let alone Parliamentary consideration has taken place. The traditional market for compromise is to be found in the committees of Parliament, where agreement can sometimes be reached over the head of the Cabinet and with considerable amendment of Government proposals. This method has been particularly important in periods of minority Governments. When the Government party or parties enjoy a safe parliamentary majority, representatives on parliamentary committees are rarely permitted to make major concessions to opposition demands.

In Denmark and Norway, the politics of compromise reached their peak just after 1945. This was only natural. Persons from all political parties, from Conservatives to Communists, had participated in the resistance movements, and there was a strong conviction that common values had proved more important than differences. Also, personal respect and personal friendships across party lines had developed. In Finland, the situation during the war had been far more complicated, especially after 1941, but at least if one excepts the Communists—who initially imagined that harvesting time had finally come—there was widespread recognition of the need for cooperation and sacrifice in order to maintain freedom and to heal the wounds of war.

The Swedish situation was different. Sweden had managed to keep out of the war and remained intact. During the war years there had been a national Government under a Social Democratic prime minister, but including also Conservatives, Farmers, and Liberals. This was in spite of the great victory by the Social Democrats in the elections of 1940, where they for the first time gained independent majorities in both houses of Parliament. As a result, many of them grew impatient with the need for catering to bourgeois wishes. The prime minister may have wanted to continue the coalition, but his party thought otherwise. Even before the end of the war, the party and the labor unions (LO) adopted a "postwar program" which was unacceptable to the non-Socialist parties but which was accepted in toto by the Communists, although they had not been consulted in advance. It appeared that the time for compromise was over. But the situation changed rapidly. Already in the 1944 elections the Social Democrats had lost some of their ascendancy, and in 1948 the Liberals more than doubled their parliamentary representation, partly but not entirely at the expense of other non-Socialist parties. Openly Socialist proposals no longer had much of a chance, and political life again became characterized by compromise rather than consistency. The welfare state was maintained and extended, but there appeared to be little prospect of wholesale changes in the economic system.

In Finland, the tradition of compromise, including even the Communists to some extent, has been laboriously preserved to the present day. But in the three other countries it has been breaking up, not completely but to an increasing extent. There were different reasons for this development.

One of the fundamental elements in the "Swedish model" was that the parties in the labor market—labor unions and employers' associations—should solve their problems by negotiation and mutual agreement with a minimum of intervention by the state. In the 1950s, blue-collar workers began to express a greater interest in obtaining old age pensions. Both individual employers and their associations were unwilling to meet workers' demands, however, in contrast to their attitude regarding wages and working conditions. As a result, it was "the other part of the Labor movement," the Social Democratic party rather than the unions, that began to play the most prominent role in the pensions question. After various developments, a system of obligatory pensions (ATP) was adopted in 1959. Success in this field whetted the appetite, and the Social Democratic government initiated legislation in an increasing number of questions of the type which formerly would have been dealt with by negotiation in the labor market. It is obvious that this added to controversy in politics.

As a matter of fact, it appears that by about 1960 there was not only in Sweden but in Denmark and Norway as well a sort of saturation with compromise solutions. Genuine ideological differences between the political parties, which had always existed but for a time had been submerged in pragmatism to such an extent that some observers believed they were gone, again surfaced. The limits had been reached for pragmatic solutions by mutual consent, at least for the time being, and it seemed necessary to make hard choices.

There was also a sort of disenchantment with compromise, on both sides. "Progressive" Social Democrats believed that development was too slow. They wanted to introduce real Socialism, and not just social security and welfare, in their own time. To do so without openly admitting it appeared to be increasingly difficult. It was necessary, in their opinion, to come out into the open and accept the increased controversy. After having been in apparent power for such a long time, their party began to be seen as "the establishment" rather than as the instrument of radical social change. Also, there was a new leadership, less influenced by the experiences of 1940-45 and with great new ambitions. In Sweden, where Tage Erlander was succeeded by Olof Palme, this change was particularly striking, but there were corresponding developments in the other countries as well.

Upheavals in 1968 were perhaps more noticeable in Sweden than in the three other countries, probably because Sweden was more Americanized than the others and thus was affected by the "Vietnam movement." And although protests were by no means as violent as in France, they represented something like a revolt by "progressive" elements against the politics of compromise, against pragmatism, and in favor of ideological politics. The "new left" managed to infiltrate the Swedish news media, and while its attitudes were quickly modified when it appeared that no social revolution was possible, its influence for a time remained anything but unimportant, especially to the extent that it alarmed active politicians and made them more prone to controversy than to compromise. In Denmark the initial protest movement also appeared to be very vigorous, but eventually difficult economic problems claimed immediate attention. And in both Finland and Norway the effect of "1968" always remained much smaller than in Sweden.

Disenchantment with compromise appeared on the other side as well. There is hardly any doubt that the emergence of Mogens Glistrup's Progress party in Denmark and its meteoric success were caused largely by disappointment among the "bourgeois" that their traditional parties, Conservatives and Liberals alike, had been so willing to conclude pacts with the Social Democrats and had not taken account of the growing tax resistance. In Norway and Finland also, parties of discontent appeared and gained a certain amount of support. This did not happen in Sweden. Although taxes were higher and tax resistance at least as strong as in the three other countries, no protest party arose, probably because Swedish non-Socialist parties had not been called upon to accept responsibility for Social Democratic or similar policies to the same extent as their brethren in Denmark and Finland. But in Sweden as well as in the other Nordic countries controversy dominated the political scene in the late 1960s and the 1970s to a much greater extent than during the preceding twenty years.

It is important to keep in mind that the tendency to increasing controversy was by no means a product of the greater—real or apparent—need for austerity but on the contrary developed at the very peak of affluence. But in any case a new situation has developed since the late 1960s. Controversy, of course, is no novelty. There was controversy not only in the 1920s, when actual disputes were perhaps more violent than they have ever been subsequently, but also in the early 1930s and as far as Sweden is concerned over the pensions question in the 1950s. But the very atmosphere in politics has changed. Disenchantment with compromise has reached the point where polarization rather than compromise is fashionable and where making concessions in order to reach agreement is regarded as immoral—perhaps not generally, but at least by large and vocal groups. Also, compromises that had been agreed upon in the past are no longer accepted as permanent solutions, but as only technical maneuvers designed to press those on the other side farther and farther back. Even in regard to social security, which at one time seemed to have been taken out of the field of political controversy by apparently final compromises, a tendency to disagreement has begun to appear—on both sides.

There are of course a number of different reasons for the change. Many of them, perhaps the greatest number, have little or nothing to do with the exigencies of the welfare state. Nor are all of them in themselves relevant to its future. But the new situation as a whole is very relevant indeed.

Some of the causes relate to persons. Labor leaders such as Thorvald Stauning and Hans Hedtoft in Denmark, Väinö Tanner and Carl-August Fagerholm in Finland, Einar Gerhardsen in Norway, Per Albin Hansson and Tage Erlander in Sweden enjoyed authority and sympathy far beyond the limits of their own parties and organizations. The same was true of several leaders on the other side, for example, Christmas Møller in Denmark, Juho Paasikivi and Urho Kekkonen in Finland, C. J. Hambro in Norway, Bertil Ohlin and Jarl Hjalmarson in Sweden. They belonged to the generation that had been active during the establishment of the welfare state, but several of them had also appeared as symbols of national unity during the Second World War. Their successors were perhaps no more extreme in their opinions, but they were obliged to make themselves known by defining their profiles under new conditions. The most typical example is the Social Democratic leader Olof Palme in Sweden, but similar personalities have emerged in the three other countries as well. Reiulf Steen in Norway is one example, and at first even Anker Jørgensen in Denmark and Kalevi Sorsa in Finland were hailed as "counterparts to Palme."

The old mechanisms of compromise are no longer effective. Ironically, one of the reasons for this is the diminishing role played by class consciousness especially in the younger generation (this has nothing to do with the rise of Marxist fashions among young intellectuals). The floating vote in elections is growing. Voters take their stand on the basis of political issues, obviously after consideration of how the outcome will affect them but often without regard to class or occupational interests. This renders it much more difficult to reach compromise by "horse trading," that is, by distributing advantages among different interest groups. In addition, for some issues the traditional distinctions of "right" and "left" are no longer relevant.

Simultaneously, it appears that the bureaucratization of popular movements such as the labor unions does not facilitate compromise either. Leaders of the old type, who were definitely *of* the people and not only *for* the people, could take greater risks and exercise more authority over their members in the interests of reaching agreement with the other side. The new leadership in organizations as well as in political parties has to prove itself all the time, especially since it is no longer possible to gain any great advantages either by bargaining or by any other means. And because organizations are appropriating to themselves some of the traditional functions of political parties, political agreement also becomes more difficult: in order to be effective it must comprise both organizations and parties. The antagonism between the Social Democratic Cabinet of Anker Jørgensen and the union leadership of Thomas Nielsen in Denmark is a case in point.

The position and role of the Communists is changing. Up to the Second World War they were unanimously regarded by all others as beyond the pale of decent politics. Even as late as the 1950s the Liberal leader Bertil Ohlin in Sweden suggested—quite unrealistically—that the Communist vote should not be considered when parliamentary majorities were calculated. In Norway and especially in Denmark the Communists had, however, been active in the resistance movement during the war. In Finland the special relationship to the Soviet Union after the war made it impossible to treat native Communists with disdain. And in Sweden Social Democratic governments in the 1970s were dependent on the Communist vote in order to push their proposals through Parliament. At the same time the appearance of the Communist parties changed. They became more and more Eurocommunist, increasingly independent of their brothers in the Soviet Union, increasingly willing to conform to democratic parliamentary procedures. But of course they still remained in opposition to established society, and the politics of compromise were anathema to them.

Another characteristic of recent decades in Scandinavia consists of populist tendencies, involving distrust of "politicians" and other elements of "the establishment." It is by no means only "the left" that is an exponent of such tendencies. In fact they are probably even stronger among a number of citizens traditionally regarded as predominantly "rightist," such as small entrepreneurs. But there are also new movements that can hardly be placed on the old right-left scale, such as environmentalists, religiously motivated peace movements, and so on. Many of these are the products of affluence: it is only when growth seems to be a permanent fact of life that it becomes fashionable to play with ideas of zero growth. It can hardly be denied that populism and distrust of established authority make it more difficult to reach compromise. Agreements have to be concluded between accredited representatives and can never be negotiated at the level of mass meetings. Populist democracy can be viable only to the extent that it is possible to apply simple, clear-cut principles which can be accepted or denied by an equally clear-cut majority. For this reason the growth of populism also goes hand in hand with the emergence (or revival) of ideology. A mass movement in which the system of representative government is nullified can say yes or no in no uncertain terms. But it is incapable of considering nuances and therefore also of negotiation. And finally, since political compromises necessitate delicate negotiations in which one possibility after another is tested before being discarded in favor of another, it cannot be pursued in public. But negotiations in closed rooms are held suspect as manipulative conspiracies.

Vastly more important than personalities, ideologies, and political mechanisms are the actual questions that have to be resolved by political means. There is not much doubt that throughout the industrialized world the 1960s and early 1970s were a period of blue-eyed optimism and trust in the possibility of unlimited economic growth. The only real problem was held to be the equitable distribution of the resources flowing so abundantly. In 1973, the year of the first oil crisis, which hit Scandinavia at least as hard as other parts of the industrialized world, these attitudes were upset. Eventually the almost forgotten concept of austerity was revived, and the welfare states were faced with the necessity of adjusting distribution to the available quantity of resources.

In all four Nordic countries, stagflation and tax resistance became serious problems. One of the symptoms was unemployment. Denmark was hit first and hardest, and public reactions were very strong to begin with, especially in politics, where the old balance was upset by the emergence of the strong protest party of Glistrup, the Progress Party. As a result, Danish politicians and the Danish public are at least looking unpleasant facts in the face. Finland conformed to the general Western European practice and accepted a comparatively high rate of unemployment, with surprisingly little protest from the public. Maybe there was relief that at least inflation was kept down, maybe the memories of the war were recent enough to restrain protest. Norway is something of a special case because of the availability of North Sea oil, although even there the economy was affected and may be so even more in the future. Norwegian policies have generally been very pragmatic and moderate under both Socialist and Conservative governments. In Sweden, optimistic beliefs remained dominant for a very long time, but by the end of the 1970s the Swedes also had come to realize that this was not a case for bridging a temporary ditch obstructing the road to paradise but a much more permanent change in the landscape.

In the 1930s Scandinavians had been among the most successful peoples in the attempts to resolve economic difficulties. Do they have a chance of equal success in the 1980s and 1990s – will they conform to the average of the industrialized world – or will they eventually find themselves in an even more difficult situation than other comparable nations? The answer will also determine their chances of maintaining political stability, or rather, since there are hardly any revolutionary tendencies, of making parliamentary democracy work about as well as before.

It does in fact not seem to be very likely that the circumstances of the 1930s will repeat themselves either in Scandinavia or anywhere else. At that time there were considerable reserves both on the supply side and in regard to demand. Raw materials were available in relative plenty even domestically, and the potential for rapid technological development was high. Because of unequal distribution of profits and other personal incomes, substantial capital formation had taken place in the private sector, and resources were thus available for profitable investments. The public sector was very small, and there was scope for enlarging it in meeting general demands. The disfavored groups in society—the so-called working classes—were numerically large and living almost at the subsistence level. They were not very far from being a proletariat. If their buying power was augmented by transfers, it would be used chiefly for acquiring goods and services that were domestically produced, so that domestic demand could be made to grow in a short period of time. The general price level had not gone up to any large extent since the First World War, and inflation did not present much of a problem. Agriculture was still an important sector of the economy. Exports played a significant role in certain parts of the economy, but even there they could largely be replaced by increased domestic consumption. Industries were not particularly specialized and could switch over to new types of production without excessive difficulties. On the whole, the role of foreign trade was limited if not marginal.

It was to economies of this type that one applied the Keynesian anticyclical policies, including "the economy of high wages." Although it is difficult to distinguish their effects from those of other circumstances, such as the growing economic nationalism and isolationism throughout the world and the demand created by the threat of war, it appears that they were comparatively successful. Scandinavian economists, especially the Swedish "Stockholm school," were internationally prominent, and some of them also exercised considerable influence over the policies of their respective national governments. These policies were also psychologically and politically attractive, since they appealed to demands for greater economic equality following in the wake of political democracy. The establishment of welfare states was favored by economic, social, and political exigencies.

Fifty years later the situation is almost entirely different. It is true that the technological potential remains high, but in this respect Western European countries are facing competition from new quarters, not only from the United States but especially from Japan and other East Asian and Southeast Asian countries. Raw materials are much more scarce and expensive. The new technologies calling for an enormously increased consumption of energy put at a disadvantage those countries that lack easy access to sufficient energy resources.

For a long time, profits and other incomes have been distributed much more equitably than fifty years ago. As a consequence, there has been a much higher consumption of services, imported perishable goods, and consumer capital goods. Another consequence is that no very considerable savings and capital formation have taken place either in the private or in the public sector. Egalitarian policies also have made it much more difficult to draw major profits from industrial investment. The public sector is already very large, as evidenced by the level of taxation, and there is considerable resistance to the higher taxes that would be indispensable in order to enlarge it further. Practically all groups and individuals in society enjoy relatively high material standards, at least in comparison to what was regarded as normal fifty years ago, and the pressure for further equalization in this respect is relatively small. Inflation, on the other hand, has become a major problem and is sometimes seen as even more serious than unemployment. Self-sufficiency in agricultural products, at least during times of peace, is achieved by a comparatively small agricultural population. International exchanges are a dominant factor in the economies of all industrialized countries. Apart from agriculture, no country would be able to maintain present standards, or anything remotely approaching them, without considerable exports and imports, and the Nordic countries provide almost extreme examples of this situation. Their industries are highly specialized and always looking for *"niches"* in the world market. And as has been pointed out in an earlier chapter, there is no coherent and uniform economic theory to deal with the situation. The public choice theorists advance interesting analyses which, however, can hardly be utilized in the quest for practically viable solutions. Neo-Keynesians, or monetarists or other supply side economists each tend to deal with some isolated element in the problem, and the solutions advocated by them are mutually contradictory. And even if one or the other of these systems were to prove theoretically superior to the others, none of them would have the same psychological and political appeal as the Keynesianism of fifty years ago. The public is apt to look with a jaundiced eye at anything involving inflation, unemployment, or/and higher taxes. Certainly no Scandinavian economists have yet found the stone of the magi.

How does all this relate to the welfare state? On the one hand, the difficulties may have been aggravated—but not created!—by the insistence on equitable distribution of assets not yet produced but seen as probably available in the near future. The welfare state, in contrast to the society existing six or seven decades earlier, has a politically inbuilt tendency to live beyond its means. On the other hand, the standard of living is still so high, the distribution of not only the necessities of life but also the trimmings is so equitable, and the public is so enlightened that it ought to be possible to gain public support for realistic policies even if they must involve a certain amount of austerity.

One particular complicating factor is related to the importance of labor market organizations and the balance between them. Until World War II employers' organizations were able to hold their own in relation to the labor unions. This was one of the reasons for the success of anticyclical policies. Even in times of expansive economic action by the public authorities, there was little danger that the wage level would get out of hand. Other inflationary tendencies were to some extent compensated by the balance in the labor market.

With increasing dependence on exports, Scandinavian industries looked for arguments favoring their claims against those of competitors in other countries. One such argument was reliability based on labor peace. But as a consequence they became more vulnerable to any threat of open labor conflicts, and this in turn made it difficult for them to resist labor demands. There is no doubt that the labor unions used this circumstance with great skill in their attempt to raise the standard of living of their members. They proved successful not only in the export industries but over the whole field by introducing the concept of "solidarity in wage policies." Moreover, the political Labor parties, working hand-in-hand with the labor unions, were in power most of the time, and this gave further impetus to union demands in the labor market. When the boom was over, unions had grown so much stronger than the representatives of capital that resistance to their demands still remained very difficult. Moreover, contrary to the practice of the 1930s, social security measures were now largely financed with employers' fees, and these were not subject to wage negotiations.

There may be a further problem in this connection. The interest and activities of industrial management in Scandinavia were and are largely subject to a fixation on wages and other labor market problems, as well as on fees and taxes. This may conceivably have detracted from their interest in industrial policy. Some large enterprises have been successful in the world market all the same, presumably because they avoided this fixation. But organizations on the management side concentrated on labor market problems rather than on ways and means for further expansion and development. In this respect, as in so many others, Scandinavia is not very different from other parts of Western Europe. Conversely, a comparison with Japan shows striking differences.

The altered situation will undoubtedly affect the future of the welfare state. The new economic problems, reinforced as they are by the negative attitude toward political compromise which had already appeared previously, must constitute a serious threat to its existence. The welfare state was established by the politics of compromise; can it survive increasing controversy? There can of course be no definite answer to such a question. But something can perhaps be gauged from an assessment of certain concrete problems that are likely to confront the Scandinavian countries in the near future.

The capacity for solving economic problems does not depend primarily on politics as long as we are dealing with mixed economies. Equally or even more important are such things as whether private (and publicly owned!) enterprises will prove able to develop sufficient vigor, imagination, and farsightedness to compete in international markets and whether parties in the labor market will realize that in many respects they have identical interests. Past experiences in these respects are not entirely encouraging. On the political side, farsightedness is even more indispensable, and perhaps not very likely to develop either. One important question in economic policy is whether each of the four Nordic countries will insist on pursuing its own path regardless of others, or at the expense of others, or whether they will prove ready to cooperate either within the Nordic entity or with the rest of Western Europe.

But social problems cannot be disregarded either; and here political responsibilities predominate. One of them is unemployment. It seems unlikely that any Western industrialized country will within the foreseeable future be able to wholly contain unemployment or even maintain full employment at the level assumed possible and desirable by Beveridge in the 1940s, that is, at about 97 percent. The Scandinavian peoples like others will have to face this fact, however shocking it may appear to those who forget that present unemployment percentages have to be calculated on a potential labor force that is much larger than what existed a few decades ago. But it is equally important to remember that the social and political effects of unemployment in a democratically governed country are dangerous indeed, whatever the causes. If the term "welfare state" is to have any meaning, the well-being of the unemployed must not be disregarded. The fact that for various reasons unemployment today tends to be more serious among the young than among the old and the middle-aged gives further emphasis to such demands. The young are the most sensitive, the least stable, and perhaps also the most vulnerable of all elements in society. But their problems can be solved only if their elders—who in Scandinavia today form the vast majority, demographically and politically speaking—are prepared to make sacrifices of one type or another in the interests of their juniors. To demand such sacrifices is not a very attractive proposition for any political party or organization. But this does not make it any less necessary.

There are other new social problems as well. The Nordic countries no longer have such a homogeneous population as before. Not only the movement of labor within Scandinavia but also immigration from outside has led to the formation of ethnic minorities, not large by international standards, but larger and more esoteric than what Scandinavians were used to in the past. This is a matter requiring political decisions: whether the primary aim should be to integrate these minorities as quickly as possible with the indigenous population or whether they should be encouraged to maintain their separate cultural traditions. The first alternative calls for a certain amount of ruthlessness, whereas the second demands great tolerance from the majority of the population—something that cannot always be created by political fiat.

One of the difficulties lies in the fact that many immigrants react very negatively to the moral permissiveness of Scandinavian society. Apart from this consideration, it is a major social question, to be politically decided, how permissive these societies should be. Obviously there must be some limit, and there is hardly any doubt that the majority of the population is in favor of more law and order. At the same time, it must be recognized that even totalitarian governments frequently find it difficult to maintain law and order, and that in any case the means employed by such governments are unacceptable to the Nordic tradition. Similar problems arise in connection with "civil disobedience" actions attempted by environmentalists and other minority groups.

A problem that bears close relationship to the principles of the welfare state is how social security is to be organized in circumstances of greater austerity. Especially Sweden, but to some extent the other three countries as well, have established systems of social "insurance" and other benefits on the assumption that they should be available to all and sundry regardless of need. This has been criticized from several sides, in Denmark not least forcefully by a leading Social Democrat, Ritt Bjerregaard, who frankly maintains that "social benefits should be given to those who are in the most difficult positions, not to others." This has been heatedly contradicted in Sweden, for instance by Professor Walter Korpi, head of the Swedish Institute for Social Research at the University of Stockholm and an active Social Democrat: social policies are to "discipline marketing forces," not merely act as "a Red Cross nurse" to the needy. Another Danish expert, Gøsta Esping Andersen, has pointed out that Scandinavian welfare policies differ from those applied elsewhere in that they have attempted to institutionalize solidarity, equality, and security. But in fact the ideals of solidarity and of equality have become more and more incompatible. The choice between different solutions, he emphasizes, will in the end depend on the balance of power in society and the result of political elections—even in Scandinavia.

There are of course many other problems facing Nordic politicians today, as well as the politicians of other industrialized Western countries. Setting aside issues of foreign policy and military security, which are mostly if not wholly independent of the problems of the welfare state, some of them appear to be related to the position of organized interest groups and "corporativism": to what extent is the power of great organizations compatible with the power of elected Parliaments and Governments in democratically governed states? Should labor unions, for instance, be entitled to nullify, by means of their legitimate powers, economic policies supported by a majority of the electorate? Is peace in the labor market possible only with Labor Governments?

How should the interest of environmental protection and those of economic growth be balanced? As has just been pointed out, it is attractive to talk about zero growth in societies with an assured growth of 5 or 6 percent per annum, but much less so when zero growth or decline is a real probability even apart from environmental considerations.

How should underprivileged minorities be protected? The voting power of such very different minority groups as families with many children, immigrants, ex-criminals, and abusers of alcohol and other drugs is almost negligible. At the same time, there are many indications that at least in Scandinavian societies it is these minorities, and not the broad strata of the population, who are in danger of suffering real hardship — in economic terms or otherwise. Again, this is a matter for political decision and involves hard choices, which have to be made within the next decade or decades.

Education is another difficult issue, where the interests of egalitarian policies and of the maintenance of quality have to be balanced. Here the four countries have followed different paths. In Sweden, where the quality of education used to be particulary high, recent tendencies have been to go to all lengths in order to avoid "elitism," while the three other countries have been more hesitant in this respect. Public opinion has on the whole supported the latter approach and been more critical of what has taken place in Sweden. But all four countries have to decide, especially now that financial resources are so scarce: will Denmark, Finland, and Norway follow Sweden's lead, or will the latter country sacrifice some of its egalitarian ideas?

Throughout the Nordic countries, women's rights began to be increasingly respected as early as the last decades of the nineteenth and the first decades of the twentieth century. In this respect, as has already been pointed out, Scandinavians were somewhat ahead of other peoples in Western Europe. On the other hand, debate about a new relationship between men and women in both private and public life — "women's lib," or parity (jämställdhet), as it is more frequently called in Scandinavia — has become more vigorous since the early 1970s. This is not at all a question of party politics. It may be a part of Liberal ideology and thus more easily accepted by parties calling themselves Liberal, but on the whole all parties pay lip service to the idea and none of them take a really fundamental interest in it. For obvious reasons, parties whose electoral results are favorable elect more women representatives (as well as more young people), whereas those on the way down tend to protect their male, and especially their older male candidates. On the other hand, there is no denying that parity is an issue that enjoys great publicity. It remains to be seen whether it, like environmental protection, is more popular in times of affluence and more easily forgotten during periods of austerity, or whether it will remain permanently in evidence.

"The new left," which was so vocal in the late 1960s and early 1970s has been little heard of in the 1980s. It appears to have been a transient movement among intellectuals, with little permanent effects on substantial matters. As far as political debate is concerned, it did, however, manage to resuscitate Marxism, which had been dormant, believed dead in Scandinavia since the 1920s. Thus there is an increasing tendency for some participants in the debate to view social and political problems, such as those just mentioned in the context of class, in the Marxist sense.

There are indications that class consciousness is stronger in Sweden than in Denmark and Norway, although incomes are in fact probably more equal in the first named country. As a consequence, voting in Swedish elections has been determined more strongly by occupation or previous occupation. Especially in Norway, issues of immediate interest have more frequently been the deciding factors. It is true that even in Sweden the same tendency has appeared, especially among the younger age groups, but since these are for demographic reasons proportionately small in numbers, the old voting habits have lingered on. While class consciousness and class resentment in Finland have stronger historical roots and have been more obviously preserved than in the three other countries, this has in fact not resulted in stable voter support of either Social Democrats or Communists. Elections in Finland have tended to result in "bourgeois" majorities even earlier than in the rest of Scandinavia, although the prevalence of coalition Governments has largely nullified the effect of changes in the relative strength of parties in Parliament. Only the presidential election of 1982 resulted in a decisive victory for the labor candidate, and there is every indication that it was Mauno Koivisto as a person, rather than his party, who attracted the voters.

Can one really distinguish between class and issues? The Marxist assumption of course is that all issues are in the last resort determined by class. But this assumption is founded on concepts of class that have certainly not been applicable in Scandinavia after the Second World War, nor in most other affluent countries. In these countries there is no "proletariat" in the Marxist sense. In fact, if there ever was a proletariat, it had already ceased to exist in the years between the two World Wars. Consequently, it is necessary to examine the issues one by one to determine which of them are such that different opinions coincide with class interests.

On the face of it, this should be true of all economic issues. Tax resistance is a universal phenomenon, but there is no denying that it is stronger in higher income groups—not the really opulent, but above all small entrepreneurs and earners of relatively high salaries. The same groups also strongly tend to appreciate freedom in economic life, and they resent state controls more than blue-collar workers do. But with increasing equality of incomes and with the growing desire of individuals from the so-called working classes to acquire their own houses and perhaps move from employee status into the class of small entrepreneurs, even these differences tend to be reduced. It is nowadays far from certain, even in Sweden, that members of labor unions enthusiastically approve of *dirigiste* policies.

Similar changes of opinion are taking place in regard to social policies. At the time when the welfare state was first established, there were still sharp differences of incomes in Scandinavian societies, and the majority of the people believed that social benefits were provided for them, as of right, at the expense of the rich. This is no longer so. The majority of the people are today conscious of the fact that they themselves have to pay for the benefits they receive and that child subventions, pensions, etc., involve redistribution between different periods in life rather than between classes. Consequently, the connection between class and issues is tenuous even in regard to social security and welfare. And when it comes to the social problems of underprivileged minorities or to questions of "law and order," restrictive attitudes are by all accounts as strong among manual workers as among the so-called middle classes, if not even stronger. Only the relatively small group of middle-class intellectuals is on the other side.

The question of "corporativism" is more complicated. Not only the labor unions, but also the unions of white-collar workers and those of persons with university degrees, producers' cooperatives in agriculture, and employers' associations still command the loyalty of the vast majority of their members. But this is becoming more and more of a matter of routine rather than one of genuine feelings of allegiance. The bureaucratization of interest organizations, especially in the labor market, makes identification more difficult than before. Quite often, union members think of the officers of their organization as "they" rather than "we." And when these officers insist on speaking for their members even in questions outside the traditional field of organization activity, it becomes increasingly obvious that they cannot always be regarded as representative. Even in the labor market itself their authority is not quite what it used to be. Wildcat strikes, often directed against concessions made in the nationwide labor agreements, are becoming less unusual, and there have even been recent cases where employees, whether blue-collar or white-collar, have concluded that it is to their advantage to deal directly with their employer rather than to trust this function to a union. Tenants' organizations insist that it is for them alone to negotiate with landlords, but protests from tenants in individual apartment houses are far from unusual. Farmers may believe, rightly or wrongly, that producers' cooperatives no longer act in their interests but have become large, bureaucratic enterprises aiming at monopoly.

Education was originally very much a class issue. In the heyday of folk high schools, there was a hunger for culture and education among those who were active in political parties or in organizations, within both the industrial and the farming population, and with growing political power they insisted on reforms that should make available to their children and grandchildren the facilities for education, perhaps especially higher education, that they themselves had missed. At that time it was common to speak of the reserve of talent that was to be found in the working classes. But once education had been made more or less *available* to all, regardless of economic status, the question of the *type* of education came to the surface. Initially, reforms in this field were also advocated on the basis of class interest: the old, authoritarian type of education had been in the interests of the ruling upper classes, the insistence on detailed knowledge and traditional intellectual skills was also for their benefit, and now "manual working class" children should be given scope for their particular capacities. Education ought to develop character and social awareness, not knowledge and skills alone. As has already been noted, these ideals influenced the educational system particularly in Sweden. It turned out that they were not consonant with the interests of any particular class. The sons and daughters of manual workers needed

factual knowledge and skills in reading, writing, and arithmetic no
less than did those of capitalists; in fact they were more and not less
dependent on schooling in these areas than were those who had the
advantage of a more intellectual environment at home. Regardless of
the merits and demerits of the new ideas, they proved to have far
less connection with class interests than the simple availability of
education to all—perhaps no connection at all.

Some advocates of greater influence and power for women indicate
that this is a question of class: the subjection of women, they maintain, is a characteristic of capitalist society and part of the tyranny
of the capitalist class. Whatever the historical truth of such ideas, it is
difficult to see any connection in modern society. In fact it is not in
the "working classes" but on the contrary in the upper middle class,
and especially among intellectuals, that parity between men and
women has been first and most easily realized. The farming population has always been in a special position, with women playing an
active, important, and respected role in life, but one mostly different
from that of men. Industrial blue-collar workers, on the other hand,
cling to traditional relationships far more than do white-collar workers, small entrepreneurs, and academically trained professionals. It is
only by the most violent stretch of imagination that one could argue
that this is exclusively or even chiefly the result of lingering traces of
capitalism. Yet it is obvious that the new economic order established
by the welfare state has been particularly favorable to low income
groups, and that these consist largely of women.

Thus, to the extent that the establishment of welfare states in
Scandinavia has reduced or almost abolished economic class distinctions—as has happened in many countries outside Scandinavia as
well—this has had a dual effect on the political situation. First, there
is no longer the old division between a working-class majority and an
upper-class minority in society. Consequently, more and more voters
tend to take up their position on the basis of issues rather than that
of occupation, economic status, class, or whatever it is to be called.
Second, class distinctions also have less and less connection with
standpoints in current issues, so that here also real political argument
tends to influence voters more than group interest—a fact which
politicians have been slow in recognizing.

Those Social Democrats in Scandinavia who regard the welfare state
only as "a whistle-stop on the way to Socialism" (Walter Korpi) can

therefore no longer count on the support of clearly distinguishable interest groups. "The will to go further" (Olof Palme) cannot be expected to develop automatically even among their traditional supporters. On the other hand, it may well gain approval among some of their traditional opponents, if the supporting arguments are cogent and convincing enough. This is democracy.

But more disquieting observations also offer themselves. The economic problems of welfare states such as those of Scandinavia loom large on the horizon already in the early 1980s, and there is no indication that they will be easily solved within the near future. In a similar situation fifty years ago, the Nordic peoples benefited from "politics of compromise" in alleviating their difficulties and ultimately overcoming them. Ideological differences were temporarily—in appearance almost permanently—shelved, not only in politics but also in labor relations. This necessitated notable concessions on all sides, but there was surprisingly little opposition to such a pragmatic approach. One reason may be that there had previously been a comparatively long period of vigorous strife, which had seemingly resulted in more defeats than victories both to labor and to management, both to the "bourgeois" and to the Socialists.

As we have seen, ideological polarization was revived at least in some of the Nordic countries just before the present difficulties surfaced. Again, this applied not only to politics but equally to labor relations. In fact there are some indications that labor unions and employers' organizations, which formerly were more pragmatic and prone to compromise than the major political parties, nowadays are the foremost advocates of controversial policies.

There is of course the possibility that all this will result in drastic change, partly or wholly disestablishing the welfare state in favor of either full Socialism or revived Capitalism. The new order may then conceivably be so successful that opposition—and thus polarization —will be overcome. But it would be rash to reject out of hand the opposite possibility, namely, that insistence by different parties and organizations on drastic and controversial changes will aggravate the problems instead of solving them. In the absence of signal success, public policies may well be frequently reversed as the electorate finds itself disillusioned, and in any one country where the politics of compromise are not revived it may become virtually impossible to pursue consistent policies giving any hope of continued prosperity.

Welfare and Equality

In 1969, Alva Myrdal presented a report on "equality" to the national congress of the Swedish Social Democratic party. It was an elaboration of ideas that she had outlined in a speech a few years earlier. The report was unanimously adopted and thus became the official policy of the party at the same time that Olof Palme took over the leadership from Tage Erlander. It consequently merits very serious attention.

No hard and fast line of distinction had ever been drawn between the welfare state and an egalitarian society founded on equality and solidarity rather than competition. From the beginning egalitarian ideas and practices had been important in the welfare state. The policies of the 1930s and the 1950s had been characterized by a leveling of economic disparities between different groups in society—or classes, as they were called by those who preferred to employ Marxist terminology. The principle of solidarity in wage policies had already been adopted by the labor unions in 1951.

But Alva Myrdal's report made a strict distinction between welfare and equality, and emphasized that past policies were not sufficient. "After the World War, when our third generation took over, the fight was expanded to aim at 'full employment and social security.' . . . Now it is time for the fourth generation to take over. It is in the line of continuously heightened aims that the labor movement now quite logically turns to equality. This means a bolder advance," she said in presenting the report. "The policy of equality is what the 1970s demand of our movement."

According to the report, equality and freedom are not opposites, but complements. Freedom—whether political, economic, or cultural freedom—must also be equitably distributed. Older ideas of liberty and equality, such as free economic competition and unregulated market economics, were expressly rejected. Liberal ideas of equality, referring chiefly to the right of competition on equal terms, neglect the fact that competition isolates the less successful from the social community. The responsibility of individuals for their own situation must be reduced to reasonable proportions. All should be seen as having an equal right to get their share of the resources of society. Equalization, which is the general principle, must be supplemented by the right to compensation in order to redress the balance in favor of "those who for some reason are badly equipped to assert themselves in the competitive struggle. Something should be done for the large groups of people who demand too little from life. There are many who refrain from taking the chances that would be most favorable from an economic point of view; they know too little about the available possibilities." So said the report.

Perhaps more important than these generalities were some of the practical conclusions drawn in the report. Salaries and wages should be changed radically in order to reduce the differential between those performing jobs that require an extensive theoretical education on the one hand and on the other hand those who have acquired knowledge or skills by practical experience only or who are obliged to make greater physical or mental efforts. In other respects too policies on wages and salaries should be strongly committed to the idea of solidarity. Public policies should consciously attempt to improve the conditions for equalization of wages and salaries. The function of public employment agencies must be reconsidered. Their primary goal must be to provide employment to those who are out of work, a less-important goal being to supply labor to industry and trade. Employees and employers should not be considered equal partners. The service provided by organs of society should be supportive of employees, whom the report designated as the weaker partner. Public employment agencies should help not only job seekers but also those employed persons in need of better and higher-paying jobs, thereby contributing to the transfer of labor to more profitable and satisfying occupations. And job satisfaction, the feeling that the work is stimulating and meaningful, would result in greater efficiency.

In education the emphasis on equality ought to mean that less importance is given to individual performance. Pedagogical development should concentrate on the problems of pupils with low performance. All teaching, including that taking place in the classroom, should be organized so as to permit pupils to participate in decision making. "The democracy of our study circles should be introduced also into the educational system organized by society," said Alva Myrdal.

The report emphasized that social policies resulted largely from the growth of the labor movement. It stressed the importance of establishing an active policy of redistribution that leveled out prosperity and abolished islands of poverty. Social investments and social consumption should be seen as important elements in these policies. In line with this tradition, social insurance must be accorded wider functions than just to protect minimum standards; it should in principle neutralize any loss of normal income.

Consumer policies should correct the results arising from the market economy. They ought to favor weak consumer groups. Information should aim at correcting and neutralizing the effects of private commercial publicity.

Much was said about "economic democracy." It was assumed that this principle should be realized through the medium of society. Economic democracy "implies that the people are able to influence the decisions of trade and industry and of private enterprises through society. Especially the influence of owners must be reduced in favor of the interests of the majority of the people." Thus, in housing, the long-range objective must be that municipal, cooperative, and other housing enterprises working in the interests of the public should become increasingly dominant.

Equalization, the report emphasizes, must be seen as a lasting tendency of social development. It cannot be "achieved" at a given time. It must be a permanent ambition permeating all political activities. It is a question not only of breaking down traditional differences of class and privilege, dating from older times, but equally of preventing the emergence of new differences. Equalization must be carried out by a true popular movement and be asserted everywhere—in every

assembly of persons, in every school, in all places of work, in all organizations, in every home.

This brief summary can give no more than a vague idea of the
force and enthusiasm expressed by Alva Myrdal and in her report.
Undoubtedly hers was a spirited attempt to revive the labor movement by pointing the way to new and drastic changes, doing away
with the remaining vestiges of hierarchy and of capitalism. Like most
appeals of this type, it was strong in its condemnations of existing
conditions, but it also included a glowing if somewhat sketchy picture of what the ideal society should be like. The question of how
the ideal society is to be achieved was hardly touched on in the report, however. The issue of economic resources was mentioned only
once, and then in order to point out the necessity of setting priorities, since everything cannot be carried out at the same time. The
focus of the report was on what should be held desirable, leaving it
to others to consider the means of realization.

Such an attitude was natural in Sweden at that time. In 1969 the
country had not yet felt the effects of any economic crisis. Permanent
and spectacular growth seemed assured. The distribution of prosperity—to use the words of Danish labor leader Thomas Nielsen quoted
at the beginning of this book—appeared to be the only important
issue. The ideas embodied in Alva Myrdal's report of 1969 represent
the climax of the Swedish social reformers' ambitions. They strongly
influenced Swedish policies and politics, serving as a guideline for
the Social Democratic Cabinets in power up to 1976 and coloring the
work of that party in opposition from 1976 to 1982.

It is more difficult to assess the effect of these ambitions in the
other Nordic countries. In all of them similar tendencies undoubtedly
appeared from time to time, for instance when Thomas Nielsen in
Denmark pleaded for "economic democracy." But it appears that
even the other Nordic labor parties, none of which was numerically
as strong as the Swedish one, hesitated before following in the foot-
steps of their Swedish friends. Also, the reforming zeal of Swedish
Cabinets in the early 1970s sometimes made them disregard traditional concepts of Nordic cooperation, e.g., in legislation. They were
unwilling to slow down and wait for their colleagues in the other
Nordic countries to catch up with them. It is characteristic that labor
politicians like Ritt Bjerregaard, at one time minister for social affairs
in Denmark, and Gro Harlem Brundtland, at one time prime minister

of Norway, have been criticized by Social Democrats in Sweden for the moderation and hesitance of their policies. The development of egalitarian ideas and practices in the Nordic countries has been much less uniform in the years after 1969 than it had been before. And this is so even if only the labor parties are considered.

In Sweden, this disparity is sometimes seen as a consequence of the differences between the Nordic countries in their foreign relations. Both Denmark and Norway are members of NATO and might consequently be subject to stronger American influence than the two others. Denmark, moreover, is a member of the European Economic Communities, and this fact could be important in determining its economic and social policies. Compared with the three other countries, Finland has a closer relationship to the Soviet Union and more important trade relations with Eastern Europe. As a matter of fact, it is, however, unlikely that these circumstances could have accounted for differences in egalitarian policies. Finland is scrupulous about dissociating domestic policies from its foreign relations. Denmark and Norway are no more willing than anybody else to copy the policies of their allies. On the contrary, it used to be said that Sweden was perhaps the most "Americanized" country in Europe, so much so that even anti-Americanism was imported from the United States. The insistence on going beyond the welfare state is on the whole an indigenous Swedish invention.

When confronted with the enthusiasm underlying Alva Myrdal's report, one cannot at first avoid the feeling that its arguments in favor of egalitarian policies are, if not universally convincing, at least very seductive. It is undoubtedly true that the rights and freedoms established by Liberal policies (here as usual the word "Liberal" is taken in its European and not in its American sense) are not equally valuable to everybody. Equality of opportunities is often very difficult to apply in practice. Freedom of the press is only indirectly valuable to those who are not in a position to express their views in public or to publish in books or periodicals what they regard as relevant facts. Opinions may vary about what news is fit to print. Equality before the law becomes a full reality only to those who know and understand the law or can afford assistance from others who possess such knowledge. Freedom of bargaining is effective only when the partners are at least roughly equal in strength. Freedom of association is sometimes a hindrance to those who would prefer to remain outside organizations. Profits from entrepreneurial undertakings are by no means always proportionate to the effort that was put into them. Educational facilities cannot always be easily used by those who are intellectually not so well equipped as others or who in their early life were not accustomed to intellectual pursuits or not encouraged to take part in them.

If you set out to establish the perfect society and are certain of possessing the wisdom that enables you to do so, it is not surprising that you want to continue beyond the welfare state. The question is how much egalitarian perfectionism you can afford in this imperfect world without running into serious problems in other respects. Alva Myrdal's report recognizes no such qualms. Enthusiasts are apt to pass lightly over such difficulties as those connected with resources or with the need to consider different objectives at the same time. But in the end they cannot be neglected, and decisions must involve difficult choices whenever more than one type of consideration comes into play.

There can be no doubt that Alva Myrdal's report of 1969 and the attitudes of the leadership of her political party were influenced by outside events taking place at about this time. The upheavals of 1968 were particularly vigorous in other countries such as the United States, France, and West Germany. But they had their counterparts in Sweden and Denmark as well, while hardly any disturbances occurred in the two other Nordic countries. In any case, the circumstances strengthened the fears of Swedish Social Democrats that they would be seen as "The Establishment" after being in power for thirty-six years. In their view this was a serious danger, among other reasons because it could benefit the Communists, and they therefore found it necessary to show that they still insisted on radical change in the existing social and economic framework of their country.

On the other hand, egalitarian efforts have always met with strong opposition whenever they were openly in evidence. This is not particular to the Nordic countries in the postwar period, nor is it in itself an argument against them, although it is a fact of life. In her speech Alva Myrdal anticipated such opposition and practically welcomed the consequent polarization. The politics of compromise, embodied in "broad-based solutions," can of course not be regarded as an end in itself.

Opposition and criticism appear in different forms. One consists of objections in principle and substance. The egalitarian argument is held to be unrealistic, especially when applied to specific, concrete measures. It is also said to run counter to other, equally or even more important principles than that of equality. This is the kind of criticism that chiefly concerns us here. But we must not entirely neglect the other kind of opposition, that which stems from vested interests, social groups, and political parties that are "counterrevolutionary" and that dig in their heels to prevent developments of which they disapprove, whether on rational or on irrational or on purely selfish grounds. For their opposition may be wholly or partly successful, and in combating it reformers may be tempted to have recourse to means running counter to the principles of liberty and democracy.

In assessing egalitarianism, it is best to deal individually with each specific issue. The general egalitarian argument may be ever so convincing; the total vision of a new type of society, never before seen in the world, may be ever so attractive. But when it comes to such concrete proposals as what is called employee funds in Sweden and economic democracy in Denmark, the general argument does not suffice. It is necessary to study the result of its practical application in a particular case and to weigh advantages and drawbacks on the basis of all possible considerations. To take one other example: what is the purpose of education? Is it only—as Alva Myrdal apparently maintained—to prepare pupils and students for decision making, and to help those with low performances? Or does it also, perhaps primarily, comprise an effort to raise the intellectual standards of society and encourage the development of knowledge and skills? In the latter case it can hardly be possible to abolish "elitism." Attempts in that direction may in fact impede the training of persons who are to carry on, for example, research and technical development. The choice is not always easy. Such analyses of issues lie outside the scope of this book. But in practical politics they are indispensable.

One of the greatest difficulties of egalitarianism is obviously to be found in international relations. No man (or woman) is an island. But nowadays no country is an island either, except in the purely geographical sense, and this has become more and more irrelevant. Even huge countries like the United States and India, which dominate a whole subcontinent, depend for their well-being on developments elsewhere. This dependence is of course even greater in small, highly developed countries like Denmark, Finland, Norway, and Sweden.

These nations made their fortune and established the economic foundations of their social security and welfare system by exporting, with reasonable profit, such goods as bacon, ball-bearings, dairy products, fertilizer, fish, paper, pulp, ships, steel, and telephonic equipment. All of these they produce in much greater quantities than their home markets can absorb. Thus for them it cannot be enough to abolish competitive attitudes at home as long as competition remains rampant abroad. Anybody who likes to do so can call this good Marxism but must add the qualification that the World Revolution appears to be as far away as it ever was.

It is all very well to say that because of egalitarian considerations nobody should be allowed to make great profits in a Nordic country. The example may be enthusiastically followed in Tanzania and other countries outside the mainstream of economic development. But this does not help the Scandinavians very much as long as the Americans, Germans, Japanese, Koreans, and Taiwanese disregard such lofty principles and in doing so manage to supply desirable goods, which are also produced in Scandinavia, at lower prices and of equal or even higher quality. The Scandinavians may suffer material losses and have to console themselves with their moral superiority alone.

Nor is it quite certain that all Scandinavians really are morally superior. When speaking of tax reform, Alva Myrdal's report pointed out that the relevant reforms could not be financed solely by increasing the burden of taxation of persons in the higher income brackets. In the transfer of resources, the emphasis must lie on indirect taxes to be paid by all. This requirement ought to be a tangible test of the willingness of the broad strata of the population to contribute to greater equality. It can hardly be maintained that such optimism has been justified. In Scandinavia as well as elsewhere, tax resistance, against both direct and indirect taxes, appears to be definitely greater than egalitarian enthusiasm. All social groups insist that the tax burden—*their* tax burden—should be reduced, although they are of course unwilling to sacrifice any advantages of their own for this purpose. Sacrifices should be made by others, and if this be not equality it is at least designated as social justice.

When the international economic climate changed in the latter part of the 1960s and the beginning of the 1970s, the economies of Denmark, Finland, and Sweden became less competitive and successful, although Norway was somewhat better off. It would be a mistake to believe that the difficulties implied diminishing efficiency as a result of the activities of the welfare state. The Nordic economies on the whole remained no less efficient than before. But the international market was becoming saturated with their products, and simultaneously other countries had greatly increased their efficiency. Thus competition had become much stiffer than before. The German miracle, let alone the Japanese miracle, put the Scandinavians into the shade.

The new problems appeared first in Denmark and Finland. These countries found themselves unable to maintain employment at the traditional level. In Denmark other parts of the welfare system also moved into the danger zone when budget deficits became increasingly high.

Sweden was less affected by economic problems until the oil crisis of 1973, which had serious consequences for all three countries. Their per capita oil consumption was high, about as high as that of Japan, and there was the additional complication that much of it consisted of household consumption which could not easily be reduced through rationalization. Swedish economic policies at this juncture were based on two assumptions: that the difficulties were only temporary and could be "bridged" by suitable measures; and that major unemployment should be regarded as the supreme evil and avoided at any cost. Consequently it was not until the latter half of the 1970s that the seriousness of the Swedish situation had become clearly visible and recognized as a more or less permanent fact of life. Countermeasures came late.

By that time Finland had recovered from the initial shock. Although unemployment remained relatively high, its economy had improved in other respects. But it was uncertain whether the improvement would be permanent. In Denmark there was no improvement and no agreement on countermeasures, only widespread realization of the problem. Because of its access to North Sea oil, Norway remained in a more comfortable situation than that of the three others.

Unavoidably, the new economic situation has influenced attitudes toward the welfare state. Resources, which at one time had appeared to be practically unlimited, have been shown to be very limited indeed. Previously existing problems such as those mentioned above appeared to be more acute when growth slowed down, and with diminishing resources it became more difficult to solve them by the means traditionally employed. In an unguarded moment Olof Palme said that "realities are our most dangerous enemy."

Naturally, there is no agreement on what caused the difficulties confronting the Nordic countries and even less on what the remedies should be. Since the 1930s most Scandinavian economists maintained that the "economy of high wages" should be regarded as one of the best stimuli for growth. They pointed out that it increased buying power and encouraged rationalization of production, thus lowering costs and prices. Now some of them are beginning to doubt whether this reasoning is any longer correct. Even when it makes actual production more economical, rationalization in its prevalent form of automation may involve problems and costs for society, for instance by creating temporary or long-term unemployment. And in a multinational economic society such as that of the modern industrialized world rationalization sometimes consists in transferring production from one country to another where conditions, including the cost of labor, are more favorable. In this case the economy of high wages and salaries entails a sort of rationalization that of course by no means increases buying power in the country where it is applied.

Heretics even revert to the previously abandoned proposition that there could be a connection between high wage and salary levels and high unemployment. If this were so, the traditional "active" labor market policies applied in Scandinavia and particularly in Sweden must also be questioned. As long as nothing more seemed to be required than to deal with a temporary slackness in the demand for labor, or with the need to transfer labor from one branch of industry to another, there were good reasons for keeping the unemployed, and particularly the young unemployed, occupied at the expense of the public with odd jobs for which there would otherwise have been little demand, or in industrial training courses. But if permanently applied, these devices could distort normal labor relations. With the removal of threats of open unemployment, it becomes easier for employee organizations to maintain higher wage and salary levels than would be warranted by the market value of the output. As a result, the demand for industrial labor has been diminished, and while apparently reducing open unemployment the traditional labor market policies could therefore indirectly contribute to the maintenance of real unemployment at a higher level than would have been reached otherwise.

As has been pointed out in an earlier chapter, it is characteristic of the situation in the 1970s and 1980s—in contrast to that of the 1930s —that inflation and unemployment often appear simultaneously in the same society. The traditional anticyclical theory consequently does not provide the requisite guidelines for economic policy. And so long as no coherent theory of the phenomenon of stagflation has been provided, politicians are consequently not in a position to be guided by economic theory, or at least not by the advice of professional economists.

In most countries including Scandinavia, the new situation is held to call for retrenchment or at least greater "austerity" with regard to public expenditure. It is generally agreed that administrative superstructures should be carefully pruned by eliminating all components that are not absolutely necessary. It is quite clear that this is not enough, however. Administrative simplification is highly desirable in itself, but it does not go very far in reducing public expenditure. Real economy measures cannot be concerned with procedures only. They must relate to the very substance of the public sector, notably to transfers and/or collective consumption.

But the altered situation involves more than merely a need for economies. If the resources of society are to be maintained or even augmented, productivity rather than equality must be the primary consideration. And the two do not always go well together. It becomes necessary to favor productive enterprises, whether privately or publicly owned, over those that find themselves in difficulties. Technical development and a high degree of sophistication in industry require an elite of skilled workers, engineers, and researchers. Since these can be trained only in a suitably adapted educational system, elitism in education can no longer be condemned. Nor is it by any means certain that so-called industrial democracy favors the development of industrial productivity. Employees' organizations have in the past frequently proved unwilling to put the interests of efficiency in the enterprise—again, whether privately or publicly owned—ahead of their own direct interest in employment opportunities and convenient working conditions.

Even over such a short period as that of the recession in the 1970s and 1980s, circumstances of this type have shown their effects in the Nordic countries. Finland early gave priority to fighting inflation at the price of relatively high unemployment. In Denmark social expenditures have been considerably reduced in spite of the fact that the Social Democratic party was in power most of the time. And when the Social Democrats returned to power in Sweden in 1982, they made it quite clear that no new social reforms could be envisaged in the foreseeable future and that it might be necessary to continue at least some of the economy measures in the social field that had been introduced by the "bourgeois" Governments.

In fact, the situation has changed drastically from that existing as late as a decade earlier. Thomas Nielsen said that "now the question is one of distributing prosperity." Will prosperity always and in all circumstances be available for distribution? As has been pointed out in an earlier chapter, this is to some extent a question of the motivations that make human beings work hard and produce successful innovations. It is quite true, as stated in Alva Myrdal's report, that economic gain is not the only important motive. But it is impossible to deny that it is one of the most important motives yet observed, and that another potent motive is the hope of acquiring power. Insistence on economic equality of results and on equality in decision making largely removes such motives. Are remaining incentives sufficient to ensure efficiency, productivity, and growth?

Resources are bound to remain finite even if the economy improves. In any case economic growth is unlikely to resume the pace that characterized the decades just after the Second World War. And with the scarcity of resources, many problems are apt to surface. What is to be meant by a just distribution cannot be determined on objective grounds, and not only different individuals but even more decidedly different social groups are likely to hold irreconcilably different attitudes. When real incomes increased rapidly, it seemed relatively easy to preach solidarity and to focus attention on those who were less favored than others. In a fundamentally changed situation all, or nearly all, may argue that they have not been sufficiently favored. Signs of such bickering, for instance in negotiations over wages, salaries, and related benefits, are already apparent. "Poverty is easier to endure when it is equally endured by all," Ernst Wigforss said in the old days. This statement was forgotten by everyone but the historians: surely poverty was gone forever! It is, however, more than doubtful whether Wigforss's phrase can be applied to reductions in prosperity—if indeed it was ever applicable to anything. As pointed out earlier, under modern conditions equality is a very expensive commodity. It can be achieved only by raising the level for some without lowering it too much for others. This is possible only if resources are ample and above all grow rapidly.

Some of the choices now confronting the welfare state and its rulers are related to the size of the public sector and its support by high and highly progressive taxes. Such taxes may very well prove counterproductive, above all from the point of view of the economic growth that guarantees the future of the welfare state. In Scandinavia it is widely assumed that such effects are already in evidence.

Also, when resources are scarce, the quest for relatively high minimum standards of living through the maintenance of social security does not necessarily fit in with measures aimed at leveling out prosperity. There are two elements in the public sector of the Scandinavian welfare states: transfers and collective consumption. Which of the two should be regarded as the most indispensable when economies must be affected?

The original purpose of welfare was undoubtedly to benefit the weaker (or less prosperous) members of society at the expense of those who were stronger and richer. It involved a sort of Robin Hood policy: take from the rich and give to the poor. From this point of view, transfers were clearly indicated. They should liberate the poor from the tyranny exercised by the threat of destitution. In the early stages of the development of the welfare state—for the first two or three generations of the labor movement, to use Alva Myrdal's words —this was the predominant objective, and transfers constituted the predominant means.

With growing general prosperity, the emphasis changed. Abject destitution was no longer an immediate and present danger. Gradually more interest was given to what Gunnar Myrdal has called "socialization of consumption," that is, collective consumption. For the less fortunate, this measure had the advantage of involving no "stigma" of poverty. Nobody need feel belittled by receiving the same benefits as everybody else; whereas they might presumably be embarrassed by being singled out for special attention and assistance. From the egalitarian point of view, this is a very essential argument. Moreover, every increase in the scope of collective consumption reduces the area available for "rationing by the pocketbook."

Finally, it appeared that transfers involve other undesirable consequences. When combined with high progressive taxes, a system of benefits determined by the level of individual or family incomes creates so-called threshold effects: an increase of personal income not only makes a family or an individual liable to pay direct taxes according to a higher rate but also deprives them of some social benefits previously enjoyed. Thus an increase in nominal income might in extreme cases lead to an actual reduction of available income. Collective consumption can by definition involve no such secondary effects, since it is at the disposal of all and sundry regardless of their incomes.

In certain fields specific arguments in favor of collective consumption have also been adduced. By reductions in the cost of public transport, people may, for instance, be encouraged to refrain from using their own automobiles in crowded urban areas. If the construction of residential housing is subsidized, not only are rents kept down, but in addition more houses are built and employment is found for persons who might otherwise be unemployed and claim the dole. Especially in Swedish political debate, this sort of reasoning has carried great weight in the past. There is probably no country in the world, not excluding the so-called Socialist countries of Eastern Europe, where collective consumption has been more widespread than in Sweden.

But there are arguments on the other side as well. Collective consumption, it is maintained, reduces the motivation for hard work and special efforts far more than does social security in the form of transfers. If the latter obviates threats from the stick of poverty, the former also takes away the carrot of abundance. Why should ordinary people labor to earn more for their pocketbooks if rationing by the pocketbook is abolished? Also, if the rules of price formation by supply and demand are put out of action in one field after another, demand may increase beyond reasonable limits. When nobody knows the real cost of their housing, collective transport, healthcare, and education, people will ask for unreasonably large and well-equipped dwellings, will travel much more than necessary, will demand hospitalization for the most trivial ailments, and will use educational facilities for simple entertainment. Although this could have seemed innocuous and even desirable at a time when the sky appeared to be the limit of public expenditures, it is hardly compatible with the strict economy called for under circumstances such as those of the 1980s.

Finally, collective consumption always involves uniformity, and uniformity almost by definition involves regimentation and restriction of individual liberties. It is all very well to say that such restrictions on the liberty of minorities in the interests of the welfare of the majority should be accepted by all. But even if this statement is taken for granted (and there may be arguments to the contrary), it applies only as long as it is obvious that the sacrifices are made by minorities exclusively and that the welfare of the majority is really involved—and we can no longer be certain of this. Especially in Sweden regimentation has gone almost as far as is possible without resorting to physical coercion. There has been considerable criticism of such Swedish phenomena in the other Nordic countries, notably in Denmark. And a German observer, Hans Magnus Enzensberger, in 1982 published a series of articles in a Liberal but not libertarian Swedish newspaper (*Dagens Nyheter*), describing what he regarded as the excessive docility of the Swedish people in its relations to public authorities. He maintained that the trust of the Swedish people in the "benevolence" of the state constituted a danger to liberty and democracy. His criticisms elicited considerable response in Sweden. There is also no doubt that the growing support given to Conservative parties in all the four Nordic countries is traceable to reaction against what is felt to be excessive regimentation, caused by insistence on collective consumption and perfect economic equality.

An example of uniformity is to be found in the educational system. Public comprehensive schools were introduced in order to guarantee equal opportunities to all children regardless of their social background. They were given practically a monopoly, especially in Sweden. After over two decades of experience it appears more than doubtful whether they have achieved their objective. Children from intellectually sophisticated families still remain more literate and more likely to go into intellectual occupations than others. At the same time, there are those who believe that the uniform educational system, as well as other uniform public institutions and arrangements, take away desirable opportunities for individual choice. Why not enable everybody—by subsidies or other transfers wherever necessary—to pay for their children's education at the school of their choice, for the sort of dwellings they desire, for health care and child care? Why subsidize the general price of foodstuffs instead of favoring families with children by giving them increased child subsidies?

From the point of view of budget makers and other political

forces, the choice of alternatives looks rather different. When budget slashing becomes necessary, experience shows that it is easier to attack transfers to persons in an insecure position, forming an element of the original welfare state, than to abolish items of collective consumption which apply to everybody and have more definite egalitarian effects. Also, from a technical and administrative standpoint, and leaving aside considerations of public morals, reduction of transfers is the simplest choice. It calls for no drastic change in procedures, and it is comparatively easy to estimate the budgetary effect, for instance, of reducing old age pensions by a given percentage, or to withdraw child subsidies from families with one child only. Political difficulties are obvious, but with a sufficiently cynical approach they can be overcome. Every group is anxious to retain its own benefits, but it appears that in a pinch most people are less enthusiastic about benefits given to others. Thus in choosing which transfers to reduce, it is possible to apply definite electoral considerations. The party in power must see to it that reductions are limited to groups that are either too small to influence the next election or else likely to vote for the opposition in any case. Obviously no such considerations are openly avowed, but this does not mean that they are not taken into account — in Scandinavia as well as elsewhere. After all, in circumstances requiring economies it is unavoidable that someone must suffer . . .

Dealing with collective consumption is more complicated. Reductions or abolishment often require administrative changes of considerable magnitude. It is difficult to estimate the budgetary effect and even more difficult to get a clear idea of how different social groups are affected. For reasons of social justice, the disappearance of items of collective consumption often has to be compensated for by increasing transfers to particularly vulnerable groups and individuals, and the consequent additional costs may be unforeseeable. Thus it may seem more expedient to lower the level of social security and maintain measures aimed at increasing equality, whatever the general standard of living.

There is of course also a third alternative, perhaps the most facile of all: the "cheese slicer" approach, taking a little here and a little there without resolving any questions of principle. This approach is particularly tempting when it is believed that only a brief period of thrift is required until circumstances again become more auspicious for expenditure-happy reformers. For a short time practically any activity can be kept going at low heat. On the other hand, if prolonged, this sort of indiscriminate cheese paring often proves disastrous. The economies achieved will almost without exception prove insufficient, while the welfare system may crumble on all sides.

It should be strongly emphasized that in the Nordic countries neither the advocates of egalitarianism, with the possible exception of a few dyed-in-the-wool Communists, nor the advocates of economy in social expenditures even consider the possibility of establishing or maintaining the system of their choice by other than democratic means. Political democracy is universally and unequivocally accepted as the overall principle. Reformers as well as critics of the welfare state believe that they can succeed by means of the democratic process, and they accept the qualification that if defeated they will have to desist, temporarily or permanently, from pursuing their ideals in practice.

The democratic process itself involves definite difficulties, however. The rigid parliamentary party systems in force in Scandinavia, as well as in other Western European countries, sometimes have the effect of distorting the expression of popular will even when one party or coalition of parties has a working majority in the legislature. Party discipline is strong, and within each party majority decisions are held to be morally binding on the minority. A majority of a majority is, however, often only a minority of the whole: 60 percent of a 60 percent majority is only a little more than one-third of the whole. But it claims to represent the will of the people. Moreover, at election time well-organized minority groups may hold the balance between parties and blackmail them for promises of new benefits or the retention of old ones. Holders of old age pensions as well as owners of small detached houses have proved adept at this procedure in the Nordic countries.

All this was of minor importance while the politics of compromise were applied, as was the case during the establishment of the welfare states of Scandinavia. When the shortage of economic resources on the one hand and high egalitarian ambitions on the other caused increasing polarization and required political decisions on highly controversial issues, a different situation arose. It may in the long run be increasingly difficult to enforce economic policies intended to benefit the whole of society if their immediate consequences involve sacrifices for influential groups, whether or not such groups constitute a majority of the people. And it is equally difficult in such circumstances to find endorsement for policies in support of relatively small, disfavored minorities.

Equality does not grow by itself. It has to be enforced against resistance not only from previously favored groups and individuals but from much broader strata of the population. There are many who will have to sacrifice what they regard as absolutely legitimate privileges, acquired for instance by free negotiations in the labor market. Nor is really widespread and strong support ensured. Egalitarian policies are largely concerned with realizing what are held to be latent, unconscious desires of the broad strata of the population. The existence of such desires is presumed rather than proved, and they could in the opinion of the reformers be brought to the surface in the future. In the meantime, however, the reformers take it upon themselves to interpret them.

How do egalitarian policies affect the working of political democracy? In their ambitions they are of course entirely democratic, and one of the characteristic elements in egalitarian thought has been to decry "elites," a term which has been identified with hierarchical tendencies, with class rule, and with "meritocracy" even when top posts in the hierarchy are accessible to all regardless of social origins. But there could be a danger that another type of elites would grow up in the process of enforcing equality—not an elite based on traditional hierarchy, but one exercising tutelage. Even if it is presumed that power is used with absolute unselfishness—and is that always the case?—its exercise must unavoidably establish a category of persons—a "new class"—with power to influence the well-being of others.

A new feature in Scandinavia is the growing distrust of politicians, which was discussed in an earlier chapter. This distrust is contrary to tradition. Until quite recently persons involved in politics as well as civil servants were highly respected for their professional activities. The change is certainly not due either to the growth of welfare states or to egalitarian policies; nor is it the result of more than the unavoidable moral shortcomings of politicians or civil servants. To a considerable extent it is probably caused by influence from the other side of the Atlantic, where negative attitudes of this type have of course existed for a long time. A contributory factor may also be the growing professionalization of politics. Career politicians are more suspect than citizens who in accordance with earlier traditions continued to pursue their original occupations while spending part of their time representing the people and their political parties in Parliament or local councils.

Whatever the cause, distrust of politicians is a complicating factor. Both measures of strict economy and the quest for perfect equality require steering and interference in matters that ordinary citizens sometimes prefer to handle themselves. Only the organs of society can determine what interference is called for and what methods are to be employed. Such decisions rest with politicians.

To be successful in a democracy that pursues egalitarian policies, politicians must win the confidence of the public. It is not enough that their party collects a sufficient number of votes at election time. They must also be able to make people firmly believe in their honesty and their good judgment. In the absence of day-to-day confidence, they may reach the point where nothing but brute force can ensure efficient steering. Part of the early success of the welfare states in Scandinavia was due to this kind of public confidence. The recent erosion of confidence has occurred at a time when even more extensive steering is envisaged.

The distrust of politicians and administrative authorities is generally acclaimed as a healthy phenomenon, resulting from more widespread education and the growth of democratic as against authoritarian traditions. But it does not facilitate enforcement of laws and regulations. Especially when it comes to the collection of revenue, tax resistance is reinforced by distrust of tax authorities.

When the public tends to regard administrative agencies as not only extraneous but also dubious, it becomes more difficult to carry out wholesale intervention in private activities. This is particularly important with regard to egalitarian policies, where such intervention cannot be avoided and where it consequently becomes necessary to give considerable power to administrators. The argument in Alva Myrdal's report concerning the function of public employment agencies provides an illustration.

Control of the administration becomes more difficult at the same time. There are many things that cannot be clearly laid down in legal rules or administered by courts of law, not even by administrative courts. Much must be left to the discretion and common sense of officials. But discretionary decisions are frequently regarded as arbitrary, especially by those who suffer rather than profit from them. Nor can such decisions be subject to any legal control. Moreover, discretionary power for administrators almost by definition reduces the scope of political democracy.

Organizations, most of which have been designated as popular movements, have always played an important role in Scandinavia. They have provided a democratic element existing alongside the general system of political elections. Most typical of these organizations are the labor unions. In many respects citizens were more apt to identify themselves with an organized interest group than with society as a whole. They were convinced that the organization would protect their interests, right or wrong, against all others.

Gradually the organizations assumed wider functions and responsibilities than before. In several fields, especially that of labor market policies, the state refrained wholly or at least partly from interference and gave organizations something like a free hand, confident that they would use their power for the benefit of society as a whole. Occasionally organizations were assigned functions as agents of the state for the execution of laws or public policy. All this appeared to be useful because the organizations enjoyed the full, solidly established confidence of their members and applied much more of direct democracy than what was held possible in the normal political framework. In this respect they were similar to the self-governing local bodies, which had other functions of the same type and which were also closer to the people than Parliament or other state authorities.

As has been pointed out before, both organizations and self-governing local bodies have in recent years become much more bureaucratic. This was partly a result of the establishment of the welfare state. Egalitarian policies can in any case do nothing to counteract such tendencies; rather, they are likely to strengthen them. If equality is the overall objective, labor unions and similar organizations cannot be permitted to work exclusively in the interests of each particular category of employees or other citizens but must coordinate their activities in the interest of society as a whole. Otherwise equality could suffer. The insistence on solidarity in wage policies is a typical example. Quite apart from its economic consequences, it can of course be realized only by means of strongly centralized wage negotiations, denying to the employees in a particular trade, let alone in a particular enterprise, the use of available opportunities to further their own particular interests. In these circumstances there can be no direct democracy. In fact workers in successful enterprises are straining at the leash, and the idea of employee funds has been designed partly with this problem in mind.

There is a similar situation in local self-government. Left to themselves, some of the local bodies, which have access to richer sources of revenue than others, would be able to adapt their services and other activities so as to meet the direct wishes of their citizens, whereas other local bodies could not accomplish this. Different political majorities prefer to give priority to different facilities and services. But if the local bodies were given a free hand, standards for citizens would come to differ sharply depending on domicile, and equality would suffer. This can be prevented only by state interference either directly by means of rules and regulations or by redistribution of local revenues or indirectly by offering the incentive of grants-in-aid for particular purposes. In either case self-government with its possibilities of something at least approaching direct democracy is given less scope.

The process of economic growth, combined with the establishment of welfare states and the leveling out of economic disparities between major social groups, has also upset traditional class structures in the Nordic countries. It is increasingly difficult to identify classes or speak of class feeling in these countries. The so-called working classes are so far from being a proletariat that their members are largely better off than some people belonging to what used to be called the middle classes: white-collar workers, shopkeepers, and other owners of small enterprises, let alone farmers. And even apart from the blurred character of distinguishing lines, the proportions are different from what they used to be. Policies appealing exclusively or even primarily to the traditional "working class," that is, to blue-collar workers, could nowadays command no numerical majorities in Scandinavian electorates. Consequently, even if the new egalitarian policies could be presented so as to appeal to the majority of the people at the outset and could be adopted by democratic means, their future maintenance could not be ensured by class power. The decisive factor would be what success they could achieve in ensuring economic growth and universally high standards of living without calling for so much "steering" that voters would feel excessively restricted in their private activities.

The welfare states of the Nordic countries have an international reputation of almost unequaled success. It has been shown in this book that such estimations are excessive but not entirely unreasonable. On the whole the welfare state has been more of a success than a failure in Denmark, Finland, Norway, and Sweden—as well as in a number of other Western industrialized countries. It is possible that it will remain a success notwithstanding its present difficulties, but this is by no means a certainty. Even in Scandinavia the welfare state may be in jeopardy. It is exposed to different, almost diametrically opposite dangers.

The establishment of welfare states in the Nordic countries coincided with spectacular growth in their economies. This growth had nothing to do with social security and welfare. It was not caused by the welfare state, but neither was it impeded by it—contrary to the forebodings of critics. But obviously the growth of resources established a safe foundation on which to build.

Another important factor was ideological. Humanitarian ideas, which for many centuries had been prevalent and in theory accepted by all sorts and conditions of men, could be invoked in favor of the new policies. Even those who opposed such policies on intellectual grounds or because of vested interests frequently had qualms of conscience about these beliefs. At the back of their minds was the fear that the aims on the other side were morally superior or at least in greater accord with the precepts of Christian religion and accepted ethical principles.

In both these respects egalitarian policies are likely to confront greater difficulties than the establishment of social security. Most experts seem to agree that economic growth of the same magnitude as that which took place in the decades immediately following the Second World War is unlikely to happen again in the Western world. There are certainly no indications that it is likely to happen again in Scandinavia, either with or without egalitarian reforms. And there is today far less consensus than formerly about basic principles of ethics, individual or social, or on religion, and what consensus there is hardly affects attitudes toward the idea of perfect equality. Egalitarianism can by no means find the same general acceptance across social groups and political parties as did humanitarian ideas.

The advocates of egalitarian policies maintain that history will repeat itself: in spite of initial controversy, it will ultimately be possible to achieve some sort of consensus in their support. This is a sign of their deep conviction that their aims are so good that in the end everybody will come to agree with them. It is the Hegelian and consequently in some respects also the Marxist approach: out of the conflict between thesis and antithesis a synthesis will emerge, more or less to the satisfaction of everybody. Recognition of probable difficulties of course establishes no conclusive argument against the possible success of the new policies. Even Alva Myrdal in presenting her 1969 report proclaimed with considerable satisfaction that it would lead to fights. In fact, at the time a considerable number of intellectual radicals were hoping for polarization, not only in a temporary phase but of a more lasting and definite nature. Many of them presumably still hope that class conflicts, which had been hidden by the politics of compromise, will finally appear in the open. In their vision the time for the social revolution has come, even though the revolution should be peaceful as far as physical violence is concerned.

Those who call for a fight, for revolutionary struggle, cannot, however, entirely disregard the risk of defeat, at least as a remote possibility. Already at present one frequently hears talk of "disestablishment of the welfare state" as soon as somebody suggests that social benefits might in some cases be marginally reduced or that some activity hitherto conducted in the public sector might conceivably be transferred to the private one. Such statements could perhaps be taken as indications of the level of political debate in Scandinavia rather than of problems confronting its welfare states. In fact they are more important than that, however: they reflect genuine if possibly unfounded fears that the continued existence of the welfare state may actually be endangered once the first steps have been taken. The unanimous public endorsement of the welfare state that characterized the 1950s and 1960s can no longer be counted upon.

In all industrialized Western countries there are some tendencies tht could justly be called reactionary with regard to social security and welfare. Such ideas are usually based on the assumption that individual liberty and individual responsibility are absolute values that cannot be seriously interfered with in the interest of social justice. Intervention by the organs of society thus should be regarded as an evil almost by definition. This kind of attitude can be observed whenever successful or otherwise favored individuals and groups are required to make severe and no longer only marginal or temporary sacrifices. In Denmark it was personified by Mogens Glistrup. On the whole, the attitude is less common and less widespread in the Nordic countries than in most others, while it would of course be a mistake to neglect it altogether. In the 1960s and early 1970s the pendulum swung very far in the direction of demands for self-sacrificing public spirit, and it may now be swinging in the other direction, perhaps farther than could have been imagined.

As is often the case, reaction could be promoted by indiscriminate perfectionism on the other side. When the ideas of the welfare state are invoked to promote excessive egalitarian ambitions, further expansion of the public sector, additional regimentation, and outright collectivism, those who are opposed to such policies may come to lose faith altogether in ideas of social responsibility, solidarity, and social security. The would-be champions of the welfare state could in the end prove more dangerous to it than extreme critics. Political polarization, which at different times seemed to be unavoidable in both Denmark and Sweden, could well work in the same direction.

Insofar as it is possible to judge the state of public opinion—a very difficult undertaking despite the prevalence of opinion polls—it appears that the people take a middle stand. There is undoubtedly polarization of political parties, so that "parties in the middle" have recently been far from successful in Scandinavia. But it hardly seems probable that changes in the party system really reflect the attitudes of the general public. The Swedish Social Democrats lost power in 1976 by "wanting to go further," as Olof Palme put it in the title of a collection of his speeches. One after another of the Swedish opinion polls have shown that those questioned, even among Social Democrats, are critical of the project of employee funds which should crown the efforts to establish "economic democracy." This was so both before and after the 1982 elections which brought the Swedish Social Democrats back into power. On the other hand, Mogens Glistrup has apparently lost most of his hold over Danish public opinion. He has now been finally convicted by the Supreme Court, sentenced to three years in prison for tax frauds, and expelled from Parliament. But even before that, his party had largely repudiated his leadership and lined up with other non-Socialist parties in Denmark. Corresponding protest parties in Finland and Norway are also becoming more or less domesticated, and no similar movement of any importance has yet appeared in Sweden.

These developments have implications for the welfare state,

especially since protests have largely been directed against regimentation, high taxes, and the expansion of the public sector. It is hardly too bold to venture the interpretation that in all four Nordic countries the majority of the peoples in the early 1980s want to maintain their welfare states, while at the same time accepting the need to reduce some benefits hitherto granted either by transfers or by collective consumption, and rather definitely resisting policies aimed at perfect egalitarian societies. They may of course change their mind later, in either direction, but so far political power seems to be out of reach both for reactionaries and for perfectionists. This does not mean that unanimity has been restored, or even that the activities of protest parties have been of no avail. The hard-liners of egalitarianism have not given up their attempts to create the perfect society by increased regimentation. On the other hand, the press and the general public have become more alert about curtailment of individual liberties. Those who used to insist that the well-being of the majority should always take preference over the liberties of the more fortunate have come to realize that those belonging to the majority are also jealous about their liberties. Although the dilemma is still unresolved and may remain so forever, there is a much greater awareness on both sides that egalitarian and libertarian arguments are equally in need of consideration.

The basic argument advanced on the previous pages can be summed up as follows. In all the Nordic countries the welfare state was established over a period of about forty years just before and after the second World War. The most dynamic element in these efforts was found in their labor movements. Developments did not proceed at quite the same speed in all the countries, nor were exactly the same solutions chosen in all of them, but on the whole they followed parallel paths.

The resulting system of social security and welfare was a source of satisfaction and pride to the Scandinavian peoples and was admired in many other countries. The warnings of early critics proved unjustified on the face of it, largely because the growth of production and prosperity was such that nobody had to make any real sacrifices for the benefit of those who profited from the system. This growth included a remarkable increase of economic equality, achieved by raising the income levels of previously disfavored groups without appreciably lowering the standards of what had been called the upper classes.

Although these achievements must be considered very successful indeed, there was no absence of social and other problems. Some of these were caused by developments without any direct relation to the welfare state, such as urbanization, industrialization, and changing moral attitudes. Some had existed all the time but had formerly been overshadowed by immediate material needs. Others, especially those concerned with administration and with relations between the governed and the governing, were at least in part connected with the interventionism inherent in the welfare state. These problems were frequently glossed over, and this may be one of the reasons why they remained almost entirely unsolved. Even when recognized, they were as a rule regarded only as flaws and not held to be serious enough to balance the advantages that had been gained. But with a more unfavorable economic climate, the maintenance of the welfare states in all four countries is becoming less easy than before, at least less easy than it was in the 1950s and the 1960s. Some parts of the system have come in for serious criticism, and some of them are being pruned. The main body remains undamaged, however, and there is widespread agreement that this is as it should be.

In Sweden as well as to a lesser extent in Denmark and the two other countries, the labor movement, which had long been the most dynamic element in political life, attempted to maintain its impetus by insisting that the time had come to go further. Social security and welfare were held to be insufficient even though they had brought about a very considerable increase in economic equality between social groups. It was argued that the time had come to establish a truly egalitarian society. This was a different proposition from the previous one. It was not founded on ideas of economic growth; rather, it was intended to make far-reaching changes in the ownership of means of production. It was based on ideas other than the humanitarian principles that had been such an important force in the establishment and maintenance of social security and welfare. Moreover, the new attempt was made at a time when the question no longer appeared to be one of distributing growing prosperity, but of creating prosperity for distribution.

It is by no means certain that the four countries will in the long run continue to march side by side. Attitudes may come to differ in the future more than they did in the past. But so far all the Scandinavian peoples are apparently still strongly attached to ideas of social security and welfare. Parties and movements attempting to dismantle the welfare state are unlikely to succeed by democratic means, and no other means are acceptable in these countries. On the other hand, the demand for perfect equality has met with but little popular acclaim. There is a marked dislike for heavy taxes, and above all Scandinavians are increasingly unwilling to sacrifice too much of their individual liberties for the establishment of the millennium. In this they are not very different from other Western peoples.

Bibliography

Bibliography

The following list of books covers the general topics of the welfare state and the welfare experiences of the Nordic societies. Although far from complete, it does indicate the abundance of literature on these subjects and should prove helpful to those who want to study them in greater depth.

Ahlberg, F., ed. *Socialhaandbogen.* 2 vols. København, 1975-76.

Aijar, J. P. *Perspective on the Welfare State.* Ajmer, 1979.

Allardt, E. *Att ha, att älska, att vara: om välfärd i Norden.* Lund, 1981.

———, ed. *Nordic Democracy.* København, 1981.

Andersen, B., et al. *Langvarigt forsorgsunderstøttede.* København, 1960.

Andersen, B. R. *Hvad er der i vejen med tryghedssystemet?* København, 1973.

———. *Nyere maalsætninger i socialpolitiken.* København, 1966.

———. *Socialpolitik i velfærdssamfundet.* København, 1966.

Andersen, C. R. *Borgeren og tryghedssystemet.* København, 1970.

———. *Grundprincipier i socialpolitiken.* København, 1971.

Andrén, N. *Modern Swedish Government.* Stockholm, 1968.

———, et al. *Svensk statsförvaltning i omdaning.* Stockholm, 1967.

Arnault, J. *Le socialisme suédois.* Paris, 1970.

Arter, D. *Bumpkin against Bigwig.* Tampere, 1978.

Back, P. E. *Det svenska partiväsendet.* Stockholm, 1967.

Berthold, H. *Sozialethische Probleme des Wohlfahrtsstaates.* Güntersloh, 1968.

Birch, R. C. *The Shaping of the Welfare State.* London, 1974.

Board, J. B. *The Government and Politics of Sweden.* Boston, 1970.

Brixtofte, P. *Krisen i det danske Samfund.* København, 1977.

Bruce, H. *The Coming of the Welfare State.* London, 1961.

Burenstam Linder, S. *Den hjärtlösa välfärdsstaten.* Stockholm, 1983.

Cappelen, H., and Ervik, A. *Sosiale opgaver.* Oslo, 1968.

Childs, M. *Sweden: The Middle Way*. New Haven, 1935.
_____. *Sweden: The Middle Way on Trial*. New Haven, 1980.
_____. *This is Democracy*. New Haven, 1938.
Christensen, B. *Det offentliges Virksomhed*. København, 1971.
Clegg, R. K. *The Welfare World*. Springfield, Ill., 1968.
Cootes, R. J. *The Making of the Welfare State*. London, 1966.
Dahl, R. A., and Lindblom, C. E. *Politics, Economics, and Welfare*. Chicago, 1976.
Dahlman, C. J., and Klevmarker, A. *Den privata konsumtionen, 1931-1975*. Stockholm, 1971.
Dahmén, E. *Ekonomisk utveckling och ekonomisk politik i Finland*. Helsinki, 1963.
Danaho, R. *Une politique active de l'emploi—l'exemple de la Suède*. Paris, 1968.
Danmark: det økonomiske Raad. *Den personlige inkomstfordeling og inkomstudjæ vningen over de offentlige finanser*. København, 1967.
Druitt, B. *The Growth of the Welfare State*. London, 1966.
Eckstein, H. *Division and Cohesion in Democracy: A Study of Norway*. Princeton, 1966.
Elder, N. C. M. *Government in Sweden: The Executive at Work*. Oxford and New York, 1970.
Elmer, Å. *Svensk socialpolitik*. Stockholm, 1980.
Elstob, E. *Sweden: A Political and Cultural History*. Totowa, N.J., 1979.
Elvander, N. *Intresseorganisationerna i dagens Sverige*. Stockholm, 1972.
_____. *Svensk arbetrarrörelse*. Stockholm, 1980.
Eriksen, K. E., et al., eds. *Norsk innenrikspolitik*. Oslo, 1972.
Faramond, G. de, ed. *Suède: la réforme permanente*. Paris, 1977.
Ferraton, H. *L'économie norvégienne et al Marché Commun*. Oslo, 1964.
_____. *Syndicalisme ouvrier et social-démocratie en Norvège*. Paris, 1960.
Fleisher, F. *The New Sweden: The Challenge of a Disciplined Democracy*. New York, 1967.
Fordelingen af levekårene. 5 vols. København, 1978-80.
Friisberg, C. *Socialpolitik i Danmark*. København, 1978.
Fry, J., ed. *Limits of the Welfare State: Critical Reviews on Post-war Sweden*. Farnborough, 1979.
Furniss, N., and Tilton, T. *The Case for the Welfare State*. Bloomington, Ind., 1977.
Fusilier, R. *Les pays nordiques*. Paris, 1965.
Galenson, W. *The Scandinavian Labor Movement*. Berkeley, 1952.
Gathorne-Hardy, G. A. A., et al. *The Scandinavian States and Finland: A Political and Economic Survey*. New York and London, 1952.
Gault, F. *Les nouveaux syndicalistes: Suède, Japon, Italie*. Paris, 1978.
Grünbaum, I., et al. *Krise i Danmark*. Roskilde, 1977.
Guldimann, T. *Die Grenzen des Wolhfahrtsstaates: am Beispiel Schwedens und der Bundesrepublik*. München, 1976.
Gunzburg, D. *Industrial Democracy Approaches in Sweden: An Australian View*. Melbourne, 1978.
Hancock, M. D. *Sweden: A Multi-party System in Transition?* Denver, 1968.
_____. *Sweden: The Politics of Post-industrial Change*. Hinsdale, Ill., 1972.
Hansen, B. *Velstand uden velfærd*. København, 1974.
Haue, H., et al. *Det ny Danmark, 1880-1980*. København, 1981.
Heckscher, E. F. *An Economic History of Sweden*. Cambridge, Mass., 1963.
Heckscher, G. *Democratie efficace*. Paris, 1957.
_____. *Swedish Public Administration at Work*. Stockholm, 1955.
Heckscher, S., ed. *Straff och rättfärdighet: ny nordisk debatt*. Stockholm, 1980.
Hecklo, H. *Modern Social Policies in Britain and Sweden*. New Haven, 1974.
Heining, P. *Die schwedische Sozialfürsorge*. Tübingen, 1961.

Henig, S., and Pinder, J., eds. *European Political Parties*. London, 1969.

Hewart, G. H. *The New Despotism*. London, 1929.

Himmelstrand, U. *Beyond Welfare Capitalism*. London, 1982.

Hoffmeyer, E., ed. *Velfærdsteori og velfærdsstat*. København, 1962.

Höjer, K. J. *Social Welfare in Sweden*. Stockholm, 1949.

_____. *Svensk socialpolitisk historia*. Stockholm, 1952.

Holgersson, L. *Socialvården: en fråga om människosyn*. Stockholm, 1977.

Holmberg, P. *Arbete och löner i Sverige*. Stockholm, 1969.

_____. *Socialpolitisk teori och praktik*. Stockholm, 1978.

Holmberg, S. *Svenska väljare*. Stockholm, 1981.

Hopkins, K. *Sweden: Focus on Post-industrialism*. Englewood, N.J., 1977.

Hudson, K. *Towards the Welfare State*. London, 1971.

Hufford, L. *Sweden: The Myth of Socialism*. London, 1973.

Huntford, R. *The New Totalitarians*. London, 1971.

Jansson, J. M. *Idé och verklighet i politiken*. Ekenäs, 1972.

Jordan, B. *Freedom and the Welfare State*. London and Boston, 1976.

Kaim-Candle, P. R. *Comparative Social Policy and Social Security: A Ten-Country Study*. London, 1973.

Kirby, D. G. *Finland in the Twentieth Century*. Minneapolis, 1979.

Knoellinger, C. E. *Labor in Finland*. Cambridge, Mass., 1960.

Koblik, S., ed. *Sweden's Development from Poverty to Affluence, 1750-1970*. Minneapolis, 1975.

Korpi, W. *The Democratic Class Struggle*. London, 1983.

_____. *Fattigdom i välfärden*. Stockholm, 1971.

_____. *The Working Class in Welfare Capitalism: Work, Unions, and Politics in Sweden*. London, 1978.

Kragh, T., and Sørensen, M. *De politiske partier og deres programmer*. København, 1972.

Kvavik, R. *Interest Groups in Norwegian Politics*. Oslo, 1982.

Lafferty, W. M. *Economic Development and the Response in Scandinavia*. Oslo, 1971.

Lansbury, R. *Swedish Social Democracy*. London, 1972.

Leion, A. *Inkomstfördelningen i Sverige*. Solna, 1970.

Lewin, L. *Governing Trade Unions*. Cambridge, Mass., 1980.

_____. *Planhushållningsdebatten*. Uppsala, 1967.

Lindbeck, A. *Swedish Economic Policy*. London, 1975.

Lindberg, O. *Urban Settlement and Income Distribution*. Umeå, 1972.

Logue, J. *Socialism and Abundance: Radical Socialism in the Danish Welfare State*. Minneapolis, 1982.

Lundberg, E. F., ed. *Svensk ekonomisk politik*. Stockholm, 1980.

Lundquist, L. *Förvaltningen i det politiska systemet*. Lund, 1971.

_____. *Means and Goals of Political Decentralization*. Lund, 1972.

_____, and Peterson, H., eds. *Byråkrati och demokrati*. Lund, 1971.

Lyngby Jensen, H. *Stauning*. Viborg, 1979.

Macarov, D. *The Design of Social Welfare*. New York, 1978.

Marjomaa, P. *Private Consumption Expenditure Patterns and Trends in Finland*. Helsinki, 1969.

Marsh, D. C. *The Future of the Welfare State*. London, 1964.

_____. *The Welfare State*. London, 1970.

Meidner, R. *Employee Investment Funds*. London, 1978.

Merkl, P., ed. *European Party Systems*. Riverside, N.Y., 1980.

Meyerson, P.-M. *The Welfare State in Crisis—the Case of Sweden*. Stockholm, 1982.

Midré, G. *Samfunnsendring og sosialpolitikk*. Oslo, 1973.

Miller, K. E. *Government and Politics in Denmark*. Boston, 1968.

Mishra, R. *Society and Social Policy*. London, 1977.
(Möller, G.) *Ett genombrott, Den svenska socialpolitiken: utvecklingslinjer och framtidsmål.* Till G. Möller. Stockholm, 1944.
Mukherjee, S. *Making Labor Markets Work: A comparison of the U. K. and Swedish Systems.* London, 1972.
Myrdal, A. *Jämlikhet. Första rapport från SAP:s oh LO:s arbetsgrupp.* Stockholm, 1969.
————, and Myrdal, G. *Kris i befolkningsfrågan.* Stockholm, 1935.
Myrdal, G. *Beyond the Welfare State.* London, 1960.
————. *Hur styrs landet?* Vol. 1. Stockholm, 1982.
Naseem, M. *The Dilemma of the Welfare State.* London, 1966.
Niklasson, H., et al. *Välfärdsteori och ekonomisk politik.* Lund, 1967.
Nilsson, L. G., et al. *Demokrati och förvaltning.* Lund, 1970.
Nordisk statistisk skriftserie. *Social Security in the Nordic Countries. Scope and Expenditures, 1978.* Stockholm, 1981.
Nordiska rådet. *Levnadsnivå och ojämlikhet i Norden.* Göteborg, 1983.
Norge, Rikstrygdeverket. *Norsk praktisk socialpolitik.* Oslo, 1976.
Norge, Sosialdepartementet. *Sosial trygghet i Norge.* Oslo, 1975.
Norges offentlige utredninger. *Maktutredningen: slutrapport.* Oslo, 1982.
Nousiainen, J. *Finlands politiska partier.* Orebro, 1960.
Nyholm, P. *Parliament, Government, and Multi-dimensional Party Relations in Finland.* Helsinki, 1972.
OECD. *Manpower Policy in Denmark.* Paris and Washington, 1974.
————. *Manpower Policy in Finland.* Paris and Washington, 1977.
————. *Manpower Policy in Norway.* Paris and Washington, 1972.
Ohlin, B. *Fri eller dirigerad ekonomi.* Uddevalla, 1936.
Oram, C. A. *Social Policy and Administration in New Zealand.* Washington, D.C., 1969.
Palm, G. *The Flight from Work.* New York, 1979.
Parent, J. *Le modèle suédois.* Paris, 1970.
Pestoff, V. *Voluntary Associations and Nordic Party Systems.* Stockholm, 1977.
Pinker, R. *Social Theory and Social Policy.* London, 1971.
Riis, T. *Les institutions politiques centrales de Danemark.* Odense, 1977.
Rintala, M. *Three Generations: The Extreme Right Wing in Finnish Politics.* Bloomington, Ind., 1962.
Roberts, D. *Victorian Origins of the British Welfare State.* New Haven, 1960.
Robson, W. A. *Welfare State and Welfare Society.* London, 1976.
Rosenthal, A. H. *The Social Programs of Sweden: A Search for Security in a Free Society.* Minneapolis, 1967.
Rustow, D. A. *The Politics of Compromise: A Study of Parties and Cabinet Government in Sweden.* Princeton, 1955.
Sandhu, M. M. *The Concept of Welfare State.* Delhi, 1975.
Schmaltz-Jørgensen, H., ed. *De politiska partierna i Norden.* Stockholm, 1970.
Schneider, E., ed. *Skandinavische Wirtschaftsprobleme im heutigen Europa.* Tübingen, 1967.
Schnitzer, M. *The Economy of Sweden: A Study of the Modern Welfare State.* New York, 1970.
————. *Income Distribution: A Comparative Study.* New York, 1974.
Scott, F. D. *Sweden: The Nation's History.* Minneapolis, 1977.
Silverman, A. D. *Selected Aspects of the Administration of Publicly Owned Housing: Great Britain, Netherlands and Sweden.* Washington, D.C., 1961.
Sleeman, J. F. *The Welfare State: Its Aims, Benefits and Costs.* London, 1973.
Socialforskningsinstituttet. *Socialreformundersøgelserne.* 2 vols. København, 1970-1972.
Socialpolitisk Forening. *Fattig i et velstandssamfund.* København, 1966.

Bibliography   261

Södersten, B., ed. *Svensk ekonomi*. Stockholm, 1970.
Spånt, R. *Den svenska inkomstfördelningens utveckling*. Stockholm, 1976.
Stauning, T. *Af Tidens Strid*. *Taler*. København, 1933.
———. *Tanker og taler*. København, 1931.
Steincke, K. K. *Minder og Meninger*. 5 vols. København, 1945-1954.
Stekke, A. J. *Politisk aktivitet og struktur*. Oslo, 1972.
Storing, J. A. *Norwegian Democracy*. Boston, 1963.
Sunesson, S. *Politik och organisation: staten och arbetarklassens organisationer*. Lund, 1974.
Sverige, Finansddepartementet. *Svensk ekonomisk tillväxt*. Stockholm, 1966.
Sverige, Statistiska Centralbyrån. *Levnadsförhållandena i Sverige*. 33 vols. Stockholm, 1976-1982.
Thomas, A. K. *Parliamentary Politics in Denmark*. Glasgow, 1973.
Thomson, A., ed. *Samhälle och riksdag*. 5 vols. Uppsala, 1966-1967.
Tinbergen, J. *Economic Policy: Principles and Design*. Amsterdam, 1956.
Tingsten, H. *The Swedish Social Democrats*. Totowa, N.J., 1973.
Titmuss, R. M. *Commitment to Welfare*. London, 1970.
———. *Essays on the Welfare State*. London, 1958.
———. *The Gift Relationship*. New York, 1971.
Toivola, A. *Vårt socialskydd i huvuddrag*. Borgå, 1973.
Törnudd, K. *The Electoral System of Finland*. London, 1968.
Uhr, C. G. *Sweden's Social Security System*. Washington, D.C., 1966.
U. N. *Organization of Social Welfare Programs: Norway*. New York, 1967.
Upton, A. F., et al. *The Communist Parties of Scandinavia and Finland*. London, 1973.
Valen, H. *Political Parties in Norway*. Oslo, 1964.
———. *Valg og politikk: et samfunn i endring*. Oslo (Gjøvik), 1981.
——— et al. *Velgere og politiske frontlinjer*. Oslo, 1972.
Verney, D. V. *Public Enterprise in Sweden*. Liverpool, 1959.
Vinde, P. *The Swedish Civil Service*. Stockholm, 1967.
Westergård Andersen, H. *Dansk politik*. København, 1966.
Wheeler, C. *White Collar Power*. *Changing Patterns of Interest Group Behavior in Sweden*. Chicago and London, 1975.
Widmaier, H. P. *Politische Ökonomie des Wohlfahrtsstaates*. Frankfurt a/M, 1974.
———. *Sozialpolitik im Wohlfahrtsstaat*. Hamburg, 1976.
Wieslander, H. *De politiska partiernas program*. Stockholm, 1968.
Wigforss, E. *Efter välfärdsstaten*. Malmö, 1956.
———. *Minnen*. 3 vols. Stockholm, 1950-1954.
Wilensky, H. *The Welfare State and Equality*. Berkeley, 1975.
Wilson, D. *The Welfare State in Sweden*. London, 1979.
Wordsworth, D. E. *Social Security and National Policy in Sweden, Yugoslavia, Japan*. Montreal, 1977.

Index

Index

There are no entries for Denmark, Finland, Norway, and Sweden, or for the welfare state because they are basic to my entire discussion and pervade it.

Gunnar Heckscher's career has spanned the academic, political, and diplomatic worlds. Born in Sweden and educated at the University of Uppsala and Cambridge University, he served as director of the Stockholm School of Social Work and Local Administration from 1941 till 1954 and as a professor of political science at the University of Stockholm from 1948 till 1965. Heckscher was elected a member of the Swedish Riksdag in 1956 and became leader of the Conservative party in 1961. During these parliamentary years he was also a member of the Consultative Assembly of the Council of Europe, and chair of its Economic Committee. In 1965 he was appointed Sweden's ambassador to India, Ceylon and Nepal, and from 1970 till 1975 he held that post in Japan and the Republic of Korea. His books include *The Study of Comparative Government and Politics* and *The Role of Small Nations: Today and Tomorrow.*